CW00432896

INTERMEDIATE LEVEL

Paper 3 (GBR)

Maintaining Financial Records

EXAM KIT

ACCA
Approved Publisher

KAPLAN

PUBLISHING

FOULKS LYNCH

British Library Cataloguing-in-Publication Data

A catalogue record for this book is available from the British Library.

Published by Kaplan Publishing Foulks Lynch
Swift House
Market Place
Wokingham
Berkshire
RG40 1AP

ISBN 1 84390 724 0

© FTC Kaplan Limited, 2006

Printed and bound in Great Britain.

Acknowledgements

We are grateful to the Association of Chartered Certified Accountants, the Chartered Institute of Management Accountants and the Institute of Chartered Accountants in England and Wales for permission to reproduce past examination questions. The answers have been prepared by Kaplan Publishing Foulks Lynch.

INTRODUCTION

This new edition of the CAT Exam Kit for 2006 has been updated and reorganised.

Packed with exam-type questions, this book will help you to successfully prepare for your exam.

- All questions are grouped by syllabus topics with separate sections for 'objective test questions' (Section 1 of this book), 'short form questions' (Section 2) and 'practice questions' (Section 3).

- All questions are of exam standard and format – this enables you to master the exam techniques.

- Mock exams are at the back of the book – try these under timed conditions and this will give you an exact idea of the way you will be tested in your examination.

If you are sitting a computer-based exam, Section 1 questions provide exam-type practice. Sections 2 and 3 questions should still be attempted to test your knowledge of each syllabus topic.

If you are sitting a paper-based exam, Sections 1, 2 and 3 questions are representative of what you will come across in your exam.

CONTENTS

INDEX TO QUESTIONS AND ANSWERS

Final accounts

Incomplete records

Sole trader accounts

Partnership accounts

SYLLABUS AND REVISION GUIDANCE

Syllabus content

Before commencing this paper, a thorough knowledge of Paper 1, *Recording Financial Transactions*, is required. Paper 3 builds on the knowledge acquired in Paper 1, enabling students to prepare final accounts for a sole trader and for partnerships. This knowledge will be further developed in Paper 6, *Drafting Financial Statements* which will enable students to prepare final accounts for limited companies.

1 Basic bookkeeping

(a) The nature and confidentiality of the business transactions

(b) Double entry bookkeeping

(c) Capital and revenue expenditure

(d) Assets, liabilities, revenue and expenses

(e) Initial trial balance

(f) Format of simple final accounts
  (i) trading account
  (ii) profit and loss account
  (iii) balance sheet

(g) The organisation's policies, regulations and timescales in the preparation of final accounts

2 Accounting standards, principles and policies

(a) Regulation

(b) Accounting standards (SSAPs and FRSs)

(c) Accounting principles
  (i) going concern
  (ii) accruals
  (iii) consistency
  (iv) prudence

(d) Accounting policies
  (i) relevance
  (ii) reliability
  (iii) comparability
  (iv) understandability

3 Fixed assets and depreciation

(a) Fixed assets
  (i) acquisitions
  (ii) asset register
  (iii) accounting treatment
  (iv) disposal
  (v) part exchange
  (vi) authorisation
  (vii) maintenance of capital records

(a) Depreciation
  (i) straight line
  (ii) reducing balance

4 Control accounts, reconciliations and errors

(a) Reconciliations
  (i) purchase ledger reconciliation
  (ii) sales ledger reconciliation
  (iii) bank reconciliation

(b) Identification of errors

    (i)   incorrect double entry

    (ii)   missing entries

    (iii) numerical errors

    (iv) insufficient information

(c) Correction of errors

    (i)   suspense account

    (ii)   journal entries

5   Adjustments to the trial balance

(a) Accruals and prepayments

(b) Depreciation

(c) Irrecoverable debts and allowances for debtors

(d) Closing stock (and stock valuation)

(e) Extended trial balance

(f) Provisions

6   Final accounts

(a) Incomplete records

(b) Sole trader accounts

    (i)   profit and loss account

    (ii)   balance sheet

(c) Partnership accounts

    (i)   profit and loss account

    (ii)   appropriation of profit

    (iii) balance sheet

    (iv) partners' capital and current accounts

Excluded topics

The following topics are specifically excluded from Paper 3:

- club accounts
- manufacturing accounts
- detailed knowledge of VAT
- tax computations
- foreign currency transactions
- goodwill arising on admission of a new partner
- cash flow statements

Planning your revision

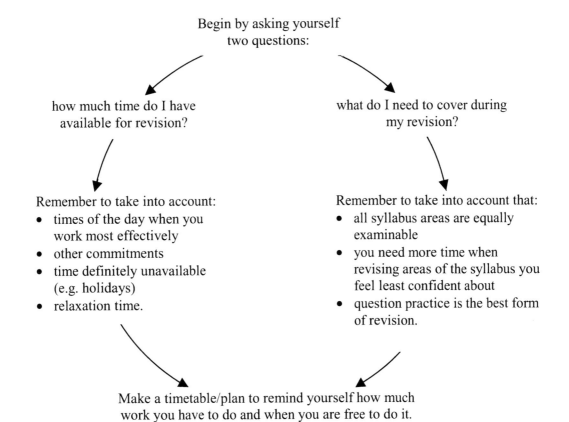

Begin by asking yourself
two questions:

how much time do I have
available for revision?

what do I need to cover during
my revision?

Remember to take into account:
- times of the day when you
  work most effectively
- other commitments
- time definitely unavailable
  (e.g. holidays)
- relaxation time.

Remember to take into account that:
- all syllabus areas are equally
  examinable
- you need more time when
  revising areas of the syllabus you
  feel least confident about
- question practice is the best form
  of revision.

Make a timetable/plan to remind yourself how much
work you have to do and when you are free to do it.
Allow some time for slippage.

Revision techniques

- Go through your notes and textbook **highlighting the important points**

- You might want to produce your own set of **summarised notes**

- **List key words** for each topic to remind you of the essential concepts

- **Practise exam-standard questions**, under timed conditions

- **Rework questions** that you got completely wrong the first time, but only when you think you know the subject better

- If you get stuck on topics, **find someone to explain** them to you (your tutor or a colleague, for example)

- **Read recent articles** on the ACCA website or in the student magazine

- **Read** good newspapers and professional journals

THE EXAM

Format of the paper-based examination

		Number of marks
Section A:	20 compulsory multiple choice questions (2 marks each)	40
Section B:	1 question that comprises 4 compulsory short-from questions (2 - 5 marks each)	15
	and 3 compulsory written questions (15 marks each)	45

Total time allowed: 2 hours   100

Format of the computer-based examination

	Number of marks
Objective test questions (mainly multiple-choice questions)	100

Total time allowed: 2 hours

Paper-based examination

Spend the first few minutes of the examination reading the paper and where you have a choice of questions, **decide which ones you will do**.

Unless you know exactly how to answer the question, spend some time **planning your answer**. Stick to the question and tailor your answer to what you are asked.

Fully explain all your points but be concise. Set out all workings clearly and neatly, and state briefly what you are doing. Don't write out the question.

If you do not understand what a question is asking, **state your assumptions**. Even if you do not answer precisely in the way the examiner hoped, you should be given some credit, if your assumptions are reasonable.

If you get stuck with a question, leave space in your answer book and return to it later.

Remember that before you finish, you must **fill in the required information** on the front of your answer booklet.

Computer-based examination

You can take a CBE at any time during the year - you do not need to wait for June and December exam sessions.

Be sure you **understand how to use the software** before you start the exam. If in doubt, ask the assessment centre staff to explain it to you. **Questions are displayed on the screen** and **answers are entered using keyboard and mouse**.

Don't panic if you realise you've answered a question incorrectly – **you can always go back and change your answer**.

At the end of the examination, **you are given a certificate showing the result** you have achieved.

Answering the questions

Multiple-choice questions: Read the questions carefully and work through any calculations required. If you don't know the answer, eliminate those options you know are incorrect and see if the answer becomes more obvious. Remember that only one answer to a multiple choice question can be right!

Objective test questions might ask for numerical answers, but could also involve paragraphs of text which require you to fill in a number of missing blanks, or for you to write a definition of a word or phrase, or to enter a formula. Others may give a definition followed by a list of possible key words relating to that description.

Essay questions: Make a quick plan in your answer book and under each main point list all the relevant facts you can think of. Then write out your answer developing each point fully. Your essay should have a clear structure; it should contain a brief introduction, a main section and a conclusion. Be concise. It is better to write a little about a lot of different points than a great deal about one or two points.

Computations: It is essential to include all your workings in your answers. Many computational questions require the use of a standard format: company profit and loss account, balance sheet and cash flow statement for example. Be sure you know these formats thoroughly before the examination and use the layouts that you see in the answers given in this book and in model answers. If you are asked to comment or make recommendations on a computation, you must do so. There are important marks to be gained here. Even if your computation contains mistakes, you may still gain marks if your reasoning is correct.

Reports, memos and other documents: Some questions ask you to present your answer in the form of a report or a memo or other document. Use the correct format - there could be easy marks to gain here.

Section 1

OBJECTIVE TEST QUESTIONS

BASIC BOOKKEEPING

1 **Consider the following statements:**

(i) 'Double entry bookkeeping' means that two sets of records are maintained.

(ii) In double entry bookkeeping we have a basic check on the accuracy of the entries, as the total value of the debit entries and the total value of the credit entries should be equal.

Are the statements true or false?

	Statement (i)	Statement (ii)
A	True	True
B	True	False
C	False	True
D	False	False

2 **Andrea started a taxi business by transferring her car, worth £5,000, into the business. What are the accounting entries required to record this?**

A	Dr	Capital	£5,000
	Cr	Car	£5,000
B	Dr	Car	£5,000
	Cr	Drawings	£5,000
C	Dr	Car	£5,000
	Cr	Capital	£5,000
D	Dr	Car	£5,000
	Cr	Bank	£5,000

3   **Jones' account is shown below:**

Jones

		£			£
1 January	Bal b/d	250	17 January	Returns out	50
12 January	Sales	1,000	28 January	Bank	800
23 January	Sales	500	31 January	Bal c/d	900
		1,750			1,750
1 February	Bal b/d	900			

What is the balance on Jones' account as at 31 January?

A   Debit £250

B   Debit £1,750

C   Debit £900

D   Credit £900

4   **Which of the following changes could not occur as a result of an entry in the bookkeeping records?**

A   Increase asset and increase liability

B   Increase asset and increase capital

C   Increase capital and increase liability

D   Increase capital and decrease liability

5   **A business has capital of £10,000. Which of the following asset and liability figures could appear in this business' balance sheet?**

A	Assets	£6,000	Liabilities	£16,000
B	Assets	£6,000	Liabilities	£4,000
C	Assets	£10,000	Liabilities	£10,000
D	Assets	£14,000	Liabilities	£4,000

6   **A business commenced with capital in cash of £1,000. Stock costing £800 (zero VAT) is purchased on credit, and half is sold for £1,000 plus VAT at 17.5%, the customer paying in cash at once.**

The accounting equation after these transactions would show:

A   Assets £1,775 less Liabilities £175 equals Capital £1,600

B   Assets £2,175 less Liabilities £975 equals Capital £1,200

C   Assets £2,575 less Liabilities £800 equals Capital £1,775

D   Assets £2,575 less Liabilities £975 equals Capital £1,600.

7   A sole trader had opening capital of £10,000 and closing capital of £4,500. During the period, the owner introduced capital of £4,000 and withdrew £8,000 for her own use.

Her profit or loss during the period was:

A   £9,500 loss

B   £1,500 loss

C   £7,500 profit

D   £17,500 profit.

8   A business sold goods to the value of £500 (net) to Harper Ltd. What would be the debit to Harper Ltd's account if VAT is payable at a rate of 17.5%?

[   ]

9   We returned goods that had a net value of £800 to Rawlins Ltd. What would be the debit to Rawlins Ltd's account if VAT is payable at a rate of 17.5%?

A   £660.00

B   £800.00

C   £940.00

D   £969.70

10   On 1 March 20X4 Andrew took out a loan for £50,000. The loan is to be repaid in five equal annual instalments, with the first repayment falling due on 1 March 20X6.

How should the balance on the loan be reported on Andrew's balance sheet as at 30 April 20X4?

A   £50,000 as a current liability

B   £50,000 as a long-term liability

C   £10,000 as a current liability and £40,000 as a long-term liability

D   £40,000 as a current liability and £10,000 as a long-term liability

11   A summary of the transactions of Ramsgate, who is registered for VAT at 17.5%, shows the following for the month of August 20X9.

Outputs   £60,000 (exclusive of VAT)   10500 DR

Inputs   £40,286 (inclusive of VAT)   6000 CR

At the beginning of the period Ramsgate owed £3,400 to HM Revenue & Customs, and during the period he has paid £2,600 to them.

At the end of the period the amount owing to HM Revenue & Customs is:

[   ]

The following information relates to questions 12 to 14.

The following information was extracted from the books of Miss Fitt at 31 December 20X8:

	£
Sales	18,955
Cost of sales	11,334
Salaries and wages	2,447
Motor expenses	664
Rent	456
Rates	120
Insurance	146
Packing expenses	276
Lighting and heating expenses	665
Sundry expenses	115
Motor vehicles	2,400
Fixtures and fittings	600
Stock as at 31 December 20X8	4,998
Debtors	4,577
Creditors	3,045
Cash in bank	3,876
Cash in hand	120
Capital	10,794

12   The current liabilities figure in the balance sheet at 31.12.X8 will be:

A   £2,939

B   £3,045

C   £3,151

D   £15,885.

13   The fixed assets figure as at 31.12.X8 will be:

14   The net profit for the year to 31.12.X8 will be:

A   £2,481

B   £2,681

C   £2,732

D   £4,940.

15   How is closing stock recorded in the bookkeeping records?

A   By a debit to stock and a credit to profit and loss

B   By a debit to profit and loss and a credit to stock

C   By a debit to stock and a credit to purchases

D   By writing the figure in a note beneath the trial balance

16   How is the closing balance on the wages account entered in the profit and loss account?

A   By a debit to wages and a credit to profit and loss

B   By a debit to profit and loss and a credit to wages

C   By a debit to profit and loss

D   By writing the total in the profit statement, the balance on wages remaining unaffected

17   How is the closing balance on the debtors account entered in the balance sheet?

A   By a debit to debtors and a credit to balance sheet

B   By a debit to balance sheet and a credit to debtors

C   By a debit to balance sheet

D   By writing the total in the balance sheet, the balance on debtors remaining unaffected

18   Which is the main concept behind making adjustments for accrued expenses?

A   Prudence

B   Going concern

C   Consistency

D   Reporting transactions as they occur

19   Which of the following best describes the entries that are made using the sales day book totals at the end of each month?

A   Debit sales with total net sales, credit sales ledger control with total gross sales and credit VAT with total VAT

B   Debit sales with total gross sales, credit sales ledger control with total net sales and credit VAT with total VAT

C   Debit sales ledger control with total net sales, debit VAT with total VAT and credit sales with total gross sales

D   Debit sales ledger control with total gross sales, credit sales with total net sales and credit VAT with total VAT

20   The payment of cash to a creditor will:

A   Increase debtors and reduce cash balance

B   ~~Reduce cash balance and reduce~~ current liabilities

C   Reduce creditors and increase purchases

D   Increase creditors and reduce cash balance.

21   To record goods returned inwards:

A   Debit sales account and credit creditors account

B   Debit returns inwards account and credit creditors account

C   Debit returns inwards account and credit debtors account

D   Debit debtors account and credit returns inwards account.

22   Which of the following best describes the entries in respect of the totals from the receipts side of the cash book?

A   Debit bank with total receipts, credit cash sales, sales ledger control and other with totals received, debit discounts allowed with total cash discount and credit sales ledger control with total cash discount

B   Debit bank with total receipts, credit cash sales, sales ledger control and other with totals received, credit discounts allowed with total cash discount and debit sales ledger control with total cash discount

C   Credit bank with total receipts, debit cash sales, sales ledger control and other with totals received, credit discounts allowed with total cash discount and debit sales ledger control with total cash discount

D   Credit bank with total receipts, debit cash sales, sales ledger control and other with totals received, debit discounts allowed with total cash discount and credit sales ledger control with total cash discount

23   Which of the following would not lead to a difference between the total of the balances on the sales ledger and the balance on the sales ledger control account?

A   An error in totalling the sales day book

B   An error in totalling the receipts column of the cash book

C   An overstatement of an entry in a debtor's account

D   An entry posted to the wrong debtor's account

24   Headington is owed £37,500 by its debtors at the start, and £39,000 at the end, of its year ended 31 December 20X8.

During the period, cash sales of £263,500 and credit sales of £357,500 were made, discounts allowed amounting to £15,750 and discounts received £21,400. Bad debts of £10,500 were written off and Headington wishes to retain its allowance for bad debts at 5% of total debtors.

The cash received in the year totalled:

☐

25   Anthony receives goods from Brad on credit terms and Anthony subsequently pays by cheque. Anthony then discovers that the goods are faulty and cancels the cheque before it is cashed by Brad.

How should Anthony record the cancellation of the cheque in his books?

A   Debit creditors   Credit returns outwards

B   Credit bank   Debit creditors

C   Debit bank   Credit creditors

D   Credit creditors   Debit returns outwards

ACCOUNTING STANDARDS, PRINCIPLES AND POLICIES

26 One of Gee plc's employees developed a new product. This has just been patented. The development costs of this product were negligible, but the patent rights are almost certainly worth many millions of pounds. Which accounting concept would prevent the company from recognising the value of this patent as a fixed asset in its balance sheet?

    A   Going concern

    B   Materiality

    C   Money measurement

    D   Prudence

27 A company sends a consignment of goods to a potential customer on a sale or return basis. How should the despatch of goods be recorded?

    A   Debit debtors and credit sales

    B   Debit sales and credit debtors

    C   Debit debtors and credit stock

    D   Make a memorandum note of the despatch until it becomes apparent that the debtor will either purchase the goods or return them

28 A few days before his year end, Colin received a claim for £30,000 following an accident caused by one of his lorries.

He accepted liability and offered to pay £15,000. His offer was rejected and legal proceedings were commenced. His legal advisor told him that when the claim goes to court he will be required to pay £20,000.

What amount should Colin provide in his year end accounts?

    A   No provision is required

    B   £15,000 should be provided

    C   £20,000 should be provided

    D   £30,000 should be provided

29 At 31 October 20X3 Maurice's balance sheet included a provision for £35,000. He has re-assessed the provision at 31 October 20X4, and has decided that at that date the provision should be £38,000.

What entry will be made in Maurice's profit and loss account for the year to 31 October 20X4?

    A   A debit of £3,000

    B   A credit of £3,000

    C   A debit of £38,000

    D   A credit of £38,000

FIXED ASSETS AND DEPRECIATION

30 If capital expenditure is incorrectly classified as revenue expenditure, how will net profit and net assets be affected?

	Net profit	Net assets
A	Understated	Understated
B	Understated	Overstated
C	Overstated	Overstated
D	Overstated	Understated

31 What is the purpose of charging depreciation in the accounts of a business?

A   To ensure that funds are available for the eventual replacement of the asset

B   To reduce the cost of the asset in the balance sheet to its estimated market value

C   To allocate the cost of the fixed asset over the accounting periods expected to benefit from its use

D   To comply with the prudence concept

32 An asset cost £100,000. It is expected to last for ten years and have a scrap value of £10,000. What is the annual depreciation charge on this asset using the straight line basis?

33 An asset cost £100,000. It is expected to last for ten years and have a scrap value of £10,000. The company is going to depreciate this asset at 20% on the reducing balance basis. What will the depreciation charge on this asset be in its second year?

A   £14,400

B   £16,000

C   £18,000

D   £20,000

34 Esther is recording the invoice for the purchase of a new fixed asset. As well as the basic cost of the asset, the invoice shows the following items:

- delivery;

- installation;

- maintenance.

Which of the costs should be treated as revenue expenditure?

A   Delivery only

B   Installation only

C   Maintenance only

D   All of the costs

35   The opening balance on Derv plc's motor vehicles at cost account was £140,000. The opening balance on depreciation of motor vehicles was £60,000. The company purchased new vehicles costing £30,000 during the year. No vehicles were sold. The company depreciates vehicles at 25% on the reducing balance basis, with a full year's depreciation in the year of acquisition and none in the year of disposal. What is the closing balance on Derv plc's depreciation of motor vehicles account?

   _____

36   A fixed asset register is:

   A   An alternative name for the fixed asset ledger account

   B   A list of the physical fixed assets rather than their financial cost

   C   A schedule of planned maintenance of fixed assets for use by the plant engineer

   D   A schedule of the cost and other information about each individual fixed asset.

37   An organisation's fixed asset register shows a net book value of £125,600. The fixed asset account in the nominal ledger shows a net book value of £135,600.

   The difference could be due to a disposed asset not having been deducted from the fixed asset ledger:

   A   With disposal proceeds of £15,000 and a profit on disposal of £5,000

   B   With disposal proceeds of £15,000 and a net book value of £5,000

   C   With disposal proceeds of £15,000 and a loss on disposal of £5,000

   D   With disposal proceeds of £5,000 and a net book value of £5,000.

38   Jane has acquired a computer for use in her business. The invoice analyses the total amount due as follows:

	£
Basic cost of computer	2,500
Additional memory	125
Maintenance for first year	250
Total	2,875

   What is the value of Jane's capital expenditure?

   A   £2,500

   B   £2,625

   C   £2,750

   D   £2,875

39   On 1 January 20X8 Wootton Ltd has a building in its books at cost £380,000, net book value £260,000.

   On 1 July 20X8 the asset is revalued at £450,000 and Wootton wishes to include that valuation in its books. Wootton's accounting policy is to depreciate buildings at 3% straight line.

   The depreciation charged to the profit and loss account is:

   _____

CONTROL ACCOUNTS, RECONCILIATIONS AND ERRORS

40   When entering invoices in the purchase day book, Elaine recorded an invoice for £126 for motor expenses as £162. The day book has been posted to the nominal ledger.

What entry will correct the error?

A   Debit   Motor expenses   £36
              Credit Creditors control   £36

B   Debit   Creditors control   £36
              Credit Motor expenses   £36

C   Debit   Motor expenses   £288
              Credit Creditors control   £288

D   Debit   Creditors control   £288
              Credit Motor expenses   £288

41   Consider the following statements about control accounts:

(i)   Control accounts can help to speed up the preparation of draft accounts by providing the balance sheet values for debtors and creditors.

(ii)   Control accounts are always used in double entry bookkeeping.

Which of the following combinations is correct?

	(i)	(ii)
A	True	False
B	True	True
C	False	True
D	False	False

The following information relates to questions 42 and 43.
Tony sold a fixed asset with a net book value of £1,500 for £1,600. The cash received was correctly recorded in the bank account, but was credited to the sales account. Tony made no entries in the fixed asset accounts in the nominal ledger in respect of the sale.

---

42   What action should be taken to ensure that the debit and credit totals of the trial balance agree?

A   Open a suspense account with a debit balance of £1,500

B   Open a suspense account with a debit balance of £1,600

C   Open a suspense account with a debit balance of £3,100

D   A suspense account is not needed as the totals will agree

---

43 If the error is not corrected before the final accounts are prepared, how will the net profit be affected?

A   Net profit will be correct

B   Net profit will be overstated by £100

C   Net profit will be overstated by £1,500

D   Net profit will be overstated by £1,600

44 When Yvonne checked the entries in her cash book with her bank statement, seven cheques with a total value of £3,259 had not been presented at her bank. Yvonne had instructed her bank to cancel two of these cheques, but did not make any entries in her cash book. The value of the cancelled cheques is £642.

What entry should Yvonne make in the bank account in her nominal ledger to correct the balance?

A   Debit £642

B   Debit £2,617

C   Credit £642

D   Credit £2,617

The following information relates to questions 45 and 46.

Jamie is preparing a reconciliation of the balance on the purchase ledger control account in the nominal ledger to the total of the list of balances on the accounts in the purchase ledger. He has discovered the following:

(i)   a debit balance on a supplier's account was listed as a credit balance;

(ii)   an invoice for £378 was entered in the purchase day book as £387.

45 Which of the errors will require an adjustment to the purchase ledger control account in the nominal ledger?

A   Neither (i) nor (ii)

B   (i) only

C   (ii) only

D   Both (i) and (ii)

46 Which of the errors will require an adjustment to the list of balances?

A   Neither (i) nor (ii)

B   (i) only

C   (ii) only

D   Both (i) and (ii)

47 Shirley has prepared the following reconciliation of the balance on the sales ledger control account in her nominal ledger to the total of the list of balances on customers' personal accounts:

	£
Balance on nominal ledger control account	35,776
less: Balance omitted from list of balances	452
	35,324
add: Sales day book undercast	900
Total of list of balances	36,224

What is the correct balance of debtors to be reported on the balance sheet?

A   £35,324

B   £35,776

C   £36,224

D   £36,676

48 The closing balance on Frank's bank account in his nominal ledger is £2,355 (debit). How should the balance be reported in Frank's final accounts?

A   As a fixed asset

B   As a current asset

C   As a current liability

D   As a long-term liability

49 In reconciling the debtors' ledger control account with the list of debtor ledger balances of Snooks Ltd, the following errors were found:

Error 1   The sales day book had been overcast by £370.

Error 2   A total of £940 from the cash receipts book had been recorded in the debtors' ledger control account as £490.

What adjustments must be made to correct the errors?

A   Credit debtors' control account £820. Decrease total of sales ledger balances by £820

B   Credit debtors' control account £820. No change in total of sales ledger balances

C   Debit debtors' control account £80. No change in total of sales ledger balances

D   Debit debtors' control account £80. Increase total of sales ledger balances by £80

50 For the month of November 20X0 Figgins Ltd's purchases totalled £225,600 with VAT of £39,480. The total of £256,080 has been credited to the creditors' ledger control account as £260,580.

Which of the following adjustments is correct?

	Control account	List of creditors' balances
A	£4,500 Cr	No adjustment
B	£4,500 Cr	Increase by £4,500
C	£29,340 Dr	No effect
D	£33,840 Dr	Increase by £4,500

51 The total of the balances on the individual suppliers' accounts in Arnold's purchase ledger is £81,649. The balance on the trade creditors control account in his nominal ledger is £76,961. He has discovered that an invoice for £4,688 has been posted twice to the correct supplier's account and that payments totalling £1,606 which he made by standing order have been omitted from his records.

What amount should be reported in Arnold's balance sheet for trade creditors?

A £72,273

B £75,355

C £76,961

D £81,649

52 The sales ledger control account at 1 May had balances of £32,750 debit and £1,275 credit. During May, sales of £125,000 were made on credit. Receipts from debtors amounted to £122,500 and cash discounts of £550 were allowed. Refunds of £1,300 were made to customers.

The closing balances at 31 May could be:

A £35,125 debit and £3,000 credit

B £35,675 debit and £2,500 credit

C £36,725 debit and £2,000 credit

D £36,725 debit and £1,000 credit.

53 Jenny has recorded the following journal entry:

Debit   Purchases   £1,500

Credit   Stationery   £1,500

What is the correct narrative for Jenny's journal entry?

A Being cash purchase of stationery

B Being credit purchase of stationery

C Being correction of error – purchases originally recorded as stationery

D Being correction of error – stationery originally recorded as purchases

54 When the purchases day book was posted to the nominal ledger, £650 for stationery was posted to the wrong side of the stationery account.Which of the following adjustments will correct the error on the stationery account?

A A debit entry of £650

B A debit entry of £1,300

C A credit entry of £650

D A credit entry of £1,300

55 One of Dawn's customers is also a supplier. It has been agreed that balances of £1,200 between the two firms should be cancelled, but no entries have yet been made.

What journal entry should be made?

A Dr Sales £1,200

Cr Purchases £1,200

Being cancellation of sales and purchases

B Dr Sales £1,200

Cr Purchases £1,200

Being cancellation of sales and purchases

C Dr Purchases Ledger Control Account £1,200

Cr Sales Ledger Control Account £1,200

Being cancellation of amounts due to and from supplier

D Dr Sales Ledger Control Account £1,200

Cr Purchase Ledger Control Account £1,200

Being cancellation of amounts due to and from supplier

56 Which of the following statements is/are correct?

(i) A separate suspense account should be opened for each error in the ledgers.

(ii) A suspense account is sometimes opened to complete postings while more information is sought on a transaction.

A Neither (i) nor (ii)

B (i) only

C (ii) only

D (i) and (ii)

57 Norma's trial balance includes a suspense account with a credit balance of £280. She has discovered that a supplier's invoice for £140 was entered twice in the purchase day book.

What is the balance on the suspense account after this error is corrected?

A Nil

B £140 credit

C £280 credit

D £420 credit

58 When Lis extracted her trial balance, the debit total exceeded the credit total by £140. A suspense account was opened while this difference was investigated. The only error which has been discovered so far is that a debit entry for £760 has been made when posting an invoice for £670.

How will the balance on the suspense account change when this error is corrected?

A It will reduce by £1,430

B It will reduce by £760

C It will reduce by £670

D It will reduce by £90

ADJUSTMENTS TO THE TRIAL BALANCE

ACCRUALS AND PREPAYMENTS

59   You are preparing the accounts for the year to 30 April 20X4 for John Moore. In March 20X4 John damaged a table belonging to one of his customers. The customer asked John to pay £1,600 to replace the table. John offered £400, which he thought was enough to pay for repairing the table. The customer refused this offer. John agrees that the damage is his fault, and he has now received a formal quotation for the repairs. The quote is for £850.

What amount should be provided in respect of the claim when preparing the accounts for the year to 30 April 20X4?

A   No provision is needed

B   £400

C   £850

D   £1,600

60   Sybil's financial year ended on 30 November 20X2. The last invoice paid for telephone calls was for £1,800. This invoice covered the three months to 31 October 20X2.

What adjustment is required when preparing the accounts for the year to 30 November 20X2?

A   A prepayment of £600

B   A prepayment of £1,200

C   An accrual of £600

D   An accrual of £1,200

The following information relates to questions 61 and 62.

A company pays an annual insurance premium. On 1 September 20X7 it paid £6,000 for the 12 months ended 31 August 20X8. On 1 September 20X8 it paid £7,200 for the 12 months ended 31 August 20X9.

61   What is the cost of insurance for the year ended 31 December 20X8?

62   What will appear in the company's balance sheet as at 31 December 20X8 in respect of insurance?

A   Accrual £2,400

B   Accrual £4,800

C   Prepayment £2,400

D   Prepayment £4,800

63 A business compiling its accounts for the year to 31 January each year, pays rent quarterly in advance on 1 January, 1 April, 1 July and 1 October each year. After remaining unchanged for some years, the rent was increased from £24,000 per year to £30,000 per year as from 1 July 20X3.

How much is the rent expense which should appear in the profit and loss account for the year ended 31 January 20X4?

☐

64 On 1 May 20X3, Blister Ltd pays a rent bill of £1,800 for the period to 30 April 20X4. What is the charge to the profit and loss account and the entry in the balance sheet for the year ended 30 November 20X3?

A £1,050 charge to profit and loss account and prepayment of £750 in the balance sheet

B £1,050 charge to profit and loss account and accrual of £750 in the balance sheet

C £1,800 charge to profit and loss account and no entry in the balance sheet

D £750 charge to profit and loss account and prepayment of £1,050 in the balance sheet

65 On 1 June 20X2, H paid an insurance invoice of £2,400 for the year to 31 May 20X3. What is the charge to the profit and loss account and the entry in the balance sheet for the year ended 31 December 20X2?

A £1,000 profit and loss account and prepayment of £1,400

B £1,400 profit and loss account and accrual of £1,000

C £1,400 profit and loss account and prepayment of £1,000

D £2,400 profit and loss account and no entry in the balance sheet

66 The electricity account for the year ended 30 June 20X3 was as follows:

	£
Opening balance for electricity accrued at 1 July 20X2	300
Payments made during the year:	
1 August 20X2 for three months to 31 July 20X2	600
1 November 20X2 for three months to 31 October 20X2	720
1 February 20X3 for three months to 31 January 20X3	900
30 June 20X3 for three months to 30 April 20X3	840

Which of the following is the appropriate entry for electricity?

	Accrued at June 20X3	*Charged to profit and loss account year ended 30 June 20X3*
A	£Nil	£3,060
B	£460	£3,320
C	£560	£3,320
D	£560	£3,420

67 At 31 March 20X3, accrued rent payable was £300. During the year ended 31 March 20X4, rent paid was £4,000, including an invoice for £1,200 for the quarter ended 30 April 20X4.

What is the profit and loss account charge for rent payable for the year ended 31 March 20X4?

A   £3,300

B   £3,900

C   £4,100

D   £4,700

68 The annual insurance premium for S Ltd for the period 1 July 20X3 to 30 June 20X4 is £13,200, which is 10% more than the previous year. Insurance premiums are paid on 1 July.

What is the profit and loss account charge for insurance for the year ended 31 December 20X3?

[   ]

69 Arlene has paid £5,520 for rent for the six-month period to 31 August 20X1.

What accrual or prepayment is required when preparing accounts for the year ended 30 June 20X1?

A   A prepayment of £920

B   A prepayment of £1,840

C   An accrual of £920

D   An accrual of £1,840

70 The last invoice Arlene received for electricity was for £1,950 and covered the three-month period to 31 May 20X1.

What accrual or prepayment is required when preparing accounts for the year ended 30 June 20X1?

A   A prepayment of £1,950

B   A prepayment of £650

C   An accrual of £1,950

D   An accrual of £650

71 The last electricity bill received by Graham was for the three-month period to 30 September 20X1. This bill was for £2,100.

What accrual or prepayment is required when preparing the accounts for the year to 30 November 20X1?

A   A prepayment of £700

B   A prepayment of £1,400

C   An accrual of £700

D   An accrual of £1,400

DEPRECIATION

The following information relates to questions 72 to 75 inclusive.

A machine that had cost of £20,000 and had accumulated depreciation of £17,200 was sold during 20X7 for £4,800. The total cost of machinery shown in the December 20X6 balance sheet was £180,000 and the related accumulated depreciation was £92,000. The company uses 10% straight line depreciation on machinery and no depreciation is charged in the year in which an asset is sold.

72   What is the balance on the accumulated depreciation account at 31/12/20X7?

        ☐

73   What is the gain or loss on disposal of the machine?

    A   A gain of £3,400

    B   A loss of £3,400

    C   A gain of £1,400

    D   A gain of £2,000

74   What is the annual depreciation for 20X7?

        ☐

75   What entries are required to record the sale of the machine in 20X7?

    A   Debit cash account with £4,800, debit the machinery account with £4,800 and credit accumulated depreciation account with £9,600

    B   Debit cash with £4,800, credit machinery with £3,400 and credit accumulated depreciation with £1,400

    C   Debit cash with £4,800, debit accumulated depreciation with £17,200 and credit machinery with £22,000

    D   Debit accumulated depreciation with £17,200, debit cash with £4,800, credit machinery with £20,000 and debit disposal with £20,000

76   Which of the following best describes the gain or loss on the disposal of a fixed asset?

    A   The amount by which management over or under chargeed depreciation for the asset

    B   The extent to which the asset's underlying value changed during its useful life

    C   The correction of forecasting errors when the asset's useful life and residual values were estimated

    D   The remaining value after depreciation has been taken into account

77   A company bought a machine on 1 October 20X2 for £52,000. The machine had an expected life of eight years and an estimated residual value of £4,000.

On 31 March 20X7, the machine was sold for £35,000. The company's year end is 31 December. The company uses the straight-line method for depreciation and it charges a full year's depreciation in the year of purchase and none in the year of sale.

What is the profit or loss on disposal of the machine?

A   Loss £13,000

B   Profit £7,000

C   Profit £10,000

D   Profit £13,000

78   At 30 September 20X2, the following balances existed in the records of Lambda:

Plant and equipment:

Cost   £860,000

Accumulated depreciation   £397,000

During the year ended 30 September 20X3, plant with a written down value of £37,000 was sold for £49,000. The plant had originally cost £80,000. Plant purchased during the year cost £180,000. It is the company's policy to charge a full year's depreciation in the year of acquisition and none in the year of sale, using a rate of 10% on the straight line basis.

What net amount should appear in Lambda's balance sheet at 30 September 20X3 for plant and equipment?

79   A business with a financial year-end 31 October buys a fixed asset on 1 July 20X3 for £126,000.

Depreciation is charged at the rate of 15% per annum on the reducing balance basis. On 30 September 20X7 the asset was sold for £54,800. It is the policy of the business to charge a proportionate amount of depreciation in both the year of acquisition and the year of disposal.

What was the loss on sale of the asset (to the nearest £)?

A   £19,792

B   £8,603

C   £7,674

D   £1,106

80   A car was purchased by a newsagent business in May 20X1 for:

	£
Cost	10,000
Road tax	150
Total	10,150

The business adopts a date of 31 December as its year end.

The car was traded in for a replacement vehicle in August 20X5 at an agreed value of £5,000.

It has been depreciated at 25% per annum on the reducing-balance method, charging a full year's depreciation in the year of purchase and none in the year of sale.

What was the profit or loss on disposal of the vehicle during the year ended December 20X5?

A Profit: £718

B Profit: £781

C Profit: £1,788

D Profit: £1,836

81 The net book value of a company's fixed assets was £200,000 at 1 August 20X2. During the year ended 31 July 20X3, the company sold fixed assets for £25,000 on which it made a loss of £5,000.

The depreciation charge for the year was £20,000. What was the net book value of fixed assets at 31 July 20X3?

```
┌──────────┐
│          │
└──────────┘
```

82 A fixed asset costing £12,500 was sold at a book loss of £4,500. Depreciation had been charged using the reducing balance, at 20% per annum since its purchase.

Which of the following correctly describes the sale proceeds and length of time for which the asset had been owned?

	Sale proceeds	*Length of ownership*
A	Cannot be calculated	Cannot be calculated
B	Cannot be calculated	Two years
C	£8,000	Cannot be calculated
D	£8,000	Two years

83 A fixed asset was purchased at the beginning of Year 1 for £2,400 and depreciated by 20% per annum by the reducing balance method. At the beginning of Year 4 it was sold for £1,200. The result of this was:

A A loss on disposal of £240.00

B A loss on disposal of £28.80

C A profit on disposal of £28.80

D A profit on disposal of £240.00.

84 A machine cost £9,000. It has an expected useful life of six years and an expected residual value of £1,000. It is to be depreciated at 30% per annum on the reducing balance basis.

A full year's depreciation is charged in the year of purchase, with none in the year of sale. During Year 4, it is sold for £3,000.

The profit or loss on disposal is:

A Loss £87

B Loss £2,000

C Profit £256

D Profit £1,200.

85 Don has sold a machine for £5,300. The machine had been bought three years previously at a cost of £10,000. At the date of sale the machine had been depreciated by £4,800.

What is the profit on disposal?

☐

BAD AND DOUBTFUL DEBTS

86 James has been advised that one of his customers has ceased trading and that it is almost certain that he will not recover the balance of £720 owed by this customer.

What entry should James make in his general ledger?

A   Dr   Debtors ledger control £720

Cr   Bad debts   £720

Being write off of bad debt

B   Dr   Bad debts   £720

Cr   Debtors ledger control   £720

Being write off of bad debt

C   Dr   Debtors ledger control £720

Cr   Bank   £720

Being write off of bad debt

D   Dr   Bank   £720

Cr   Debtors ledger control   £720

Being write off of bad debt

87 Gordon Ltd's debtors owe the company a total of £80,000 at the year end. These include £900 of long overdue debts that might still be recoverable, but for which the company has created an allowance for bad debts. The company has also made an allowance of £1,582, which is 2% of the other debtors' balances. What best describes Gordon Ltd's bad debt allowance as at its year end?

A   A specific allowance of £900 and a general allowance of £1,582

B   A specific allowance of £1,582 and a general allowance of £900

C   A specific allowance of £2,482

D   A general allowance of £2,482

88 At 31 March Sally was owed £47,744 by her customers. At the same date her allowance for doubtful debts was £3,500.

How should these balances be reported on Sally's balance sheet at 31 March?

A   £44,244 as a current asset

B   £3,500 as a current asset and £47,744 as a current liability

C   £47,744 as a current asset and £3,500 as a current liability

D   £51,244 as a current asset

The following information relates to questions 89 and 90.

Derwent plc's bad debt and allowance for bad debt account is as follows:

Bad debt and allowance for bad debt

		£			£
	Debtors	2,400	1/1/X1	Bal b/d	800
31/12/X1	Bal c/d	900	31/12/X1	Profit and loss	2,500
		3,300			3,300
			1/1/X2	Bal b/d	900

The gross amount owed by Derwent plc's debtors at 31 December 20X1 is £40,000.

89   **What is the value of bad debts that were actually discovered to be irrecoverable during the year?**

☐

90   **What debtors' figure should be shown in the balance sheet?**

   A   £35,800

   B   £36,600

   C   £39,100

   D   £39,200

91   **A company has been notified that a debtor has been declared bankrupt. The company had allowed for this doubtful debt in full. Which of the following is the correct double entry?**

	Debit	*Credit*
A	Bad and doubtful debts account	The debtor
B	The debtor	Bad and doubtful debts account
C	Allowance for doubtful debts	The debtor
D	The debtor	Allowance for doubtful debts

92   **The turnover in a company was £2 million and its debtors were 5% of turnover. The company wishes to have an allowance for doubtful debts of 4% of debtors, which would make the allowance one-third higher than the current allowance.**

   How will the profit for the period be affected by the change in allowance?

   A   Profit will be reduced by £1,000

   B   Profit will be increased by £1,000

   C   Profit will be reduced by £1,333

   D   Profit will be increased by £1,333

93 The allowance for doubtful debts in the ledger of B Ltd at 31 October 20X1 was £9,000. During the year ended 31 October 20X2, bad debts of £5,000 were written off.

Debtor balances at 31 October 20X2 were £120,000 and the company policy is to have a general allowance of 5%.

What is the charge for bad and doubtful debts in the profit and loss account for the year ended 31 October 20X2?

94 During the year ended 31 December 20X9 Follands' sales totalled £3,000,000, its debtors amounting to 4% of sales for the year.

Follands wishes to maintain its bad debt allowance at 3% of debtors, and discovers that the allowance as a result is 25% higher than it was a year before.

During the year specific bad debts of £3,200 were written off and bad debts (written off three years previously) of £150 were recovered.

What is the net charge for bad and doubtful debts for the year ended 31 December 20X9?

95 At the beginning of its accounting period a business has debtors of £13,720 after deducting a specific allowance of £350 and a general allowance against 2% of the remainder.

At the year end debtors, before any allowances, amount to £17,500. No specific allowance is to be made, but the general allowance is to be increased to 3% of debtors.

What is the charge or credit in the profit and loss account in relation to bad debts for the year?

A £525 Dr

B £175 Dr

C £105 Cr

D £99 Cr

96 A bad debt written off two years ago is unexpectedly recovered and entered in the sales ledger column in the cash book.

What adjustment, if any, will be necessary – assuming that the receipt was treated as sales ledger cash?

	Debit	*Credit*
A	Bad debts account	Sales ledger control account
B	Sales ledger control account	Bad debts account
C	Suspense account	Bad debts account
D	No adjustment will be necessary	

97 An increase in the allowance for doubtful debts results in:

A A decrease in current liabilities

B An increase in net profit

C An increase in working capital

D A decrease in working capital.

98 **At 30 September 20X4, Z Ltd had an allowance for doubtful debts of £37,000.**

During the year ended 30 September 20X5 the company wrote off debts totalling £18,000, and at the end of the year it is decided that the allowance for doubtful debts should be £20,000.

What should be included in the profit and loss account for bad and doubtful debts?

A £35,000 debit

B £1,000 debit

C £38,000 debit

D £1,000 credit

CLOSING STOCK (AND STOCK VALUATION)

99 **LMN plc has just published its financial statements, which show a gross profit for the year of £6.5 million. A major error in the stock valuation has just been discovered. The opening stock is overstated by £1.3 million, and the closing stock has been understated by £1.6 million. What should be LMN plc's correct gross profit for the year?**

A £3.5m

B £6.2m

C £6.8m

D £9.4m

100 **Nigel has closing stock which cost £38,750. This includes some damaged items which cost £3,660.**

It will cost Nigel £450 to repair these. He will be able to sell them for £1,500 after the repairs are completed.

What is the correct value of Nigel's closing stock?

A £35,090

B £36,140

C £36,590

D £38,750

101 **Kieron is an antiques dealer. His stock includes a clock which cost £15,800.**

Kieron expects to spend £700 on repairing the clock which will mean that he will be able to sell it for £26,000.

At what value should the clock be included in Kieron's stock?

A £15,100

B £15,800

C £25,300

D £26,000

102 Colin made a mistake in his calculations which resulted in the value of his closing stock at 30 April 2004 being overstated by £900. The value was calculated correctly at 30 April 2005.

What was the effect of the error on the profit reported in Colin's accounts for each of the two years?

	2004	*2005*
A	Overstated by £900	Not affected
B	Overstated by £900	Understated by £900
C	Understated by £900	Not affected
D	Understated by £900	Overstated by £900

103 When she prepared her draft accounts, Wilma included her closing stock at a value of £21,870. She has just found out that some items valued at £2,150 had not been included in the calculation.

How will net profit and net assets be affected when the stock value is corrected?

	Net profit	*Net assets*
A	Reduced by £2,150	Reduced by £2,150
B	Reduced by £2,150	Increased by £2,150
C	Increased by £2,150	Reduced by £2,150
D	Increased by £2,150	Increased by £2,150

104 Ossie is completing his extended trial balance.

Into which columns should he extend the entries for closing stock?

	Profit and loss columns	*Balance sheet columns*
A	Debit	Debit
B	Debit	Credit
C	Credit	Debit
D	Credit	Credit

105 Percy Pilbeam is a book wholesaler. On each sale, commission of 4% is payable to the selling agent.

The following information is available in respect of total stocks of three of his most popular titles at his financial year-end:

	Cost £	*Selling price* £
Henry VII – Shakespeare	2,280	2,900
Dissuasion – Jane Armstrong-Siddeley	4,080	4,000
Pilgrim's Painful Progress – John Bunion	1,280	1,300

What is the total value of these stocks in Percy's balance sheet?

106 Suresh & co sell three products — Basic, Super and Luxury. The following information was available at the year end:

	Basic £ per unit	Super £ per unit	Luxury £ per unit
Original cost	6	9	18
Estimated selling price	9	12	15
Selling and distribution costs	1	4	5
	Units	Units	Units
Units in stock	200	250	150

The value of stock at the year end should be:

A £4,200

B £4,700

C £5,700

D £6,150.

107 Arlene valued her stock at 30 June 20X1 at its cost of £22,960. This includes some items that cost £1,950 which have been hard to sell. Arlene intends to have these items repacked at a cost of £400. She can then sell them for £900.

What will be the value of closing stock in Arlene's accounts at 30 June 20X1?

A £22,960

B £21,910

C £21,510

D £21,010

108 At 30 November 20X1 Kim's stock was valued at its cost of £22,700. This includes items costing £1,300 which have been superseded by an updated design. Kim will be able to sell these items through an agent for £700. The agent's commission will be 10% of selling price.

What is the value of closing stock on 30 November 20X1?

☐

EXTENDED TRIAL BALANCE

The following information refers to questions 109 to 121.

When answering questions 109 to 121, you are to assume that you are preparing the accounts of Arnold Baker for the year to 31 October 20X2. Arnold's extended trial balance has been partially completed and is shown on the following page.

On the extended trial balance each intersection of a column and a row represents a cell. Each cell is referenced by the combination of the relevant column letter and row number. For example, the Returns Inward figure of £2,248 is located in cell B7. You should use this method to identify cells when answering questions 109 to 121.

You are not required to insert any additional figures onto the extended trial balance.

	A	B	C	D	E	F	G	H	I	J	K
1	**Arnold Baker – Trial balance as at 31 October 20X2**	Balances per ledger		Journal entries		Post TB adjustments		Profit and loss account		Balance sheet	
2		Dr	Cr	Dr	Cr	Dr	Cr	Dr	Cr	Dr	Cr
3		£	£	£	£	£	£	£	£	£	£
4											
5											
6	Sales		422,656								
7	Returns inward	2,248									
8	Purchases	271,538									
9	Returns outwards		922								
10	Stock at 1.11.X1	11,669									
11	Wages	37,010									
12	Rent	14,800									
13	Machinery repairs	1,249									
14	Advertising	7,228									
15	Electricity	7,385									
16	Stationery	1,256									
17	Telephone	4,820									
18	Motor expenses	5,576									
19	Insurance	4,285			279						
20	Website costs	936									
21	Postage	670									
22	Fixed assets at cost										
23	Machinery	210,500									
24	Motor vehicles	105,000									
25	Accumulated depreciation at 1.1.1.X1										
26	Machinery		83,270								
27	Motor vehicles		51,450								
28	Trade debtors	47,825									
29	Allowance for doubtful debts as at 1.11.X1		5,200								
30	Bank account		2,278								
31	Trade creditors		51,742								
32	Capital account as at 1.11.X1		138,477								
33	Drawings	22,000									
34											
35	Accruals										
36	Prepayments										
37	Closing stock										
38	Depreciation charge Machinery										
39	Motor vehicles										
40											
41	Totals	755,995	755,995								
42	Result for year										

109 Arnold provides for doubtful debts on the basis of the length of time the debt has been outstanding. The aged debtors analysis and the related allowances are:

Age of debt	Allowance required	Balances at 31.10.X2
Less than 30 days	Nil	£27,825
30 days to 59 days	5% of balances	£13,800
60 days and over	80% of balances	£6,200

What adjustment should be made to the allowance for doubtful debts?

A   An increase of £450

B   A decrease of £450

C   An increase of £5,650

D   A decrease of £5,650

110 Arnold charges depreciation on motor vehicles at 30% per annum on a reducing balance basis.

What is the depreciation charge for motor vehicles for the year to 31 October 20X2?

A   £15,435

B   £16,065

C   £31,500

D   £46,935

111 Arnold charges depreciation on machinery on the straight line basis over 10 years.

What is the depreciation charge for machinery for the year to 31 October 20X2?

[   ]

112 Into which cells should the following journal entry be posted?

Dr   Advertising   £400

    Cr   Trade Creditors   £400

A   D14 and E14

B   D31 and E14

C   D14 and E31

D   D31 and E31

113 Into which cells should a prepayment of rent be posted?

A   F12 and G12

B   F36 and G36

C   F36 and G12

D   F12 and G36

114   Into which cells should the entries for closing stock be posted?

    A ✗   F37 and G37

    B   H37 and K37

    C   H37 and J37

    D   I37 and K37

115   Into which cells should the entries for depreciation of motor vehicles be posted?

    A   F27 and G27

    B   F39 and G39

    C   F27 and G39

    D   F39 and G27

116   When completing the extended trial balance, which is the correct cell for the extension of the trade creditors account?

    A   H31

    B   I31

    C   J31

    D   K31

117   When completing the extended trial balance, which is the correct cell for the extension of accruals?

    A   H35

    B   I35

    C   J35

    D   K35

118   When completing the extended trial balance, which are the correct cells for the extension of closing stock?

    A   H37 and I37

    B   H37 and K37

    C   I37 and J37

    D   I37 and K37

119   When the extended trial balance on the following page is completed, which of the following is the correct extension for website costs?

    A   £657 in cell H20

    B   £657 in cell I20

    C   £1,215 in cell H20

    D   £1,215 in cell I20

120 Assume that the extended trial balance has been extended, but the result for the year has not yet been calculated.

The totals of the profit and loss account and the palance sheet columns are:

Profit and loss account		**Balance sheet**	
Dr	*Cr*	*Dr*	*Cr*
£473,954	£485,889	£172,544	£160,609

Which of the following is the correct result for the year?

A   A loss of £11,935

B   A loss of £11,944

C   A profit of £11,944

D   A profit of £11,935

121 If the extended trial balance had been completed and the result was a loss, into which cells would the result be entered?

A   H42 and J42

B   I42 and J42

C   H42 and K42

D   I42 and K42

The following information relates to questions 122 to 134.

When answering questions 122 to 134, you are to assume that you are preparing the accounts of William Hayes for the year to 31 March 20X8. William's extended trial balance has been partially completed and is shown on the following page.

On the extended trial balance, each intersection of a column and a row represents a cell. Each cell is referenced by the combination of the relevant column letter and row number. For example, the motor expenses figure of £2,850 is located in cell B12. You should use this method to identify cells when answering your questions.

Note: You are not required to insert any additional figures onto the extended trial balance.

A	B	C	D	E	F	G	H	I	J	K
William Hayes – Trial balance as at 31 March 20X8	Balances per ledger		Journal entries		Post TB adjustments		Profit and loss account		Balance sheet	
	Dr	Cr	Dr	Cr	Dr	Cr	Dr	Cr	Dr	Cr
Sales		273,000		189						✓
Returns inward	572									
Purchases	148,500									
Returns outwards		275								
Stock at 1.4.X7	9,500									
Wages	41,700									
Repairs	9,100									
Light and heat	3,700									
Stationery	1,127									
Motor expenses	2,850									
Bad debt expense	600									
Fixed assets at cost:										
Motor vehicles	22,500									
Equipment	61,950									
Accumulated depreciation at 1.4.X7										
Motor vehicles		9,844								
Equipment		22,113								
Debtors ledger control a/c	26,375									
Allowance for doubtful debts as at 1.4.X7		1,950								
Bank account	4,260									
Cash in hand	171									
Creditors ledger control account		24,400								
Capital account as at 1.4.X7		14,371								
Drawings	13,200									
Suspense		152	189							
Discount allowed										
Accountancy fees										
Closing stock										
Depreciation for year										
Accruals										
Prepayments										
Totals	346,105	346,105								
Profit for year										

122 The total sales as recorded in the Sales Day Book for December 20X7 were £27,645. During posting this had been entered as £27,456 in the Sales Account in the General Ledger.

What adjustment should be made to sales?

A   An increase of £27,645

B   A decrease of £27,645

C   An increase of £189

D   A decrease of £189

123 On 22 March 20X8, following an agreement with your client, a customer had paid £2,500 in full settlement of an outstanding balance of £2,537. The bookkeeper had correctly entered £2,500 in the cash account, and had also entered £2,537 in both the sales ledger control account and the customer's account in the sales ledger.

What adjustment should be made?

A   Dr Discount allowed £37   Cr Suspense £37

B   Dr Suspense £37   Cr Discount allowed £37

C   Dr Bad debt expenses £37   Cr Debtors ledger control £37

D   Dr Debtors ledger control £37   Cr Bad debt expense £37

124 Your client, William Hayes, has provided the following additional information:

Customers are allowed one month's credit. The Sales Ledger balances have been analysed according to the length of time the debt has been outstanding. The analysis is as follows:

Length of time debt outstanding		Allowance required
Less than 30 days	£18,205	No allowance
31 – 60 days	£4,960	5%
61 days and over	£3,210	50%

Note: A balance of £250 which has been outstanding for 70 days is regarded as irrecoverable.

What entries are required in the extended trial balance to make the required adjustment for the doubtful debts allowance?

A   £222 in cells F13 and G21

B   £222 in cells F21 and G13

C   £1,728 in cells F13 and G21

D   £1,728 in cells F21 and G13

125 Depreciation is charged as follows: motor vehicles 25% per annum, reducing balance. Equipment to be written off over seven years, on a straight line basis.

Note: A full year's depreciation is charged in the year of acquisition of an asset, but no allowance is made in the year of disposal.

What is the depreciation charge for the year?

A   £12,014

B   £3,164

C   £8,850

D   £12,656

126   Into which cells should the journal entries be posted to correct an error whereby an invoice for electricity has been charged to the motor expenses account?

   A   D10 and E10

   B   D12 and E10

   C   D12 and E12

   D   D10 and E12

127   Into which cells should a prepayment of car insurance be posted?

   A   F33 and G33

   B   F33 and G12

   C   F12 and G33

   D   F12 and G12

128   Into which cells should the entries for closing stock be posted?

   A   F30 and G30

   B   H30 and K30

   C   H30 and J30

   D   I30 and K30

129   Into which cells should the entries for depreciation of motor vehicles be posted?

   A   F31 and G31

   B   F18 and G31

   C   F18 and G18

   D   F31 and G18

130   When completing the extended trial balance, which is the correct cell for the extension of accruals?

   ☐

131   When completing the extended trial balance, which are the correct cells for the extension of closing stock?

   A   H30 and I30

   B   H30 and K30

   C   I30 and K30

   D   I30 and J30

132   When the extended trial balance is completed, which of the following is the correct extension for sales?

   A   £273,189 in cell H3

   B   £273,189 in cell I3

   C   £272,811 in cell I3

   D   £272,811 in cell H3

133   Assume that the extended trial balance has been extended, but the result for the year has not yet been calculated.

The totals of the profit and loss account and the balance sheet columns are:

Profit and loss account		Balance sheet	
Dr	*Cr*	*Dr*	*Cr*
£231,816	£281,917	£136,778	£86,677

Which of the following is the correct result for the year?

A   A loss of £50,101

B   A loss of £50,001

C   A profit of £50,001

D   A profit of £50,101

134   The extended trial balance has been completed and suppose the result was a profit. Into which cells would the result be entered?

A   H35 and J35

B   I35 and J35

C   H35 and K35

D   I35 and K35

The following information relates to questions 135 to 146.

When answering questions 135 to 146, you are to assume that you are preparing the accounts of Arnold Cathcart for the year to 31 May 20X9. Arnold's extended trial balance has been partially completed and is shown on the following page.

On the extended trial balance each intersection of a column and a row represents a cell. Each cell is referenced by the combination of the relevant column letter and row number. For example, the Stationery figure of £1,673 is located in cell B15. You should use this method to identify cells when answering your questions.

Note: You are not required to insert any additional figures onto the extended trial balance.

Arnold Cathcart – Trial balance as at 31 May 20X9	Balances per ledger		Journal entries		Post TB adjustments		Profit and loss account		Balance sheet	
	Dr	Cr	Dr	Cr	Dr	Cr	Dr	Cr	Dr	Cr
	£	£	£	£	£	£	£	£	£	£
Sales		764,000								
Returns inward	4,758									
Purchases	529,750									
Returns outward		4,256								
Stock at 1.6.X8	39,238									
Wages	93,453		5,200				8653			
Equipment repairs	16,555			2500						
Advertising	3,138									
Bad debts	1,136		750							
Electricity	9,796									
Stationery	1,673									
Vehicle expenses	12,582									
Fixed assets at cost:										
Motor vehicles	75,950									
Equipment	156,500		2500							
Accumulated depreciation at 1.6.X8										
Motor vehicles		45,570		7595						
Equipment		109,950		2345						
Debtors	112,230			750						
Allowance for doubtful debts as at 1.6.X8		4,650								
Bank account		32,573								
Cash in hand	250									
Creditors		84,877								
Capital account as at 1.6.X8		38,693								
Drawings	27,560			5,200						
Accruals										
Prepayments				✓		✓				
Closing stock							✓		✓	
Depreciation charge										
Totals	1,084,569	1,084,569								
Result for year							✓		✓	

135 In October 20X8 an invoice for £2,500 in respect of a new fork lift truck had been posted to equipment repairs. This should have been treated as capital expenditure on equipment.

Into which cells should the journal entry be posted?

A   D11 and E11

B   D19 and E19

C   D19 and E11

D   D11 and E19

136 Depreciation for the year is to be charged on the following basis:

Motor vehicles: 25% per annum, reducing balance

Equipment: To be written off over 10 years, on a straight line basis

Note: A full year's depreciation is charged in the year of acquisition of an asset, but no allowance is made in the year of disposal.

What is the depreciation charge for the year?

A   £7,595

B   £23,495

C   £15,900

D   £45,570

137 On the last day of May 20X9 stock had been valued at its cost of £38,785. This valuation includes slow moving items which had cost £7,650. It is proposed to organise a special sale to sell these goods directly to the public. The expected sale value of these goods is £5,900. The costs of organising this special sale are expected to be £690.

What is the value of closing stock?

```

```

138 The debtors' balances have been analysed according to the length of time the debt has been outstanding. The analysis is as follows:

	£
Less than 30 days	85,652
31 – 60 days	21,400
61 days and over	5,178
Total per trial balance at 31 May 20X9	£112,230

The doubtful debt allowance is calculated as follows:

Length of time debt has been outstanding	*Allowance required*
Less than 30 days	No allowance
31 – 60 days	7% of outstanding balances
61 days and over	75% of outstanding balances

A customer who had not dealt with the firm for 18 months had gone out of business in February 20X9. The customer owes Arnold Cathcart £750. None of this is expected to be recovered.

What is the additional allowance for doubtful debts?

‾‾‾‾‾‾‾‾

139 **The last invoice received for electricity was for the three months ended 30 April 20X9. On the basis of past experience the electricity bill for the three months ended 31 July 20X9 is expected to be £2,850.**

What is the accrual for electricity at 31 May 20X9?

A   £950

B   £2,850

C   £712

D   £713

140 **Vehicle insurance of £2,472 for the year to 30 November 20X9 has been paid.**

What is the accrual/prepayment for vehicle insurance at 31 May 20X9?

A   £2,472 prepaid

B   £2,472 accrued

C   £1,236 prepaid

D   £1,236 accrued

141 **A customer who had not dealt with the firm for 18 months had gone out of business in February 20X9. The customer owes Arnold Cathcart £750. None of this is expected to be recovered.**

Into which cells should the journal entry to write off the bad debt be posted?

A   D13 and E23

B   D24 and E23

C   D33 and E13

D   D23 and E13

142 **When completing the extended trial balance, which is the correct cell for the extension of prepayments?**

‾‾‾‾‾‾‾‾

143 **When completing the extended trial balance, what are the correct cells for the extension of closing stock?**

A   H33 and I33

B   H33 and K33

C   I33 and J33

D   I33 and K33

144 When the extended trial balance is completed, which of the following is the correct extension for wages?

A £98,653 in cell H10

B £98,653 in cell I10

C £88,253 in cell H10

D £88,253 in cell I10

145 Assume that the trial balance has been extended and that the totals are as follows:

Profit and loss account		Balance sheet	
Dr	Cr	Dr	Cr
£738,907	£804,601	£406,621	£340,927

What is the result for the year?

A A loss of £65,694

B A loss of £65,685

C A profit of £65,694

D A profit of £65,685

146 If the result were a profit, into which cells would the result be entered?

A H40 and J40

B I40 and J40

C H40 and K40

D I40 and K40

The following information relates to questions 147 to 151.

The following trial balance has been extracted from the books of T Ltd as at 30 June 20X8.

	£	£
Administrative costs	19,000 ✓	
Bank overdraft		800
Cost of sales	166,900 ✓	
Fixed assets (cost)	540,000	
Fixed assets (depreciation)	~~150,000~~ ✓	150 000
Loan (repayable 20Y5)		100,000
Profit and loss		37,000
Purchase ledger control	~~19,200~~	19200
Sales		495,000
Sales ledger control	3700	37,00
Selling expenses	19,200	
Share capital		70,000
Stock as at 30 June 20X8	15,100	
Suspense	111 800	~~192,400~~
	932,200	932,200
	763900	875700

The directors requested an immediate investigation into the reason for the large difference in the trial balance totals and discovered the following problems:

(i)   The balance on the suspense account is the difference between the two trial balance columns.

(ii)   The company's inexperienced bookkeeper entered some of the account balances in the wrong column of the trial balance.

(iii)   The £14,000 balance on interest expense account has been omitted from the trial balance altogether.

(iv)   The depreciation charge of £60,000 has been correctly entered in the relevant fixed asset accounts, but was not debited to the cost of sales account.

(v)   The sales day book for June 20X8 was undercast by £5,000.

(vi)   A refund of £1,000 for defective stationery was debited to both the bank account and to the administration costs account.

147   Identify the balances that are on the wrong side of the trial balance.

A   Bank overdraft, fixed assets (cost), purchase ledger control

B   Cost of sales, loan, sales ledger control

C   Fixed assets (depreciation), sales, share capital

D   Fixed assets (depreciation), purchase ledger control, sales ledger control

148   Which of the following entries would correct the omission of the interest balance?

A   Debit interest expense, credit loan

B   Debit loan, credit interest expense

C   Debit interest expense, credit suspense

D   Debit suspense, credit interest expense

149   Which of the following entries would correct the omission of the depreciation?

A   Debit cost of sales, credit suspense

B   Debit suspense, credit cost of sales

C   Debit cost of sales, credit fixed assets (depreciation)

D   Debit fixed assets (depreciation), credit cost of sales

150   Which of the following entries would correct the undercast of the sales day book?

A   Debit sales ledger control, credit suspense

B   Debit suspense, credit sales

C   Debit sales, credit sales ledger control

D   Debit sales ledger control, credit sales

151 Which of the following entries would correct the posting error in stationery?

A   Debit administration £1,000, credit bank £1,000

B   Debit bank £1,000, credit administration £1,000

C   Debit suspense £1,000, credit administration £1,000

D   Debit suspense £2,000, credit administration £2,000

152 The trial balance of C Limited did not agree, and a suspense account was opened for the difference. Checking in the bookkeeping system revealed a number of errors:

Error

1   £4,600 paid for motor van repairs was correctly treated in the cash book, but was credited to motor vehicles asset account.

2   £360 received from Brown, a customer, was credited in error to the account of Green.

3   £9,500 paid for rent was debited to the rent account as £5,900.

4   The total of the discount allowed column in the cash book had been debited in error to the discounts received account.

5   No entries had been made to record a cash sale of £100.

Which of the errors above would require an entry to the suspense account as part of the process of correcting them?

A   Errors 3 and 4 only

B   Errors 1 and 3 only

C   Errors 2 and 5 only

D   Errors 2 and 3 only

153 The trial balance totals of Gamma at 30 September 20X3 are:

Debit   £992,640

Credit   £1,026,480

Which TWO of the following possible errors could, when corrected, cause the trial balance to agree?

Error

1   A payment of £6,160 for rent has not been entered in the accounts.

2   The balance on the motor expenses account £27,680 has incorrectly been listed in the trial balance as a credit.

3   £6,160 proceeds from the sale of a motor vehicle have been posted to the debit of motor vehicles asset account.

4   The balance of £21,520 on the rent receivable account has been omitted from the trial balance.

A   Errors 1 and 2

B   Errors 2 and 3

C   Errors 2 and 4

D   Errors 3 and 4

154 The trial balance of Delta Limited did not agree, and a suspense account was opened for the difference. The following errors were subsequently found:

Error

1 A cash refund due to customer A was correctly treated in the cash book and then credited to the sales ledger account of customer B.

2 The sale of goods to a director for £300 was recorded by debiting sales revenue account and crediting the director's current account.

3 The total of the discount received column in the cash book had been credited in error to the discount allowed account.

4 Some of the cash received from customers had been used to pay sundry expenses before banking the money.

5 £5,800 paid for plant repairs was correctly treated in the cash book and then credited to plant and equipment asset account.

Which of the above errors would require an entry to the suspense account as part of the process of correcting them?

A Errors 1, 3 and 5 only

B Errors 1, 2 and 5 only

C Errors 1 and 5 only

D Errors 3 and 4 only

155 A trial balance includes a suspense account. Opening stock of £31,763 had been entered on the credit side of the trial balance as £31,673. The trial balance itself had been undercast on the debit side by £90.

What net entry will be made in the suspense account to correct these errors?

A £63,436 Dr

B £63,436 Cr

C £63,526 Dr

D £63,526 Cr

156 A suspense account was opened when a trial balance failed to agree. The following errors were later discovered:

Error

1 A gas bill of £420 had been recorded in the Gas account as £240.

2 Discount of £50 given to a customer had been credited to Discounts Received.

3 Interest received of £70 had been entered in the bank account only.

The original balance on the suspense account was:

A Debit £210

B Credit £210

C Debit £160

D Credit £160.

157 A trial balance has been extracted and a suspense account opened. One error relates to the misposting of an amount of £200, being discounts received from suppliers, to the wrong side of the discounts account.

What will be the correcting journal entry?

A   Dr Discounts account £200, Cr Suspense account £200

B   Dr Suspense account £200, Cr Discounts account £200

C   Dr Discounts account £400, Cr Suspense account £400

D   Dr Suspense account £400, Cr Discounts account £400

158 Which of the following will not cause an entry to be made in a suspense account?

A   Drawings shown on the credit side of the trial balance

B   Discounts allowed shown on the debit side of the trial balance

C   Omission of a bad debt written off from the trial balance

D   The entry of cash in hand (£1,680) on the trial balance as £1,860

159 Jones, a sole trader, has extracted a trial balance and needs to insert a suspense account to make it balance. He has discovered the following errors:

Error
1   Opening stock of £1,475 has been listed in the trial balance as a credit balance of £1,745.
2   The sales for November (£5,390 inclusive of VAT) had been correctly entered in the control account and the sales account, but no entry had been made in the VAT account. The amount entered in the sales account was £4,600.
3   The opening accrual for telephone charges of £190 had been brought forward on the wrong side of the telephone expense account.

What was the suspense account balance that Jones inserted into the trial balance?

A   £2,050 Dr

B   £2,050 Cr

C   £2,840 Dr

D   £2,840 Cr

160 An accountant is attempting to resolve a suspense account difference. One of the errors relates to the misposting of an amount of £3,079 of VAT on purchases to the wrong side of the VAT account.

What will be the correcting entry?

A   Debit VAT account £6,158, Credit Suspense account £6,158

B   Debit Suspense account £6,158, Credit VAT account £6,158

C   Debit VAT account £3,079, Credit Suspense account £3,079

D   Debit Suspense account £3,079, Credit VAT account £3,079

161 **A suspense account shows a credit balance of £130.**

This could be due to:

A   omitting a sale of £130 from the sales ledger

B   recording a purchase of £130 twice in the purchases account

C   failing to write off a bad debt of £130

D   recording an electricity bill paid of £65 by debiting the bank account and crediting the electricity account.

162 **Kim's bookkeeper has posted an invoice for motor repairs to the motor vehicles at cost account.**

What term is used to describe this type of error?

A   Error of omission

B   Error of commission

C   Error of principle

D   Error of transposition

The following information relates to questions 163 to 165.

When answering questions 163 to 165, you are to assume that you are preparing the year end accounts of Sam Jones for the year to 30 November 20X1. Sam's extended trial balance has been partially completed and is shown at the end of this section.

You are not required to insert any additional figures onto the extended trial balance.

---

163 **Sam calculates the doubtful debts allowance on the basis of the debt's age. The analysis of debtor's balances at 30 November 20X1, and the related allowance is:**

Length of time debt has been outstanding	Allowance required	Balances at 30.11.X1 £
Less then 30 days	Nil	28,900
30 days to 59 days	8% of balances	11,700
60 days and over	75% of balances	4,900

What adjustment should be made to the allowance for doubtful debts?

A   A decrease of £589

B   An increase of £589

C   A decrease of £4,611

D   An increase of £4,611

164 **Sam charges depreciation on equipment over seven years on the straight line basis.**

What is the depreciation charge for the year ended 30 November 20X1 for equipment?

```
┌──────────┐
│          │
└──────────┘
```

---

165 Sam charges depreciation on motor vehicles at 30% per annum on the reducing balance basis.

What is the depreciation charge for the year ended 30 November 20X1 for motor vehicles?

A   £5,439

B   £5,661

C   £11,100

D   £16,761

166 When Ossie completed his extended trial balance the totals were:

Profit and loss columns		Balance sheet columns	
Debit	Credit	Debit	Credit
£	£	£	£
129,685	136,894	149,212	142,003

What is Ossie's profit or loss for the period?

A   A loss of £7,209

B   A loss of £12,318

C   A profit of £7,209

D   A profit of £12,318

FINAL ACCOUNTS

167 Which of the following items should be included in current assets?

(i)   Assets that are not intended to be converted into cash

(ii) Assets that will be converted into cash in the long term

(iii) Assets that will be converted into cash in the near future

A   (i) only

B   (ii) only

C   (iii) only

D   (ii) and (iii)

168 On 1 November 2004 Leah took out a business development loan of £30,000.

The loan is to be repaid in 10 equal six-monthly instalments. Leah made the first repayment of £3,000 on 1 May 2005.

How should the outstanding balance of £27,000 be reported on Leah's balance sheet at 31 May 2005?

	Current liability	Long-term liability
A	Nil	£27,000
B	£6,000	£21,000
C	£21,000	£6,000
D	£27,000	Nil

169 Darren is a secondhand car dealer. If a car develops a fault within 30 days of the sale, Darren will repair it free of charge.

At 30 April 2004 Darren had made a provision for repairs of £2,500. At 30 April 2005 he calculated that his provision should be £2,000.

What entry should be made for the provision in Darren's profit and loss account for the year to 30 April 2005?

A   A charge of £500

B   A credit of £500

C   A charge of £2,000

D   A credit of £2,000

170 Which one of the following statements correctly describes the difference between current liabilities and long-term liabilities?

A   Current liabilities are amounts which it is currently known must be paid, while long-term liabilities are amounts which might need to be paid in the long term

B   Current liabilities are amounts which must be paid within the next year, while long-term liabilities are amounts which must be paid in more than one year

C   Current liabilities are amounts under a certain value, while long-term liabilities are amounts greater than that value

D   Current liabilities are amounts for which there is currently a known value, while the value of long-term liabilities requires confirmation

171 Jennifer is preparing her year end accounts and she has to deal with a prepayment for rent.

Which of the following statements is correct?

A   The prepayment will increase the charge to the profit and loss account

B   The prepayment will reduce the charge to the profit and loss account

C   The prepayment has no effect on the profit and loss account

D   The prepayment will only affect the profit and loss account

172   When he prepared his draft accounts, Ralph included £1,400 as an accrual for rent for two months. However, he should have provided for only one month's rent.

How will Ralph's current liabilities be affected when he adjusts the accrual?

A   Reduced by £1,400

B   Increased by £1,400

C   Reduced by £700

D   Increased by £700

INCOMPLETE RECORDS

The following information relates to questions 173 to 177.

Carol has been in business as a freelance graphics designer for several years. She does not use the double entry system to maintain detailed bookkeeping records. Instead, she analyses cash receipts and payments on a spreadsheet. She also keeps track of the amounts due from customers and owing to creditors by means of a simple computerised record.

Carol's opening balance sheet, as at 31 December 20X8, is as follows:

	Cost	Accumulated depreciation	Net book value
	£	£	£
Furniture	800	200	600
Computer	2,800	1,225	1,575
Printer	1,500	656	844
	5,100	2,081	3,019
		£	£
Current assets			
Stocks of stationery and printer consumables		550	
Debtors		800	
Bank		700	
		2,050	
Current liabilities			
Creditors		70	
			1,980
			4,999
Long-term liabilities			
Bank loan			2,400
			2,599
Capital			2,599

Carol's analysis of cash receipts and payments for the year ended 31 December 20X9 was as follows:

	Receipts £		Payments £
Received from clients	28,000	Drawings	24,000
Additional loan	2,000	Bank interest	400
		Suppliers of stationery and printer consumables	1,800
		Sundry expenses	600
	30,000		26,800

Carol's closing stock of stationery cost £900. Her debtors owed £1,300 and she owed £200 to her suppliers. Furniture is depreciated at 25% straight line and the computer and printer at 25% reducing balance.

173 **What is Carol's sales figure for the year?**

174 **What is Carol's purchases figure for the year?**

175 **What is Carol's depreciation charge for the year?**

A £755

B £805

C £1,225

D £1,275

176 **What is Carol's capital at the year end?**

177 **What is Carol's profit for the year?**

A £1,115

B £25,115

C £26,599

D £27,714

178 Pat does not keep a full set of business records, but the following information is available for the month of June 20X9:

	£
Trade debtors, 1 June 20X9	800
Trade debtors, 30 June 20X9	550
Credit sales	6,800
Cash received from debtors	6,730
Bad debt written off	40
General allowance for doubtful debts set up at 30 June 20X9	100

Assuming no other transactions, how much discount was allowed to customers during the month?

A   £240

B   £280

C   £340

D   £380

179 A business commenced with a bank balance of £3,250; it subsequently purchased goods on credit for £10,000; gross profit mark-up was 120%; half the goods were sold for cash, less cash discount of 5%; all takings were banked.

The resulting net profit was:

☐

180 There is £100 in the cash till at the year end at F Ltd, but the accountant has discovered that some cash has been stolen.

At the beginning of the year there was £50 in the cash till and debtors were £2,000. Total sales in the year were £230,000. Debtors at the end of the year were £3,000. Cheques banked from credit sales were £160,000 and cash sales of £50,000 have been banked.

How much cash was stolen during the year?

☐

181 Which of the following items should be included in the calculation of gross profit?

A   Carriage inwards

B   Carriage outwards

C   Early settlement discount allowed

D   Early settlement discount received

182 Which of the following correctly calculates cost of sales?

A   Purchases + Opening stock + Closing stock

B   Purchases – Opening stock + Closing stock

C   Purchases – Opening stock – Closing stock

D   Purchases + Opening stock – Closing stock

183 Tina is preparing her accounts for the year to 30 September 20X4 using an extended trial balance. After extending and completing the extended trial balance, the totals are:

Profit and loss columns		Balance sheet columns	
Dr	Cr	Dr	Cr
£	£	£	£
148,990	136,909	149,608	161,689

What is Tina's profit or loss for the year to 30 September 20X4?

A   Profit of £12,081

B   Loss of £12,081

C   Profit of £12,699

D   Loss of £12,699

184 In the year to 31 August 20X4 Jermaine received £29,860 from his customers. At 31 August 20X4 he was still owed £15,865. A year earlier he was owed £16,528.

What is the value of Jermaine's sales for the year to 31 August 20X4?

A   £29,197

B   £29,860

C   £30,523

D   £45,725

185 Paolo is a sole proprietor whose accounting records are incomplete. All the sales are cash sales and during the month £50,000 was banked, including £5,000 from the sale of a business car.

He paid £12,000 wages in cash from the till and withdrew £2,000 per month as drawings. The cash in the till at the beginning and end of the month was £300 and £400 respectively. There were no other payments in the month.

What were the sales for the month?

A   £58,900

B   £59,100

C   £63,900

D   £64,100

PARTNERSHIP ACCOUNTS

186 Which of the following statements is/are correct?

(i)   Salaries paid to partners should be charged to the profit and loss account.

(ii)   Each partner's current account must have a credit balance.

A   (i) only

B   (i) and (ii)

C   (ii) only

D   Neither (i) nor (ii)

187   Albert and David are in partnership, sharing profits and losses in the ratio 3:2. Under the terms of the partnership agreement, David is entitled to a salary of £8,000. The partnership profit and loss account for the year to 30 November 20X4 reported a profit of £16,000.

What is Albert's share of the profit?

A   £3,200

B   £4,800

C   £9,600

D   £11,200

The following information relates to questions 188 to 190.

Hub Design has three partners: Mary, Jenny and Agnes. The three share profits equally after interest on capital at 5% and Jenny's partnership salary of £8,000. The partners' account balances are shown below:

	Mary	Jenny	Agnes	Total
Capital	£20,000	£15,000	£40,000	£75,000
Current	£100,000	£80,000	£110,000	£290,000
Drawings	£30,000	£35,000	£40,000	£105,000

No interest is paid on current account balances.

The net profit for the year ended 31 December 20X6 is £170,000.

188   What will the balance sheet as at 31 December 20X6 show as the total for owners' equity?

189   What will each partner receive as a share of residual profit?

190   What total profit will Jenny receive for the year ended 31 December 20X6?

Section 2

SHORT-FORM QUESTIONS

1 You have been asked to help a new trainee with questions she has regarding her studies. She had difficulty in distinguishing between capital and revenue expenditure.

Required:

Define these terms and give two examples of each. **(4 marks)**

2 A new trainee in your firm is having difficulty understanding basic accounting, in particular the distinction between assets and liabilities.

Required:

Define 'asset' and 'liability' and give one example of each. **(3 marks)**

3 A member of your staff is attending a course on finance for non-financial managers and is having difficulty in understanding the purpose of a balance sheet.

Required:

State clearly what a balance sheet shows and outline the purpose of this financial statement.
(2 marks)

4 The ASB's Statement of Principles outlines the characteristics of information as relevance, reliability, comparability and understandability.

Required:

Explain, with examples, what is meant by each of these terms. **(4 marks)**

5 Where an item of stock has a net realisable value which is less than its cost, and the NRV is used in the valuation, what accounting concept is applied? **(2 marks)**

6 A friend of yours has recently received her first set of financial accounts from her accountant for her first year of trading. She says she does not understand why on the balance sheet there are terms like accruals and prepayments.

Required:

Explain which accounting concept has been applied here and the purpose of this principle when drafting first accounts. **(3 marks)**

7   A member of your company's marketing department is concerned about the amount of information she is asked to provide each time accounts are being prepared. When you spoke to her about this, you mentioned the importance of Financial Reporting Standards and she asked you what purpose these serve.

Required:

State the basic purpose of Financial Reporting Standards.   **(2 marks)**

8   The ASB's Statement of Principles notes that that financial statements are intended to provide information to a 'wide range of users'.

Required:

Identify two different users of financial statements, and their respective needs.   **(3 marks)**

9   When preparing final accounts the principle of consistency needs to be applied so that the information possesses the characteristics of comparability.

Required:

Explain how the treatment of both stocks and depreciation need to comply with this concept.
                                                                                   (4 marks)

10   The final accounts for your company include a note which states: 'these accounts have been prepared on the going concern basis'.

Required:

Briefly explain what is meant by 'going concern basis'.   **(3 marks)**

11   You are an accounting technician working in a practice and one of your clients asks what are the main factors which cause assets to depreciate.

Required:

Briefly explain these factors giving appropriate examples for each.   **(4 marks)**

12   A friend of yours is in business as a motor mechanic and has little knowledge of accounting.

Required:

Explain how depreciation is shown in the final accounts he receives from his accountant each year-end.   **(2 marks)**

13   Your friend, the self-employed motor mechanic, has recently purchased and installed an automatic ramp. The cost of the ramp inclusive of VAT was £14,100 and installation charges were £1,645, also inclusive of VAT. The business is registered for VAT. He asks what amount he should capitalise for this transaction.

Required:

Briefly explain to him what value needs to be capitalised.   **(3 marks)**

14 You are an accounting technician working for a firm of chartered certified accountants. One of your clients uses high tech machine tools which have a short life as they soon become outdated. The client asks which method of depreciation would be suitable for these assets?

Required:

Briefly explain which method you would recommend. **(2 marks)**

15 Your friend, the self-employed motor mechanic, has recently disposed of an old set of ramps from his garage. He is unsure how he can calculate whether he has made a profit or loss on the disposal of this asset.

Required:

Briefly explain to him what factors he would need to account for in calculating the profit or loss on sale. **(4 marks)**

16 You are an accounting technician working in a practice and are currently working on a set of incomplete records. A section of the client file shows details of its opening and closing creditors, payments to creditors, discounts received and purchase returns. You need to determine the figure for purchases.

Required:

Briefly explain your procedure to determine the value of purchases. **(2 marks)**

17 You are helping a friend, a self-employed hairdresser, with her financial record keeping. You notice that she has posted the purchase of a new set of adjustable chairs for the salon to the repairs account. You bring this error to her attention.

Required:

Briefly explain what type of error this is and why it is important to correct this posting in the accounts. **(3 marks)**

18 You are currently working on a set of monthly accounts for a client who requires the figures the following day. The trial balance fails to agree by a relatively small amount.

Required:

Briefly explain what action you would take so that you could proceed to draft the set of accounts for the month end. **(2 marks)**

19 You work as an accounting technician for a small firm, transporting agricultural produce. Your manager, who is not an accountant, suggests that the business updates its accounting package. He notices that one of the features in a package, recently demonstrated by a supplier, includes the use of a sales ledger control account.

Required:

Briefly explain to him how such a control account can be an aid to management. **(3 marks)**

20 A friend of yours, in business as an hotelier, says whenever she receives a bank statement the balance rarely agrees with that shown in her cashbook.

Required:

Briefly explain the reason for such differences. **(3 marks)**

21 A new trainee in your office is working on a set of accounts for a client whose business comprises solely credit sales. The opening provision for bad debts is shown as £2,100, whereas the closing provision needs to be £1,650. Your colleague is wondering how this needs to be dealt with in the final accounts.

Required:

Briefly explain to him how this would be shown in the profit and loss account and how it would affect the balance sheet. **(2 marks)**

22 The stock sheet of a business retailing children's clothes showed a batch of summer t-shirts at a cost of £300. It seems clear that these will be later included in a sale and will be expected to realise £180.

Required:

Briefly explain at what value they should be correctly shown in the stock valuation and what principle it is based upon. **(2 marks)**

23 Your neighbour recently started his own business. He wishes to keep costs as low as possible, and intends to prepare his own year end accounts. He read that accounts should be prepared using the accruals principle, but he does not know what this means.

Required:

Briefly explain the accruals principle and how it is applied when preparing year end accounts. **(4 marks)**

24 A new trainee in your office is working on a set of accounts for a client. He is preparing the extended trial balance (ETB). A motor vehicle has been disposed of in the year and he has been given the amount of accumulated depreciation to date on the vehicle. He is unsure what entries to make on the ETB for this adjustment.

Required:

Briefly explain to him the entries that need to be made for this accumulated depreciation to date. **(3 marks)**

25 You are working on a set of incomplete records for a client whose business is based solely on credit sales. Your file contains details of opening and closing debtors, receipts from debtors, discounts allowed, bad debt written off and sales returns.

Required:

Briefly explain what procedure you would use to determine the sales figure for the year.

(2 marks)

26   A significant difference between the balance sheet of a sole trader and that of a partnership is that a partnership's balance sheet includes the partners' current accounts.

Required:

Explain what entries are made to a partner's current account and what a closing credit balance would represent.   **(2 marks)**

27   The final accounts of a sole trader showed total expenditure in excess of income, resulting in a loss for the year.

Required:

Briefly explain how this loss would affect the sole trader's capital account.   **(2 marks)**

28   A friend of yours has recently opened a children's clothes shop and is setting her selling prices. She says she does not understand the difference between the terms 'mark up' and 'margin'.

Required:

Briefly explain how mark up differs from margin.   **(2 marks)**

29   Two motor vehicles are purchased on credit. The details are as follows:

(a)   Van £12,000 + VAT at 17½%

(b)   Car £9,000 + VAT at 17½%.

Required:

Show how these would be recorded in ledger accounts by means of journal entries.

(4 marks)

30   If a customer, whose amount owing had been written off, subsequently paid later in the year, how would you account for the payment?   **(3 marks)**

31   If a company decided it needed a china coffee set to use to entertain potential customers, and it took a suitable one from the stock in the warehouse, how would you record this in the books of the company?   **(2 marks)**

32   List the details recorded in the fixed asset register in respect of fixed assets, excluding depreciation and disposals. Indicate where the relevant information may be found for the purpose of compiling the register.   **(4 marks)**

33   Work out the annual depreciation charge for five years, for a fixed asset costing £15,000, to be depreciated at a rate of 25% using the reducing balance method.   **(4 marks)**

34   Explain the difference between non-current assets and current assets.   **(4 marks)**

35   Briefly explain the purpose of the depreciation charge in the income statement.   **(2 marks)**

36   State the main reason for preparing a balance sheet.   **(2 marks)**

37   Explain the main purpose of a trial balance.   **(2 marks)**

38   Briefly explain the differences between a bad debt and a doubtful debt and the accounting treatment of each.   **(4 marks)**

39   State what is meant by the term 'accounting policies'.   **(2 marks)**

40   Explain why both a debit entry and a credit entry are used to record each transaction and give an example of a transaction and the entries required.   **(4 marks)**

41   Give three reasons why there may be a difference between the assets listed on the fixed asset register and the physical presence of assets.   **(3 marks)**

42   Give two examples of each of the following:

(i)   errors which will be detected by extracting a trial balance; and   **(2 marks)**

(ii)   errors which will NOT be detected by extracting a trial balance.   **(2 marks)**

43   Briefly describe a partner's capital account and a partner's current account, and identify one transaction which would be recorded in the capital account and one transaction which would be recorded in the current account.   **(4 marks)**

44   Identify, and briefly explain, the basic accounting principle which requires prepayments to be included in final accounts.   **(3 marks)**

45   Identify four items of data that would normally be recorded in a fixed asset register, and state why each item is required.   **(4 marks)**

Section 3

PRACTICE QUESTIONS

BASIC BOOKKEEPING

1   CAMERON FINDLAY

Cameron Findlay opens his fishing tackle shop on 1 June 20X8. During that month he notes the following business transactions:

(a)   Paid £1,500 into a business bank account.

(b)   Paid one month's rent of £230.

(c)   Purchased rods for £420, by cheque.

(d)   Purchased nets for £180, by cheque.

(e)   Sold some of the rods for £240 cash.

(f)   Purchased live bait for £10, by cheque.

(g)   Sold live bait for £16.

(h)   Purchased flies for £80, by cheque.

(i)   Paid shop assistant's wages of £95.

(j)   Sold some of the flies for £50.

(k)   Paid sundry expenses of £10.

Required:

Record the above transactions in appropriate ledger accounts and bring down a balance on each account at the end of the period.   **(15 marks)**

2   JOHN FRY AND JAYNE GARNETT

(i)   On 14 April 20X5 John Fry set up a business in which he sold frozen fish, meat and vegetable dishes from door to door in a specially adapted van. His transactions for the first two weeks of trading were as follows:

     (a)   Paid £10,000 of redundancy money into a business bank account.

     (b)   Used £3,600 to buy a second hand van by writing a cheque.

     (c)   Spent £1,700 by cheque having the van converted as a travelling deep freeze.

     (d)   Paid £400 in cash for his first assignment of frozen food.

     (e)   Received £110 of cheques and £80 of cash for sales in his first week of trading.

     (f)   Spent £260 in cash on a back up freezer in which to store additional stocks.

(g)   Paid £190 in cash for additional stock.

(h)   Received £170 of cheques and £50 of cash for sales in his second week of trading.

(i)   Paid his next door neighbour £40 in cash as wages for help in moving stock from the freezer to the van.

(j)   Withdrew £60 in cash from the business bank account as living expenses.

Required:

Fill in the boxes with the balance carried down on the following accounts:

Cash and bank account

Capital account

Van account

Purchases account

Sales account

Freezer account

Wages

Drawings

(8 marks)

Tutorial note: You may find it helpful (and useful practice) to answer this question by entering these transactions in the appropriate ledger accounts. Then calculate a balance on each ledger account.

(ii)   You are the accountant for a small retail business that has just changed ownership. The new owner, Jayne Garnett, has been examining the past two years' financial statements of the business and has enquired of you why the profit figure appears in both the balance sheet and the profit and loss account.

Required:

Write a memorandum to Jayne Garnett explaining how profit links the balance sheet and the profit and loss account.   **(7 marks)**

(Total: 15 marks)

3   ROBERT DEMPSTER

Robert Dempster runs a wholesale business supplying small medical items to chemists' shops, sports clubs and local businesses. All his transactions are on credit. His transactions in the first month of trading are listed below.

(a)   Opened a bank account in the name of Surgical Supplies and deposited £10,000.

(b)   Bought a delivery van for £4,000 from Vans Galore Ltd.

(c) Bought bandages, sticking plasters and lint from Surgiplast Ltd for £150.

(d) Sold bandages and one box of antiseptic cream to Woodside Rugby Club for £65.

(e) Paid Vans Galore £2,000 and Surgiplast Ltd £150.

(f) Received a cheque for £65 from Woodside Rugby Club.

(g) Paid Robert Dempster's private electricity bill of £130.

Required:

(i) Complete the following bank account.

Cash at bank account

		$			$
(a)	Capital	10,000	....	Vans Galore	....
....	Woodside Rugby Club	65	......	Surgiplast Ltd	
				......	
		———	(g)	....	130
		10,065		Balance c/d	....
		———			———
Balance b/d		....			10,065
					———

(5 marks)

Note that there are no entries in the bank account for items (b), (c) and as these were credit transactions.

(ii) Fill in the gaps in the following sentences to explain the principles behind the treatment of (g) above.

The ....concept is the principle underlying the treatment of the owner's private expenses paid by the business. This concept requires the transactions of a ....to be recorded separately from those of the ....of a business. Consequently, this payment could not be analysed as 'electricity' as it is not the electricity expense of the business. It may be thought of as a withdrawal of cash from the business by the owner. **(10 marks)**

(iii) Given below are a number of typical examples of business expenditure:

(a) Rent of a warehouse

(b) Purchase of premises for a factory

(c) Fitting out of the factory for production purposes

(d) Legal fees incurred in purchasing the factory

(e) Legal fees incurred in drawing up a rental contract for the warehouse

(f) Wages of the owner's son

(g) Purchase of cars in order to resell them

(h) Purchase of a car for the use of the sales manager

(i) Business rates on the warehouse

(j) Business rates on the factory

Required:

Classify each of these items as either capital expenditure or revenue expenditure.

(5 marks)

(Total: 15 marks)

4 WILSON'S BANK ACCOUNT

Wilson is preparing his bank reconciliation at 31 May 2005. His bank statement shows a balance of £228 cash at the bank. The balance on the bank account in his nominal ledger is £113 (credit).

He has noted the following reasons for the difference:

(i) Cheque number 958602 was incorrectly recorded in Wilson's cash book as £760. The cheque was correctly debited on the bank statement on 2 May as £670.

(ii) Bank charges of £428 were debited by the bank on 4 May.

(iii) A customer's cheque for £320 was returned by Wilson's bank in May as the customer had insufficient funds in his account. Wilson has not recorded the return of the cheque in his records.

(iv) The bank has incorrectly credited Wilson's account with interest of £220. This is interest on a deposit account held by Wilson personally. The bank had not corrected the error by 31 May.

(v) A lodgement of £850 entered in Wilson's cash book on 31 May was credited on the bank statement on 3 June.

(vi) Five cheques have not yet been presented at the bank. These are:

Cheque No.	Amount	
	£	
956784	625	see note (vii)
956892	326	
958452	469	
958541	22	
958668	187	
	1,629	

(vii) Cheque number 956784 was lost in the post and was cancelled. Wilson has not recorded the cancellation of the cheque.

Required:

(a) Show Wilson's nominal ledger bank account including the necessary correcting entries.

(*Note:* You MUST present your answer in a format which clearly indicates whether each entry is a debit or a credit.)   **(6 marks)**

(b) Prepare a reconciliation of the bank statement balance to the corrected nominal ledger balance.   **(7 marks)**

(c) Indicate how the bank balance will be reported in Wilson's final accounts.   **(2 marks)**

(Total: 15 marks)

5   PETER PINDO

Peter Pindo has the following transactions in his first month of trading. He is registered for VAT which is payable at a rate of 17.5%.

(a)   Peter pays £41,000 into the business bank account.

(b)   He makes sales of £3,600 on credit plus VAT.

(c)   Purchases totalling £6,674 including VAT are made for cash.

(d)   Cash sales of £2,640 plus VAT are made.

(e)   Purchases on credit of £3,200 plus VAT are made.

(f)   There are further credit sales of £3,369 plus VAT.

(g)   Cash received from debtors totalled £3,110.00.

(h)   Cash paid to suppliers totalled £2,650.00.

Required:

Record all of these transactions in the ledger accounts of Peter Pindo's business. **(15 marks)**

6   PROFIT AND LOSS ACCOUNT

Required:

Prepare a profit and loss account from the following ledger accounts by closing off the accounts and showing the resulting capital account balance carried forward. Use an initial capital introduced of £10,000 as the starting point on the capital account.

Sales account

	£		£
P&L a/c		Cash at bank account	12,000
		Debtors	43,000
	55,000		
			55,000

Purchases account

	£		£
Trade creditors	23,100	P&L a/c	
Trade creditors	8,500		
			31,600
	31,600		

Loan interest account

	£		£
Interest element of loan repayment	125	P&L a/c	
			125
	125		

Sundry expenses account

	£		£
Cash at bank account	50	Journal 1	10
	—	P&L a/c	
	50		—
	—		50

Motor expenses account

	£		£
Cash at bank account	360	P&L a/c	
	—		—
	360		360
	—		—

Wages account

	£		£
Cash at bank account	970	P&L a/c	
	—		—
	970		970
	—		—

Drawings account

	£		£
Cash at bank account	200	Capital a/c	
Cash at bank account	100		—
	—		300
	300		—
	—		

Owner's capital account

	£		£

(15 marks)

7 GRAHAM WINSTON

Graham Winston started his business on 1 March 20X5. His first month's transactions are listed below:

(1) Introduces £5,000 into the business current account and brings his van, worth £4,600 into the business.

(2) Buys goods for resale costing £3,000 on credit.

(3) Sells goods for £2,000 on credit.

(4) Sells goods for cash of £1,400.

(5) Pays wages of £120, and sundry expenses of £36.

(6) Buys goods costing £1,800 on credit.

(7)   Sells goods for £6,300 on credit.

(8)   Pays rent of £175 and motor expenses of £44.

(9)   Receives £1,500 from debtors and pays £3,000 to creditors.

(10)   Draws £300 from the bank account for his personal expenses.

Required:

(a)   Record Graham Winston's transactions in appropriate ledger accounts.

(b)   Prepare a trading and profit and loss account for the month to 31 March 20X5 and a balance sheet at that date by.

   (i)   transferring all income and expense account balances to the profit and loss account; and

   (ii)   bringing down a balance on all balance sheet accounts and presenting these in the balance sheet.

(c)   Close off the drawings account and the profit and loss account to the capital account.

(25 marks)

8   IVES LTD

Given below are the purchases day book and payments cash book for Ives Ltd for 16th February 20X5.

Purchases day book

Date	Supplier	Cheque no.	Ledger ref.	Total		VAT		Stock purchases	
16 Feb	Haworth & Sons	2261	29	223	20	33	24	189	96
	JT Liverpool	10472	41	169	32	25	21	144	11
	GL Kertin	123	38	58	48	8	70	49	78
	Slutar Ltd	CN992	55	(16)	(75)	(2)	(49)	(14)	(26)
	Moore Brothers	8816	45	117	29	17	46	99	83
	Channer Ltd	19552	23	621	74	92	59	529	15
	AKC Ltd	CN113	15	(41)	(57)	(6)	(19)	(35)	(38)
				1,131	71	168	52	963	19

Payments cash book

Date	Narrative	Cheque no.	Folio ref. (PL)	Bank		Purchases ledger		Discounts received	
16 Feb	Slutar Ltd	013971	55	118	30	118	30	6	23
	Channer Ltd	013972	23	559	29	559	29		
	Tutors & Sons	013973	59	229	35	229	35		
	E Riordan	013974	52	182	49	182	49	9	60
	Cook Associates	013975	24	60	27	60	27		
	JT Liverpool	013976	41	281	59	281	59	14	82
				1,431	29	1,431	29	30	65

You are required to write up the transactions for the day in the nominal ledger and purchases ledger accounts that are given below.

Nominal ledger accounts

Purchases

	£		£
15 Feb Balance b/d	28,890.31		

Creditors ledger control

	£		£
		15 Feb Balance b/d	17,275.49

VAT

	£		£
		15 Feb Balance b/d	1,008.37

Discounts received

	£		£
		15 Feb Balance b/d	165.27

Purchases ledger

AKC Ltd   **015**

	£		£
		15 Feb Balance b/d	118.39

Channer Ltd   **023**

	£		£
		15 Feb Balance b/d	1,072.59

Cook Associates   **024**

	£		£
		15 Feb Balance b/d	60.27

Haworth & Sons   **029**

	£		£
		15 Feb Balance b/d	471.72

GL Kertin			**038**
£			£
	15 Feb	Balance b/d	–

JT Liverpool			**041**
£			£
	15 Feb	Balance b/d	612.93

Moore Brothers			**045**
£			£
	15 Feb	Balance b/d	92.69

E Riordan			**052**
£			£
	15 Feb	Balance b/d	192.09

Slutar Ltd			**055**
£			£
	15 Feb	Balance b/d	236.71

Tutors & Sons			**059**
£			£
	15 Feb	Balance b/d	229.35

(15 marks)

9 VICTORIA LTD

Given below are the sales day book and cash receipts book for Victoria Ltd for the week ended 3 August 20X8.

Required:

Write up the nominal ledger and sales ledger accounts given from these day books.

Sales day book

Date	Invoice no.	Customer name	S/L ref.	Gross £	VAT £	Net £
July 30	5102	Cameron Ass	045	48.18	7.17	41.01
30	5103	AM McGee	027	159.30	23.72	135.58
31	5104	Peter Rover	026	142.03	21.15	120.88
Aug 1	5105	Olivia Consultants	015	82.47	12.28	70.19
1	5106	Monty Dee	003	61.48	9.15	52.33
2	5107	Roberts Partners	007	153.20	22.81	130.39
2	5108	Anna Pargeter	019	221.78	33.03	188.75
2	5109	Stephen Williams & Co	001	69.00	10.27	58.73
3	5110	Owens Ltd	036	159.36	23.73	135.63
3	5111	Clive Brown	035	62.70	9.33	53.37
				1,159.50	172.64	986.86

Receipts cash book

Date	Narrative	Folio ref.	Bank		VAT		Retail sales		Debtors		Discounts allowed	
30 July	Anna Pargeter	019	198	17					198	17	6	13
	Imogen Jones	009	73	20					73	20		
31 July	Cameron Ass	045	37	40					37	40		
	Phillipa Steven	032	116	78					116	78		
1 Aug	Owens Ltd	036	211	31					211	31	6	53
2 Aug	Monty Dee	003	73	50					73	50		
	AM McGee	027	185	31					185	31	5	23
3 Aug	Roberts Partners	007	111	62					111	62		
			1,007	29					1,007	29	17	89

Nominal ledger

Sales

	£		£
		30 July Balance b/d	24,379.20

Debtors ledger control

	£		£
30 July Balance b/d	1,683.08		

Discounts allowed

	£		£
30 July Balance b/d	138.30		

VAT

	£		£
		30 July Balance b/d	352.69

Sales ledger

	Stephen Williams & Co	**001**
	£	£
30 July Balance b/d	38.20	

	Monty Dee	**003**
	£	£
30 July Balance b/d	73.50	

	Roberts Partners	**007**
	£	£
30 July Balance b/d	279.30	

	Imogen Jones	**009**
	£	£
30 July Balance b/d	137.23	

	Olivia Consultants	**015**
	£	£
30 July Balance b/d	42.61	

	Anna Pargeter	**019**
	£	£
30 July Balance b/d	198.17	

	Peter Rover	**026**
	£	£
30 July Balance b/d	296.38	

	AM McGee	**027**
	£	£
30 July Balance b/d	335.28	

	Phillipa Steven	**032**
	£	£
30 July Balance b/d	116.78	

	Clive Brown	**035**
	£	£
30 July Balance b/d	35.10	

Owens Ltd		036
	£	£
30 July Balance b/d	512.74	

Cameron Associates		045
	£	£
30 July Balance b/d	335.28	

(15 marks)

10   MICHAEL MOORE

Below are extracts from the books of prime entry of Michael Moore.

	Purchase day book		**Sales day book**	
Suppliers of goods for resale	£	*Customers*		£
Simon	340	Jill		750
Jake	603	Vivienne		312
Francis	224	Jill		620
Simon	801	Angela		55
Francis	180	Susan		400
Joseph	75	Vivienne		370
	2,223			2,507

Cash receipts book

Details	Total	Debtors	Capital introduced	Loan	Discounts allowed
	£	£	£	£	£
Vivienne	312	312			
Proprietor	100		100		
Susan	396	396			4
Jill	620	620			
Shiretown bank	1,000			1,000	
	2,428	1,328	100	1,000	4

Cash payments book

Details	Total	Creditors	Rent	Fixed assets	Discounts received
	£	£	£	£	£
Simon	340	340			
Jake	600	600			3
Property Holdings Ltd	210		210		
Office Suppliers Ltd	950			950	
	2,100	940	210	950	3

Required:

(a) Post the totals from the day books and the cash books to the general ledger accounts. Bring down a balance on the debtors ledger control account and the creditors ledger control account. **(5 marks)**

(b) Post the individual invoices, cash receipts and payments in respect of debtors and creditors and discounts allowed and received to the debtors ledger and creditors ledger. Bring down a balance on the personal account of each debtor and creditor. **(10 marks)**

(c) Prepare a list of debtors' balances from the debtors ledger and a list of creditors' balances from the creditors ledger. **(5 marks)**

(d) Compare the lists of balances prepared in (c) with the balances on the control accounts in (a). They should agree; otherwise a reconciliation is required. **(5 marks)**

(Total: 25 marks)

11 SETTLEMENT DISCOUNTS

(i) A business receives an invoice for stock totalling £600 with a 3% settlement discount for early payment.

The same business sends an invoice to one of its customers for £900 with a 3% settlement discount if it is paid before the settlement date.

Both discounts were taken.

Required:

Using T accounts, record all the transactions above from initial invoices through to payment and dealing with the settlement discounts. Ignore VAT. **(12 marks)**

(ii) Given below are a list of typical assets that might be found in a business.

Required:

Fill in the boxes by stating whether each of these assets would be classified as a fixed asset or a current asset.

(a) Cars for use by the sales team

(b) Computers for resale

(c) Computers for use in the accounting department

(d) Monies owed by a customer

(e) Goods in the warehouse awaiting sale

(f) Office furniture

(g) Deposit held in the Bank

(3 marks)

(Total: 15 marks)

ACCOUNTING STANDARDS, PRINCIPLES AND POLICIES

12   FUNDAMENTAL CONCEPTS

The use of certain concepts is fundamental to the preparation of accounts.

The fundamental concepts are referred to as:

- the going concern concept;

- the accruals concept;

- the consistency concept; and

- the prudence concept.

You are required to explain any THREE of these concepts, using an example to identify the importance of the concept.   **(15 marks)**

13   PROBLEMS

In preparing the accounts of your company, you are faced with a number of problems. These are summarised below:

(a)   The long-term future success of the company is extremely uncertain.

(b)   One of the owners of the company has invested his drawings in some stocks and shares.

(c)   At the year end, an amount is outstanding for electricity that has been consumed during the accounting period.

(d)   All the fixed assets of the company would now cost a great deal more than they did when they were originally purchased.

(e)   During the year, the company purchased £10 worth of pencils; these had all been issued from stock and were still in use at the end of the year.

Required:

Prepare notes for each of the above points explaining:

(i)   which accounting rule the accountant should follow in dealing with each of the above problems; and

(ii)   briefly what each rule means.   **(15 marks)**

FIXED ASSETS AND DEPRECIATION

14   MEAD

Mead is a sole trader with a 31 December year end. He purchased a car on 1 January 20X3 at a cost of £12,000. He estimates that its useful life is four years, after which he will trade it in for £2,400. The annual depreciation charge is to be calculated using the straight line method.

Required:

Write up the motor car cost and provision for depreciation accounts and the depreciation expense account for the first three years, bringing down a balance on each account at the end of each year.   **(15 marks)**

15   CASTINGS AND CO LTD

(i)   The following fixed assets have been purchased, on credit, by Castings and Co Ltd.

A machine with a useful life of seven years, costing £35,000, from A Denton on 10 January 20X4. This will be located in factory number two and is given the asset number FZAD123.

On 20 April 20X4, a car with a useful life of four years from C Dealer Ltd. The cost of the car was £7,500 and it will be used by N Smith. It is to be given the asset number SICD456

All fixed assets are depreciated on a straight line basis.

Required:

Ignoring VAT, show how the purchases above would be recorded in the general ledger and the fixed asset register.   **(10 marks)**

(ii)   James Banner begins a business as a second hand book seller on 1 February 20X7. His first week's transactions are listed below:

(a)   Deposit £5,000 in a business bank account as the opening capital.

(b)   Purchase books for £600, by cheque.

(c)   Sell books for £800 cash.

(d)   Pay rent of £500, by cheque.

(e)   Buy a second hand van for £2,000, by cheque.

Required:

For each of these transactions indicate which ledger account would be debited and which would be credited in the table given below:

Transactions	Account to be debited	Account to be credited
(a)		
(b)		
(c)		
(d)		
(e)		

(5 marks)

(Total: 15 marks)

16   MILTON LTD

Milton Ltd have three machines, all of which have an estimated useful life of five years and are to be depreciated on a straight line basis. Details of the machines are given below.

Compressor XTI was purchased for £5,600 on 16 February 20X2 from Mean Machines Ltd. It is located at the Walmely factory and has a residual value of £1,000.

Scrivenor was purchased on 1 January 20X3 from Jentools plc at a cost of £11,600. It has a residual value of £1,000 and is also located at the Walmely factory.

Excelsior ZXY was purchased on 30 June 20X6 for the Chipping Norton site. It cost £7,000 and has a nil residual value.

Required:

Complete the fixed asset register showing the details that would appear for the year to 31 December 20X6.

Note: You are expected to calculate brought forward figures; assume a full year's depreciation in the year of purchase of a fixed asset.

Fixed asset register

Class/Group of assets:			
Register prepared as at close of business:			
Asset:	*1*	*2*	*3*
Acquisition date			
Further description, if any:			
Location:			
Estimated life (years):			
Estimated residual value:			
Depreciation method:			
Cost:			
Depreciation b/d:			
Current year's depreciation:			
C/d figures:			
Cost:			
Accumulated depreciation:			
(All figures to be recorded to the nearest £)			

(15 marks)

17   MEMORANDUM

Your manager wishes to ensure that clients are advised on an ongoing basis. He has asked you to advise William Hayes on the implications of the following proposed transaction.

Your client has identified an opportunity to develop his business by manufacturing certain products. For this he would need to buy a machine which will have an expected life of 10 years. He has received a quotation for the machine as follows:

Selling Price of Machine	£70,000
Delivery and Installation	£3,500
Commissioning Costs	£1,500
Annual Maintenance Costs	£3,500

Required:

(a)   Explain the difference between capital and revenue expenditure, and how each type of expenditure affects the accounts of a business.   **(6 marks)**

(b)   Indicate:

    (i)   which of the costs of the machine are capital costs, and which are revenue costs; **(4 marks)**

    (ii)   what the annual charge against profit will be.   **(3 marks)**

Note: Marks will be awarded for use of an acceptable memorandum format.   **(2 marks)**

(Total: 15 marks)

18   PURPOSE OF FIXED ASSET REGISTER

The Information Technology section of your firm is developing a software package to replace the Fixed Asset Register which is currently maintained manually. You have received the following memo requesting your assistance:

MEMO

From: Information Technology Section

To: Trainee Accountant

Re: Development of Computerised Fixed Asset Register

We are in the process of developing a software package to replace the existing Fixed Asset Register. Could you assist us by clarifying the purpose of a Fixed Asset Register and the information to be recorded in it?

It would be helpful if you could illustrate how the information is currently recorded in the ledger using the following data and assumptions:

The year end is 31 July 20X9, and the depreciation policy is that assets are depreciated at a rate of 15% per annum on the reducing balance basis. A full year's depreciation is provided in the year of acquisition of an asset, and no depreciation is provided in the year of disposal.

    ASSET 1

    Acquired   May 20X7

    Cost   £22,000

    Sold   31 May 20X9 in part exchange for Asset 2

    Part exchange value   £13,700

    ASSET 2   Amount paid by cheque: £15,800

Thank you.

Required:

(a)   Write a memo to the IT section which:

    (i)   states the purpose of a fixed asset register;   **(1 mark)**

    (ii)   indicates four items of information which would normally be included in a fixed asset register and states the purpose of each of these items of information.

(6 marks)

(b)   As an appendix to your memo prepare:

(i)   the asset cost account for the year to 31 July 20X9;   **(5 marks)**

(ii)   the provision for depreciation account for the year to 31 July 20X9;   **(4 marks)**

(iii)   the asset disposal account for the year to 31 July 20X9.   **(4 marks)**

(Total: 20 marks)

19   SARAH LUKE

Sarah Luke has recently commenced trading. She is about to purchase a machine which will cost £45,000 and wants to know how this cost will affect her profit.

Required:

In preparation for your meeting with Sarah, prepare brief notes which:

(i)   identify the concept under which depreciation is charged in the profit and loss account;

(1 mark)

(ii)   explain why this concept requires depreciation to be charged in the profit and loss account;   **(2 marks)**

(iii)   identify four methods for calculating the annual depreciation charge;   **(4 marks)**

(iv)   identify four items of information which are required to calculate the annual depreciation charge;   **(4 marks)**

(v)   indicate whether each of the following costs would be treated as capital expenditure or revenue expenditure:

•   cost of machine

•   delivery cost

•   installation cost

•   annual maintenance cost.   **(4 marks)**

(Total: 15 marks)

20   GARY CAMPBELL

(a)   Gary Campbell wants better information about the fixed assets he uses in his business. He has been told that he should keep a fixed asset register, but is unsure what this is.

Required:

(i)   Give two reasons for keeping a fixed asset register.   **(2 marks)**

(ii)   Identify four items of information which would normally be included in a fixed asset register.   **(2 marks)**

(iii)   For each of the four items of information you have identified in (ii), state why the information is required.   **(4 marks)**

(b)   Gary has also asked for a demonstration of the ledger entries which will be made when a fixed asset is traded in. He has suggested that the following data should be used:

Machine traded in:

Cost	£42,000
Depreciation to date of trade in	£25,200
Trade in value	£17,500
New machine:	
Loan raised	£26,000
Balance of cost (paid to supplier by cheque)	£8,000

Required:

(i)   What is the profit or loss on disposal of the machine traded in?   **(1 mark)**

(ii)   Show how these transactions will be recorded in the Machinery Cost account, clearly indicating whether each entry is a debit or credit entry.   **(6 marks)**

(Total: 15 marks)

21   JIM

At 1 October 20X2 Jim had fixed assets as follows:

	Land £	Buildings £	Machinery £
Cost	85,000	120,500	74,800
Accumulated depreciation	nil	28,920	35,600

Jim's policy is to provide for a full year's depreciation in the year of acquisition, but no provision is made in the year of disposal. Depreciation is provided at the following rates:

Land   Nil

Buildings   Written off over 25 years, on the straight line basis

Machinery   20% per annum, on the reducing balance basis

During the year to 30 September 20X3, Jim added an extension to the buildings at a cost of £6,800. He also acquired a new machine, by paying the dealer £9,000 by cheque and trading in an old machine for £5,500. The machine traded in had been acquired in January 20X0 at a cost of £11,000. Jim has asked why depreciation is not charged on the land, but is charged on other fixed assets.

Required:

(a)   As at 30 September 20X3, calculate:

(i)   the total value of Jim's fixed assets, before deducting depreciation;   **(3 marks)**
(ii)   the total accumulated depreciation on fixed assets;   **(4 marks)**
(iii)   the total net book value of fixed assets.   **(1 mark)**

(b)   Calculate the profit or loss on the machine which was traded in.   **(3 marks)**

(c)   Draft brief notes which explain why depreciation should be charged on the fixed assets other than land.   **(4 marks)**

(Total: 15 marks)

CONTROL ACCOUNTS, RECONCILIATIONS AND ERRORS

22   ELIZABETH

At 30 November 20X4, the balance on the debtors control account in Elizabeth's nominal ledger was £39,982. The total of the list of balances on the debtors' personal accounts was £39,614. Elizabeth has discovered the following errors:

(i)   An invoice for £288 was entered correctly in the nominal ledger, but no entry was made in the personal account.

(ii)   A payment of £1,300 was accepted in full settlement of a balance of £1,309. No entry was made to record the discount.

(iii)   A credit note issued to a credit customer for £120 was incorrectly treated as an invoice.

(iv)   An addition error on a personal account meant that the balance was understated by £27.

(v)   A customer lodged a payment of £325 directly to Elizabeth's bank account. The balance on the personal account was adjusted, but no entry was made in the nominal ledger.

(vi)   An invoice for £644 was posted as £466 in the nominal ledger.

(vii)   A credit balance of £47 on a customer's account was treated as a debit balance.

Required:

(a)   Show the debtors control account, including the necessary correcting entries and the corrected balance.   **(6 marks)**

(b)   Prepare a reconciliation of the list of balances to the corrected balance on the debtors control account.   **(7 marks)**

(c)   State the correct debtor's balance for inclusion in the final accounts and indicate where it should be reported on the balance sheet.   **(2 marks)**

(Total: 15 marks)

23   A NUMBER OF ERRORS

Given below are details of a number of errors discovered in the accounting records of an organisation. Explain the effect of each of these errors and how they should be rectified.

(a)   A payment to a creditor, M James, was incorrectly posted to the account of M Jones.

(b)   A bill from the electricity company was not entered into the purchases day book.

(c)   A credit note from a supplier was posted to the wrong side of the supplier's personal account.

(d)   The net of VAT column of the purchases day book was over cast.

(e)   The purchases ledger column of the cash payments book was under cast.

(f)   The discount received column total of the cash payments book was credited to the discounts allowed account in the nominal ledger.

(g)   A purchase invoice total has been entered into the purchases day book before deducting the trade discount.   **(21 marks)**

24   GRIFFIN LTD

The accountant of Griffin Ltd has discovered the following errors and omissions from the accounting records for the last month:

(a)   A purchase invoice from T Harris for £179.36 including VAT was entered into the personal account of Harris Ltd.

(b)   A credit note for £32.64 from ZZ Ltd for zero rated goods was entered into the purchases day book as £23.64.

(c)   An invoice from Price Ltd was omitted from the purchases day book in error. The invoice was for £168.26 plus VAT at 17.5%.

(d)   The total of the heat and light column in the purchases day book, £247.31 was incorrectly debited to the telephone account in the nominal ledger.

(e)   The total of the discount received column on one page of the purchases day book, £17.39, was not posted at all to the nominal ledger.

(f)   A contra entry is to be made for £126.37 between the purchase ledger account of T Thomas and the sales ledger account of T Thomas.

Required:

Write up the transfer journal for Griffin Ltd showing in full all of the entries required in the nominal ledger and the purchases ledger to amend these errors and omissions. The transfer journal should include a narrative explaining each of the entries. All of these errors are to be amended on 3 June 20X7.   **(18 marks)**

25   PETTY CASH

(a)   On 1 August 20X4 £73.42 of cash was put into the petty cash box to top it up to the imprest amount of £200 and on 8 August a further £114.37 was put into the box in cash. Cash payments during the week ending 7 August 20X4 were evidenced by the following vouchers.

Petty cash voucher		No.279....
Date.... *1 Aug X4* ...		
	AMOUNT	
For what required	£	p
Tea, coffee, biscuits	11	78
Signature.... *J. Small*		
Authorised. *Petty Cashier* ...		

Petty cash voucher		No.280.....
Date.... *1 Aug X4* ...		
	AMOUNT	
For what required	£	p
Taxi	3	90
Signature.... *P. Printer*		
Authorised. *Petty Cashier* ...		

Petty cash voucher		No.281....
Date.... *2 Aug X4* ...		
	AMOUNT	
For what required	£	p
Window cleaner	26	00
Signature.... *J. Small*		
Authorised. *Petty Cashier* ...		

Petty cash voucher		No.282.....
Date.... *3 Aug X4* ...		
	AMOUNT	
For what required	£	p
Client lunch (including VAT)	27	90
Signature.... *R. Illingworth*		
Authorised. *Petty Cashier* ...		

Petty cash voucher	No.283		
Date....3 Aug X4			
	AMOUNT		
For what required		£	p
Stamps		11	00
Signature....J. Small			
Authorised. Petty Cashier			

Petty cash voucher	No.284		
Date......4 Aug X4			
	AMOUNT		
For what required		£	p
Boxfiles		12	49
Paper		7	00
(inc VAT)			
Signature....T Semper			
Authorised. Petty Cashier			

Required:

Complete the petty cash book for the first week in August 20X4 by filling in the shaded boxes overleaf. **(10 marks)**

(b)   Droid Electronics Ltd operates a petty cash system with an imprest of £200 which is replenished on the last day of each month.

Required:

Describe briefly how the petty cash imprest system of Droid Electronics Ltd would operate in a typical month. (Ignore detailed authorisation procedures.)   **(5 marks)**

(Total: 15 marks)

PETTY CASH BOOK

Date 20X4	Receipts £	Voucher/ reference no	Details	Total payment £	VAT £	Office expenses £	Travel expenses £	Postage £	Stationery £	Sundry £
1 Aug	....		Balance b/d							
1 Aug	73.42		Cash from bank							
1 Aug		279	Refreshments	11 78		11 78				
1 Aug		280	Taxi	3 90			3 90			
2 Aug		281	Window cleaners	26 00		26 00				
3 Aug		282	Client lunch	....	....					......
3 Aug		283	Stamps	11 00				11 00		
4 Aug		284	Stationery	....	....				....	
4 Aug		285	Rail fare	12 00			12 00			
4 Aug		286	Stamps	2 30				2 30		
				....	....	37 78	15 90	13 30	....	......
7 Aug	200		Balance c/d	....						
				200 00						
7 Aug	....		Balance b/d							
8 Aug	....		Cash from bank							

26   STRONTIUM AND CO

Strontium and Co maintain a petty cash book on which a balance is brought down each week before topping up the imprest amount of £100. A petty cash account is also kept in the nominal ledger.

In June 20X5, the total receipts and payments in the petty cash book of Strontium and Co are:

RECEIPTS	PAYMENTS			
Cash from bank £	Total £	Cleaning £	Travel and subsistence £	Sundry expenses £
83	92	24	48	20

Required:

Show the entries that would be made in the nominal ledger in respect of:

(a)   the payments; and

(b)   the receipt

and state which book of prime entry would generally be used to make the posting.

(8 marks)

27   CONTROL ACCOUNTS

One of your colleagues has asked for your assistance. He is preparing the annual accounts for a client, but cannot agree the balances on the sales ledger and purchases ledger control accounts with the listing of the individual account balances.

The sales ledger control account balance is £35,748, while the listing of individual customer account balances is £34,874.

The purchases ledger control account balance is £22,372, while the listing of individual supplier account balances is £21,022.

His investigations have revealed the following:

(i)   A sales invoice for £2,570 had been posted to the customer's account as £2,750.

(ii)   One of the customers is also a supplier. During the year it had been agreed that balances to the value of £750 should be set off against each other. The relevant personal accounts had been updated, but no other action had been taken.

(iii)   According to the cash book discounts allowed to customers totalled £328. These amounts had been correctly posted to the personal accounts, but the total had not been posted from the cash book to the nominal ledger.

(iv)   The total value of invoices in the sales day book had been incorrectly calculated on two occasions. In one case the total was understated by £53, and on the other occasion the total had been overstated by £29.

(v)   £427 received from Spaks Ltd had been posted to the personal account of Sparks and Co.

(vi)   Goods to the value of £2,100 had been returned to a supplier, and a credit note received. The credit note had been correctly recorded in the supplier's account, but had not been recorded in the purchases returns book.

(vii) Payments made to a supplier by standing order totalling £1,800 had been omitted entirely from the records.

(viii) A balance of £279 due to a supplier had been included in the list of balances as £297.

(ix) A debit balance on a supplier's account had been listed as a credit balance. The balance was £741.

Required:

(a) Make the necessary postings to the sales ledger control account, and calculate the correct balance for inclusion in the client's annual accounts. **(6 marks)**

(b) Reconcile the listing of the individual customer account balances to the updated balance on the sales ledger control account. **(1 mark)**

(c) Make the necessary postings to the purchases ledger control account, and calculate the correct balance for inclusion in the client's annual accounts. **(5 marks)**

(d) Reconcile the listing of the individual supplier account balances to the updated balance on the purchases ledger control account. **(3 marks)**

(Total: 15 marks)

28 BANK RECONCILIATION

When preparing a bank reconciliation for a client, you have noted that:

- the balance on the bank account in the nominal ledger is £2,983 debit;

- the balance on the bank statement is £9,820 overdrawn;

- cheques totalling £2,187 have not yet been cleared by the bank;

- lodgements totalling £15,200 have not been credited by the bank;

- a cheque for £400, drawn on your client's personal account, has been debited by the bank to the business account;

- a cheque which was recorded in the cheque journal with a value of £2,870 has been correctly debited on the bank statement as £2,780;

- a customer has paid £1,500 directly to the bank account (this payment has not been recorded in your client's books);

- standing orders to a total value of £780 have been paid by the bank, but have not been recorded in your client's books;

- the bank has charged £200 for bank fees (this has not been recorded in your client's daybooks).

Required:

(a) Show the bank account as it would appear after making the necessary adjustments.

(*Note:* You must clearly indicate which entries are debits and which are credits.)

(8 marks)

(b) Prepare the bank reconciliation statement. **(7 marks)**

(Total: 15 marks)

29 JUDITH KELLY

Judith Kelly has extracted and listed the balances on her customers' personal accounts, but the total of the list does not agree with the balance on the sales ledger control account in her nominal ledger.

You have obtained the following information from an examination of her records:

(i)   the total of the list of balances is £122,409;

(ii)   the balance on the sales ledger control account in the nominal ledger is £120,539;

(iii)   an account balance of £7,540 (debit) has been included in the list as £5,740 (debit);

(iv)   goods with a value of £2,648 were returned by a customer, and a credit note was issued. The credit note was posted to the personal account, but no other entries were made;

(v)   a credit balance of £3,289 has been included in the list as a debit balance;

(vi)   Judith agreed to accept a payment of £9,000 in full settlement of a balance of £9,010 due by a customer. The balance on the personal account was cleared, but the discount has not been recorded in the nominal ledger;

(vii)   a credit balance of £500 has been omitted from the list;

(viii)   during the year, one of Judith's customers went into liquidation. The balance due (£750) was written off in the personal ledger, but no entries were made in the nominal.

Required:

(a)   Show the sales ledger control account as it would appear after making the necessary correcting entries.   **(7 marks)**

(*Note*: You must use a format which clearly indicates whether your entries are debit or credit entries.)

(b)   Show the necessary adjustments to the list of balances.   **(8 marks)**

(Total: 15 marks)

30 A CLIENT (1)

You have been completing the year end accounts of a client and have the following data:

(i)   Total creditors balances   –   per control account   £42,578
                                   –   per list of balances   £44,833

(ii)   A credit note for £372 has been received from a supplier but has not been recorded in the Purchases Returns Book.

(iii)   A credit balance of £2,597 has been included in the list of balances as £2,579.

(iv)   Standing order payments to a supplier totalling £3,000 have not been recorded in the cash book.

(v)   An account with a debit balance of £700 has been included in the list of balances as a credit balance.

(vi)   A supplier has agreed to write off a balance of £27 as discount. The necessary entry has been made in the supplier's account, but no other entry has been made.

(vii)   An error was made in totalling the invoices in the purchases day book. The total was undercast by £900.

Required:

(a) Complete the following Creditors Control Account, incorporating the adjustments required in respect of the information above. **(5 marks)**

(b) Complete the following reconciliation of the list of the balances to the revised balance on the control account. **(4 marks)**

(Total: 9 marks)

Creditors control account

	£			£
....	....	(i)	Balance b/f	42,578
....	....	....		....
....	....			
Balance c/f	....			
	....			....

Reconciliation of the list of balances

	£	
(i) Creditors balances per list of balances		44,833
Add:		....
		....
Less:	.....	
....	......	
....	......	....
		....

---

31 SYLVIA AVERY

You are preparing accounts for Sylvia Avery for the year to 30 November 20X2. At that date, the bank current account in Sylvia's nominal ledger had a credit balance of £15,503, while the bank statement showed cash at bank of £3,628.

You have obtained the following information from an examination of Sylvia's records:

(i) A cheque paid to a supplier for £4,595 has been recorded in the nominal ledger as £5,495.

(ii) Cheques written by Sylvia in November totalling £22,865 were presented at the bank in December.

(iii) A lodgement for £5,634 made on 29 November was credited on the bank statement on 2 December.

(iv) A customer's cheque for £400 which had been lodged on 18 November was not honoured by the drawer's bank. Sylvia's bank had debited the cheque on her statement on 25 November.

(v) Standing orders with a total value of £3,600 had been debited on the bank statement during the year, but had not been included in Sylvia's records.

(vi) Included on the current account statement is a lodgement for £5,000. This should have been credited to Sylvia's deposit account.

Required:

(a)   Show the nominal ledger bank account including the necessary correcting entries.

(6 marks)

Note: You MUST present your answer in a format which clearly indicates whether your corrections are debit or credit entries.

(b)   Prepare a bank reconciliation statement as at 30 November 20X2.   **(7 marks)**

(c)   State the amount of the bank balance, which will be reported in Sylvia's Balance Sheet as at 30 November 20X2, indicating whether it will be reported as an asset or a liability.   **(2 marks)**

(Total: 15 marks)

32   TINA

The balance on the purchase ledger control account in Tina's nominal ledger is £48,395. The total of the listing of the balances in the personal ledger is £46,644.

On checking, Tina found the following reasons for the difference:

(i)   a cheque for £4,300 was paid to a supplier in full settlement of an invoice for £4,320. The discount was recorded in the personal account, but was not recorded in the nominal ledger;

(ii)   the purchase day book total for June was overcast by £90;

(iii)   the total of cheques issued to suppliers was £78,056, but was posted to the control account as £78,065;

(iv)   an invoice for £459 was entirely omitted from the books;

(v)   a credit balance of £870 on a supplier's account was included in the listing as a debit balance of £780.

Required:

(a)   Show the purchase ledger control account, including any necessary correcting entries.

(5 marks)

Note: You must use a format which clearly shows whether each entry is a debit or a credit entry.

(b)   Show the reconciliation of the listing of the balances on the personal accounts to the corrected purchase ledger control account balance.   **(5 marks)**

(c)   State the creditor's balance to be reported on Tina's balance sheet, indicating how the balance will be reported.   **(2 marks)**

(d)   Indicate three reasons why a purchase ledger control account is prepared.   **(3 marks)**

(Total: 15 marks)

33   HOWARD

Howard calculated his net profit for the year as £75,886, but is not sure how to treat the £90 (debit) balance on the suspense account. Control accounts are not maintained.

On reviewing Howard's records you note that:

(i)   a cash sale for £900 was recorded in the cash book, but no other entry was made;

(ii)   the purchase daybook was undercast by £900;

(iii)   a cheque paid to a supplier was correctly entered in the cash book as £540, but £450 was posted to the supplier's account;

(iv)   a cheque received from a customer for £11,700 was accepted in full settlement of a balance of £11,790. No entries were made for the discount;

(v)   travel expenses include a payment of £405 for Howard's holiday.

Required:

(a)   Indicate whether or not Howard's calculation of net profit was affected by each of the errors, and calculate his corrected net profit for the year.   **(8 marks)**

(b)   Show Howard's suspense account including the correction of the errors.

(Note: You MUST present your answer in a format which clearly indicates whether each entry is a debit or a credit.)   **(5 marks)**

(c)   Indicate which of the errors are an example of:

- an error of transposition;

- an error of omission;

- an arithmetical error;

- an error of principle.   **(2 marks)**
                                                                (Total: 15 marks)

ADJUSTMENTS TO THE TRIAL BALANCE

ACCRUALS AND PREPAYMENTS

34   GAS, ELECTRICITY AND RENT

(a)   A company powers some of its machinery by gas. Accounts are prepared to the 30 June each year. On 1 July 20X5 there was an accrual brought down in the gas account of £650. Bills were received as follows:

Invoice date	Amount £	Quarter end to which bill relates
15.9.20X5	1,200	31.8.20X5
14.12.20X5	1,750	30.11.20X5
18.3.20X6	1,695	28.2.20X6
14.6.20X6	1,560	31.5.20X6

At 30 June 20X6 a reading was taken of the gas meter and an estimated charge for the month of June was computed at £480.

Required:

Write up a ledger account for gas and show the transfer to the profit and loss account.
                                                                (7 marks)

(b)   The electricity account for A Trader for the year ended 31 December 20X7 appears in the general ledger as:

Electricity account

20X7		£		£
8 Mar	Purchases day book	120		
7 Jun	Purchases day book	96		
10 Sep	Purchases day book	72		
8 Dec	Purchases day book	108		
		396		

The bill received after the year end is shown below:

Southern Electric				
Our Service Address is: 14 Broad Road, Hendon, London, H5 6GF			You can contact us on: Tel: 020 8623 0991 Fax: 020 8665 8761	
A Trader 22 Boundary Road London H14 5ON				1220 9/3/20X8

Meter reading		Units	Unit	Amount
Present	Previous	used	price	£
E 144202	C 143140	1062	9.51p	101.00
Standing charge		1/12/X7 TO 28/02/X8		25.00
				126.00
		VAT at 17½ %		22.05
Payment due by 15 Mar 20X8				148.05
VAT Reg No. 431 3363 81				

Required:

How much should be estimated as being the charge for electricity consumed in December? What would thus be the expense for the year?   **(4 marks)**

(c)   A business received rental income of £2,000, relating to the six months to 31 March 20X4, on 30 June 20X4. At its year end of 30 September 20X4 the next six-monthly rental of £1,500 had not been received.

Required:

Write up the ledger account for rental income for the year ended 30 September 20X4.

(4 marks)

(Total: 15 marks)

35   XY

At 1 October 20X5, the following balances were brought forward in the ledger accounts of XY:

Rent payable account	Dr	£1,500
Electricity account	Cr	£800
Interest receivable account	Dr	£300
Provision for doubtful debts account	Cr	£4,800

You are told the following:

- Rent is payable quarterly in advance on the last day of November, February, May and August, at the rate of £6,000 per annum.

- Electricity is paid as follows:

5 November 20X5	£1,000 (for the period to 31 October 20X5)
10 February 20X6	£1,300 (for the period to 31 January 20X6)
8 May 20X6	£1,500 (for the period to 30 April 20X6)
7 August 20X6	£1,100 (for the period to 31 July 20X6)

  At 30 September 20X6, the electricity meter shows that £900 has been consumed since the last bill was received.

- Interest was received during the year as follows:

  | 2 October 20X5 | £250 (for the six months to 30 September 20X5) |
  | 3 April 20X6 | £600 (for the six months to 31 March 20X6) |

  You estimate that interest of £300 is accrued at 30 September 20X6.

- At 30 September 20X6, the balance of debtors amounts to £125,000. The provision for doubtful debts is to be amended to 5% of debtors.

Required:

(a) Write up the ledger accounts for:

  (i) rent payable;

  (ii) electricity;

  (iii) interest receivable;

  (iv) provision for doubtful debts

  and bring down the balances at 30 September 20X6. **(11 marks)**

(b) State the meaning of EACH of the four balances brought down on the accounts at 30 September 20X6, AND show how they should be treated in the balance sheet at 30 September 20X6. **(4 marks)**

(Total: 15 marks)

36 RBD

The ledger of RBD & Co included the following ledger balances:

	1 June 20X0 £	31 May 20X1 £
Rents receivable: prepayments	463	517
Rent and rates payable: prepayments	1,246	1,509
accruals	315	382
Creditors	5,258	4,720
Provision for discounts on creditors	106	94

During the year ended 31 May 20X1 the following transactions had arisen:

	£
Rents received by cheque	4,058
Rent paid by cheque	7,491
Rates paid by cheque	2,805
Creditors paid by cheque	75,181
Discounts received from creditors	1,043
Purchases on credit	to be derived

Required:

Post and balance the appropriate accounts for the year ended 31 May 20X1, deriving the transfer entries to the profit and loss account where applicable. **(15 marks)**

37   PDS

PDS operates a manual bookkeeping system. An examination of the accounts paid for motor expenses reveals the following:

Petrol	(paid one month in arrears) to June X7	£1,225
	June 20X7 account received and paid July X7	£165
Car insurance	(started 1 October 20X6) for year to 30 September X7	£1,200
Car licenses	(paid September 20X6) for six months to 31 March 20X7	£80
	(paid March 20X7) for year to 31 March 20X8	£140

Servicing and repairs accounts amounted to £1,500 for work carried out and invoiced in the period to 30 June 20X7. An invoice for £350 was received in August 20X7 for work carried out in June 20X7.

You are required:

(a)   to make the appropriate entries in the motor expenses account for the year ended 30 June 20X7;

(b)   to balance off the account as at that date using an accruals account and a prepayments account;

(c)   to make the opening entries in the motor expenses account as at 1 July 20X7.

(15 marks)

DEPRECIATION

38   SPANNERS LTD

Spanners Ltd has a car it wishes to dispose of. The car cost £12,000 and has accumulated depreciation of £5,000. The car is sold for £4,000.

Required:

(a)   Work out whether there is a profit or a loss on disposal.   **(3 marks)**

(b)   Show all the entries in the general ledger T-accounts.   **(7 marks)**

(c)   Explain why an organisation charges depreciation on fixed assets and the accounting concepts and principles which govern the charging of depreciation.   **(5 marks)**

(Total: 15 marks)

39   SBJ

SBJ's fixed asset register gives the cost and depreciation to date for every fixed asset held by the company. Prior to charging depreciation for 20X4, the total net book value of all fixed assets on the register at 31 December 20X4, was £147,500.

At the same date, the fixed asset accounts in the nominal ledger showed the following balances:

	Cost	Depreciation to date
	£	£
Motor vehicles	48,000	12,000
Plant and machinery	120,000	30,000
Office equipment	27,500	7,500

You are told that:

(i) An item of plant costing £30,000 has been sold for £23,500 during 20X4. The loss on disposal was £800. No entries have been made for this disposal in the nominal ledger, but the asset has been removed from the fixed asset register.

(ii) A motor car was purchased on 1 October 20X4, and correctly recorded in the nominal ledger. Its cost was as follows:

List price of vehicle	£24,000
Trade discount	20%
VAT added at 17.5%	
Insurance	£360
Vehicle licence (road fund) tax	£130
Painting of company name	£100 (No VAT)

The vehicle has not been entered in the fixed asset register.

(iii) Office equipment was purchased during 20X4, entered on the fixed asset register, but not in the nominal ledger. Until the omission can be investigated fully, its cost is deemed to be the difference between the balances on the fixed asset register and the nominal ledger at 31 December 20X4 (prior to charging depreciation for the year).

(iv) Depreciation for 20X4 is to be charged as follows:

- on motor vehicles, at 25% per annum straight line on an actual time basis;

- on plant and machinery, at 10% per annum straight line, with a full year's depreciation in the year of purchase;

- on office equipment, at 10% per annum reducing balance, with a full year's depreciation in the year of purchase.

You are required:

(a) to calculate the correct balances at 31 December 20X4, for cost and depreciation to date on the three fixed asset accounts in the nominal ledger (prior to the charging of depreciation for 20X4);   **(11 marks)**

(b) to calculate the depreciation for each class of fixed asset for 20X4.   **(4 marks)**

(Total: 15 marks)

40   DIAMOND PLC

Diamond plc is a trading company making up its accounts regularly to 31 December each year.

At 1 January 20X5 the following balances existed in the records of Diamond plc.

	£000
Freehold land – cost	1,000
Freehold buildings – cost	500
Aggregate depreciation provided on buildings to 31.12.X4	210
Office equipment – cost	40
Aggregate depreciation provided on office equipment to 31.12.X4	24

The company's depreciation policies are as follows:

Freehold land – no depreciation.

Freehold buildings – depreciation provided at 2% per annum on cost on the straight-line basis.

Office equipment – depreciation provided at 12½% per annum on the straight-line basis.

A full year's depreciation is charged in the year of acquisition of all assets and none in the year of disposal.

During the two years to 31 December 20X6 the following transactions took place:

1   Year ended 31 December 20X5:

    (a)   10 June   Office equipment purchased for £16,000. This equipment was to replace some old items which were given in part exchange. Their agreed part exchange value was £4,000. They had originally cost £8,000 and their book value was £1,000. The company paid the balance of £12,000 in cash.

    (b)   8 October   An extension was made to the building at a cost of £50,000.

2   Year ended 31 December 20X6:

    1 March   Office equipment which had cost £8,000 and with a written-down value of £2,000 was sold for £3,000.

Required:

Write up the necessary ledger accounts to record these transactions for the *two* years ended 31 December 20X6. (Separate cost and aggregate depreciation accounts are required – you should *not* combine cost and depreciation in a single account.)

(15 marks)

41   A CLIENT (2)

You are finalising the accounts of a client for the year to 30 April 20X4. During the year the client acquired a new motor vehicle. In the working papers you note the following:

- The new motor vehicle was purchased on 15 October 20X3 and was financed by a loan of £9,000 and a trade in allowance of £10,500 on a car which had been purchased for £15,000 on 17 September 20X2.

- Depreciation on motor vehicles is provided on a straight line basis at a rate of 20% per annum.

- Assets are depreciated from the beginning of the month following their acquisition. A full month's depreciation is charged in the month of disposal of an asset.

- The balances brought forward at 1 May 20X3 were:

	Cost	Accumulated depreciation
Motor vehicles	£37,200	£15,890

Required:

(a)   Calculate the accumulated depreciation as at 15 October 20X3 on the car traded in.

(4 marks)

(b)   Calculate the profit or loss arising on the disposal of the car traded in.   **(4 marks)**

(c)   Calculate the depreciation charge on Motor Vehicles for the year to 30 April 20X4.

(4 marks)

(d)   Prepare the Motor Vehicles at Cost account for the year to 30 April 20X4.   **(5 marks)**

(Total: 17 marks)

Note: In part (d) you MUST use a format which clearly identifies the debit and credit entries.

42   DEBBIE FRASER

Debbie Fraser prepares her accounts to 31 October each year. During the year to 31 October 20X3, she traded in her old car which she had purchased in November 20X0 for £12,800. She receive a trade in allowance of £6,500 and paid a cheque for £8,200 to the dealer for the new car.

Debbie's policy is to provide for depreciation on motor vehicles at a rate of 25% per annum on the reducing balance basis. She charges a full year's depreciation in the year of purchase, and no charge is made in the year of disposal.

Required:

(a)   Calculate the amount of depreciation which will be charged in the accounts for the year to 31 October 20X3 for the new car.   **(2 marks)**

(b)   Calculate the profit or loss on the disposal of the old car.   **(4 marks)**

(c)   How will the profit or loss on the disposal of the old car be dealt with in Debbie's accounts for the year to 31 October 20X3?   **(2 marks)**

(d)   Show Debbie's motor vehicles at cost account for the year to 31 October 20X3.

   (5 marks)

   (*Note*: You must use a format which clearly indicates whether your entries are debits or credits.)

(e)   Briefly explain the difference between the reducing balance method and the straight line method of providing for depreciation.   **(2 marks)**

   (Total: 15 marks)

BAD AND DOUBTFUL DEBTS

43   DOUBTFUL DEBTS

You are given the following balances at 1 January 20X1:

Debtors	£10,000
Bank overdraft	£5,000
Provision for doubtful debts	£400

You ascertain the following information:

	£
Sales for the year 20X1 (all on credit)	100,000
Sales returns for the year 20X1	1,000
Receipts from customers during 20X1	90,000
Bad debts written off during 20X1	500
Discounts allowed during 20X1	400

At the end of 20X1 the provision for doubtful debts is required to be 5% of debtors, after making a specific provision for a debt of £200 from a customer who has gone bankrupt.

	£
Sales for the year 20X2 (90% on credit)	100,000
Sales returns for the year 20X2 (90% relating to credit customers)	2,000
Receipts from credit customers during 20X2	95,000
Debtor balances settled by contra against creditor balances during 20X2	3,000
Bad debts written off during 20X2 (including 50% of the debt due from the customer who had gone bankrupt, the other 50% having been received in cash during 20X2)	1,500
Discounts allowed during 20X2	500

At the end of 20X2 the provision for doubtful debts is still required to be 5% of debtors.

You are required to write up the debtors and provision for doubtful debts accounts for 20X1 and 20X2, bringing down the balances at the end of each year and showing in those accounts the double entry for each item. **(10 marks)**

44 BAD DEBT TRAINING

You are preparing to train a new member of staff on the topic of bad and doubtful debts. You have the following data:

Aged analysis of debtors:	£
0–30 days	42,700
31–60 days	18,728
Over 60 days	4,836
Total debtors	66,264

These balances include a balance of £900 which has been outstanding for nine months. The customer has recently ceased trading and the debt will not be recovered.

The policy is to provide for doubtful debts on the following basis:

0–30 days	1% of balances
31–60 days	25% of balances
Over 60 days	75% of balances
Provision for doubtful debts brought forward	£8,200

Required:

(a) Calculate:

    (i) the provision for doubtful debts carried forward; **(5 marks)**

    (ii) the movement in the provision for doubtful debts; **(2 marks)**

    (iii) the total charge or credit for bad and doubtful debts which will be reported in the Profit and Loss Account. **(3 marks)**

(b) Indicate and briefly explain the accounting concept under which a provision for bad and doubtful debts is made. **(3 marks)**

(c) Briefly explain what is meant by a bad debt and doubtful debt. **(2 marks)**

(Total: 15 marks)

CLOSING STOCK (AND STOCK VALUATION)

45 DEBTS AND STOCK

You are preparing the year end accounts for a client who buys and sells industrial machinery. You are dealing with bad debts and closing stock.

(a) **Bad and doubtful debts**

Included in the debtors balance is an amount of £3,574 which has been outstanding for just over a year. Your client has decided to write this balance off.

Provision for doubtful debts is to be made as follows:

6% of balances which have been outstanding for between 30 and 59 days;

50% of balances which have been outstanding for 60 days or more.

At the end of the previous year the provision for doubtful debts was £4,516.

The debtors balances, including the irrecoverable balance of £3,574, have been analysed as follows:

Age of debt	Balance
	£
Less than 30 days	36,591
30 days to 59 days	18,700
60 days and over	9,722
Total debtors	65,013

Required:

(i) Briefly explain the difference between a bad debt and a doubtful debt.

(2 marks)

(ii) Calculate the total charge to the profit and loss account for the year in respect of bad and doubtful debts and the value to be reported in the balance sheet for debtors. **(6 marks)**

(b) **Closing stock**

At the year end, your client had three machines in stock. Details of the machines are:

Machine type	Packing machine	Industrial press	Fork lift truck
	£	£	£
Cost	5,890	11,670	3,926
Expected sales value	5,500	14,900	4,200
Expenses of sale	200	475	720

Required:

(i) Briefly state the basic rule to be applied to the valuation of stock. **(2 marks)**
(ii) Calculate the value of closing stock to be reported in the balance sheet.

(5 marks)
(Total: 15 marks)

46   IMELDA FROST

(a)   Imelda Frost had debtors of £2,849 at 31 March 20X5. During the year ended 31 March 20X6 she undertakes the following transactions:

	£
Credit sales	37,088
Cash sales	3,220
Cheques received from debtors	35,764
Bad debts written off	1,217
Cheque received from a debt written off in 20X4	380

Required:

Write up the debtors ledger control account and bad debts expense account of Imelda Frost for the year to 31 March 20X6.   **(8 marks)**

(b)   Imelda has the following stock items at the year end

Item	Raw materials costs	Labour costs	Production overheads	NRV
	£	£	£	£
A	500	800	800	2,600
B	1,000	-	-	1,100
C	500	800	800	1,950

Required:

At what amount will stock be stated in the balance sheet?   **(7 marks)**

(Total: 15 marks)

47   P, Q & R

(a)   A firm buys and sells two models, P and Q. The following unit costs are available (all figures are in £s and all the costs are borne by the firm):

	P	Q
Purchase cost	100	200
Delivery costs from supplier	20	30
Delivery costs to customers	22	40
Packaging costs	15	18
Selling price	150	300

Required:

Calculate the figure to be included in closing stock for a unit of each model. **(6 marks)**

(b)   A firm has the following transactions with its product R:

Year 1

Opening stock: Nil

Buys 10 units at £300 per unit

Buys 12 units at £250 per unit

Sells 8 units at £400 per unit

Buys 6 units at £200 per unit

Sells 12 units at £400 per unit

Year 2

Buys 10 units at £200 per unit

Sells 5 units at £400 per unit

Buys 12 units at £150 per unit

Sells 25 units at £400 per unit

Required:

Calculate on an item by item basis for both Year 1 and Year 2:

(i)   the closing stock;

(ii)   the sales;

(iii)   the cost of sales;

(iv)   the gross profit

using the FIFO method of stock valuation. Present all workings clearly.   **(9 marks)**

(Total: 15 marks)

48   THOMAS BROWN AND PARTNERS

Thomas Brown & Partners, a firm of practising accountants, has several clients who are retail distributors of the Allgush Paint Spray guns.

The current price list of Gushing Sprayers Ltd, manufacturers, quotes the following wholesale prices for the Allgush Paint Spray guns:

Grade A distributors	£500 each
Grade B distributors	£550 each
Grade C distributors	£600 each

The current normal retail price of the Allgush Paint Spray gun is £750.

Thomas Brown & Partners are currently advising some of their clients concerning the valuation of stock in trade of Allgush Paint Spray guns.

(a)   **Charles Gray – Grade B distributor**

On 30 April 20X1, 15 Allgush Paint Spray guns were in stock, including one gun which was slightly damaged and expected to sell at half the normal retail price. Charles Gray considers that this gun should remain in stock at cost price until it is sold.

K Peacock, a customer of Charles Gray, was expected to purchase a spray gun on 30 April 20X1, but no agreement was reached owing to the customer being involved in a road accident and expected to remain in hospital until late May 20X1.

Charles Gray argues that he is entitled to regard this as a sale during the year ended 30 April 20X1.

(b)   **Jean Kim – Grade C distributor**

On 31 May 20X1 22 Allgush Paint Spray guns were in stock. Unfortunately Jean Kim's business is suffering a serious cash flow crisis. It is very doubtful that the business will survive and therefore a public auction of the stock is likely. Reliable sources suggest that the spray guns may be auctioned for £510 each; auction fees and expenses are expected to total £300.

Jean Kim has requested advice as to the basis upon which her stock should be valued at 31 May 20X1.

(c)   **Peter Fox – Grade A distributor**

Peter Fox now considers that stock valuations should be related to selling prices because of the growing uncertainties of the market for spray guns.

Alternatively, Peter Fox has suggested that he uses the cost prices applicable to Grade C distributors as the basis for stock valuations – 'after all this will establish consistency with Grade C distributors'.

Required:

Prepare a brief report to the partners which they can use in advising each of Charles Gray, Jean Kim and Peter Fox concerning the valuation of their stock.

Note that the report should include references to appropriate accounting concepts.

(15 marks)

49   STOCK LETTER

A client has recently received the accounts which you prepared in respect of his first year's trading. He has contacted you saying that he is concerned about the treatment of stock. He is aware that the value applied to closing stock in the accounts will affect the reported profit. He has queried how his stock has been valued, claiming that 'the profit is understated because stock will be sold for much more than the amount shown in the accounts'. From your working papers you have selected one stock item to illustrate how stock is valued. The stock movements and purchase prices for that item were:

Date	Purchases quantity	Unit price £	Sales quantity
Jan	120	17.00	
Apr	170	17.50	
May			120
June	180	17.80	
July			185
Aug	100	18.00	
Sept			120
	570		425

Required:

(a)   Calculate the closing stock value which would be included in the accounts in respect of this item using the FIFO basis.   **(3 marks)**

(b)   Prepare a letter to your client which briefly but clearly explains:

(i)   why selling price is not used to value stock;   **(2 marks)**

(ii)   the relevant accounting concept used when valuing stock;   **(4 marks)**

(iii)   how the FIFO method of valuation applies this concept to the valuation of stock;   **(2 marks)**

(iv)   how the valuation of stock affects reported profit.   **(2 marks)**

Marks are awarded for use of an acceptable letter format.   **(2 marks)**

(Total: 15 marks)

50 JAMES BARTON

James Barton has prepared draft accounts for his first three months of trading which ended on 31 May 20X1. He has asked for your advice about the valuation of his closing stock. In drafting his accounts he has valued stock at its anticipated selling price of £95 per unit. He says that he knows that this is incorrect, but as the price at which he bought the stock has changed continually this was the only constant value he could apply.

He has provided the following information about his purchases and sales:

Month	Purchases		Sales	
	Quantity (units)	Price per unit £	Quantity (units)	Price per unit £
March	1,500	62	900	95
April	1,600	65	1,200	95
May	1,900	67	2,500	95

Required:

(a)   Prepare discussion notes for a meeting with James which briefly but clearly:

- explain why stock should not be valued at selling price;   **(2 marks)**

- state the basic rule which is applied when valuing stock;   **(2 marks)**

- explain the FIFO method of valuing stock.   **(2 marks)**

(b)   Using the FIFO method, calculate the value of the closing stock.

(4 marks)

(c)   Calculate the gross profit which would be reported in James' accounts.   **(5 marks)**

(Total: 15 marks)

51 ANNE LOUGHLIN

One of your clients, Anne Loughlin, is an interior designer. At 30 November 20X2 she had some paintings and fabric in stock. She has provided the following information:

Paintings

There were three paintings in stock at 30 November.

The first was bought on 22 October 20X2 at a cost of £700. It will need to be reframed at a cost of £150. Anne is confident that she will then be able to sell it for at least £1,000.

The second was bought on 15 March 20X2 for £850. It is a certified original work by an increasingly popular artist. Other similar paintings by this artist are currently selling for over £2,500.

Anne bought the third on 10 November 20X2. She thought it was an original work and paid £900. She has now found out that it is a good copy. Similar copies are currently being sold for £400.

Fabric

Anne has one type of fabric in stock, and you have already agreed that the FIFO method should be used to value this stock.

Anne made the following purchases during November:

Date	Quantity in metres	Price per metre
11th November	200	£10.00
19th November	120	£11.00
23rd November	90	£9.50

She used the fabric as follows:

Date	Quantity in metres
14th November	180
22nd November	60
28th November	70

Anne had no fabric in stock at the beginning of November.

Required:

(a)   State, and briefly explain, the basic rule which is applied when valuing stock.

(3 marks)

(b)   Calculate the closing stock value of:

     (i)   paintings; **(4 marks)**

     (ii)   fabric. **(6 marks)**

(c)   Identify two methods other than FIFO used to value stock. **(2 marks)**

(Total: 15 marks)

EXTENDED TRIAL BALANCE

52   SAMANTHA WRIGHT

The transactions for Samantha Wright's first month of trading are listed below:

(1)   Deposited £10,000 in a business bank account.

(2)   Paid one month's rent of £140.

(3)   Bought goods for cash of £730.

(4)   Bought a van for £4,050 cash.

(5)   Sold goods on credit for £2,575.

(6)   Bought goods on credit for £1,912.

(7)   Paid wages of £370.

(8)   Sold goods on credit for £2,316.

(9)   Took £700 in drawings.

(10)   Sold goods for £380 cash.

(11)   Received £2,575 from debtors.

Required:

(a)   Record these transactions in ledger accounts and balance each account. **(10 marks)**

(b)   Prepare a trial balance from the ledger accounts. **(5 marks)**

(Total: 15 marks)

53   RAMSEY

The following figures have been extracted from the books of Ramsey as at 31 December 20X8:

	Trial balance as at 31 Dec 20X8	
	Dr	Cr
	£	£
Capital		24,860
Sales		94,360
Purchases	48,910	
Fixed assets, at cost	32,750	
Provision for depreciation		11,500
Debtors	17,190	
Bank	18,100	
Creditors		11,075
Stock at 1 Jan 20X8	8,620	
Rent	4,200	
Electricity	2,150	
Drawings	9,875	
	141,795	141,795

The following additional information is provided:

(a)   The stock at 31 December 20X8 is £9,180.

(b)   Depreciation for the year is to be charged at 10% of the cost of the fixed assets.

(c)   Rent of £300 is prepaid for 20X9.

(d)   Electricity of £250 is still owing on 31 December 20X8.

Required:

Prepare an extended trial balance for Ramsey as at 31 December 20X8 showing clearly the profit for the year.   **(15 marks)**

54   JANE SIMPSON

Jane Simpson, a retail trader, has been trying to keep her own accounting records and has extracted the following list of balances as at 30 April 20X9 from her accounts prior to the preparation of the annual accounts and balance sheet by James Lang, an accountant and your employer.

	£
Fixtures and fittings	5,000
Motor vehicles	4,000
Stock in trade	12,000
Trade debtors	7,000
Balance at bank (asset)	1,700
Trade creditors	6,900
Sales	132,000
Cost of sales	79,200
Establishment and administrative expenses	11,800
Sales and distribution expenses	33,500
Drawings	9,700
Capital	30,000

In reviewing the information, James Lang makes a number of discoveries which he passes on to you.

MEMORANDUM

From: James Lang

To: You

Date:

Subject: Accounts for Jane Simpson for year ended 30 April 20X9

Can you do some initial work on the enclosed accounts? I think there are some errors. In particular I have discovered:

(i)   an entry in the cash book for the purchase of fixtures and fittings on 1 February 20X9 costing £4,500 has not been posted to the ledger;

(ii)   a credit sale of £4,700 in March 20X9 was included correctly in the posting to the sales account, but recorded as £4,200 in the debtor's account;

(iii)   goods costing £600 withdrawn by Jane Simpson for her own use have not been recorded in the accounts. This should be treated as a reduction in the figure for purchases.

Required:

(a)   Prepare Jane Simpson's uncorrected trial balance as at 30 April 20X9, including a suspense account as the balancing figure.   **(5 marks)**

(b)   Prepare journal entries for the errors discovered.   **(6 marks)**

(c)   Prepare a new trial balance showing the corrected amounts.   **(4 marks)**

(Total: 15 marks)

55   JEFFREY

Jeffrey's trial balance at 30 September 20X4 is shown below.

	Dr £	Cr £
Capital at 1 October 20X3		30,217
Stock at 1 October 20X3	12,560	
Debtors	12,880	
Creditors and accruals		6,561
Bank	4,754	
Sales		90,560
Returns inward	375	
Purchases	72,674	
Carriage inwards	974	
Wages	4,684	
Rent	3,200	
Stationery	382	
Travel	749	
Telephone	853	
General expenses	753	
Drawings	12,500	
	127,338	127,338

The value of Jeffrey's stock at 30 September 20X4 was £11,875.

Jeffrey has discovered the following errors in the postings:

(i)   An invoice for carriage inwards was posted to the returns inwards account. The invoice was for £264.

(ii)   A credit sale invoice for £560 was posted as £650.

(iii)   The telephone bill for the three months to 30 September 20X4, which was received after the year end, has not been included. The bill is for £297.

Required:

(a)   Indicate which of the balances in the trial balance will be changed by the correction of the errors, and calculate the corrected balances.   **(6 marks)**

(b)   Based on the corrected trial balance, calculate:

        (i)   the gross profit and the net profit for the year to 30 September 20X4; **(7 marks)**

        (ii)   the capital balance at 30 September 20X4.   **(2 marks)**

                                                                     (Total: 15 marks)

FINAL ACCOUNTS

INCOMPLETE RECORDS

56   ERASMUS LTD

(a)   A bathroom fitting business has had its closing stock destroyed by fire.

        Last year's accounts showed stock to be £35,000. Sales for the year were £300,000, whilst total credit purchases were £190,000. A mark-up of 50% was applied to purchases.

        Required:

        Find the closing stock figure.   **(8 marks)**

(b)   A trial balance for Erasmus Ltd is extracted. Debit balances total £165,100; credit balances £157,590. The difference is posted to a suspense account.

        Checks are made to discover the reasons for the errors and the following errors are discovered:

        (1)   No entry has been made for a cash receipt of £600 from a debtor.

        (2)   Salaries totalling £3,600 have been posted to travelling expenses.

        (3)   A debit balance on sundry expenses, £860, has been included on the trial balance as a credit balance.

(4)   The purchases account has not been totalled correctly. The debit column should have been £345,000 and not £357,200.

(5)   Cash sales receipts have been debited to cash as £3,460 and credited to sales as £6,430. The correct amount is £4,360.

Required:

(i)   Open a suspense account and show how it can be cleared.   **(5 marks)**

(ii)   For those errors not recorded in the suspense account, state the type of error discovered.   **(2 marks)**

                                                                     (Total: 15 marks)

57 YATTON

Yatton does not keep proper books of account. You ascertain that his bank payments and receipts during the year to 31 December 20X8 were as follows:

Bank account

	£		£
Balance 1 Jan 20X8	800	Cash withdrawn	200
Cheques for sales	2,500	Purchases	2,500
Cash banked	3,000	Expenses	800
		Drawings	1,300
		Delivery van (bought 1 Oct 20X8)	1,000
		Balance 31 Dec 20X8	500
	6,300		6,300

From a cash notebook you ascertain that:

	£
Cash in hand 1 January 20X8	70
Cash takings	5,200
Purchases paid in cash	400
Expenses paid in cash	500
Cash in hand 31 December 20X8	30
Drawings by proprietor in cash	unknown

You discover that assets and liabilities were as follows:

	1 Jan 20X8 £	31 Dec 20X8 £
Debtors	300	450
Trade creditors	800	900
Expense creditors	100	150
Stock on hand	1,400	1,700

Yatton says that he has no hope of receiving an amount of £100 due from one customer and that a provision of 10% of debtors would be prudent. Depreciation on the van is to be provided at the rate of 20% per annum.

Required:

Prepare a trading and profit and loss account for the year to 31 December 20X8 and a balance sheet at that date.

(20 marks)

58   JULIE GRAY

One of your clients, Julie Gray, has prepared a draft trading and profit and loss account for her first year of trading. She knows that she has made a number of errors and has asked for your help.

Her draft trading and profit and loss account is set out below, together with some additional information:

Julie Gray
Trading and Profit and Loss Account as at 31 October 20X2

	£	£
Sales		375,680
Purchases	254,000	
Closing stock	32,580	286,580
		89,100
Expenses:		
Wages	37,600	
Motor expenses	9,780	
Telephone	4,660	
Stationery	3,590	
Advertising	15,470	
Loan costs	19,500	
Settlement discounts (net)	1,900	
Trade discounts received	(10,200)	82,300
Net profit		6,800

Additional information:

(i)   When she commenced trading, Julie purchased equipment for £75,000. She expected to use this equipment for five years, and then sell it for £5,000.

(ii)   Julie obtained a loan for the full cost of the equipment. This is being repaid over five years in equal monthly instalments of £1,625 including interest. The capital balance outstanding at 31 October 20X2 was £60,000.

(iii) Julie receives 5% trade discount on all her purchases. She has valued closing stock at cost before trade discount.

(iv) Julie has still to receive invoices from suppliers for some costs. She has included estimated amounts to 31 October 20X2 for these.

Required:

(a)   Identify FOUR errors in the draft accounts.   **(8 marks)**

(b)   Indicate how these items would appear if they had been correctly treated in the accounts.   **(4 marks)**

(c)   Show how the net profit for the year would be affected by the correction of each of the errors.   **(3 marks)**

(Total: 15 marks)

59 PETER ROBIN

You have been asked to go and help a client, Peter Robin, who set up in business on 1 April 20X7, and who is unsure whether he is recording his transactions correctly. His sales are normally for cash but he occasionally allows credit to regular customers – these sales are registered through the till when the customer pays. He pays many of his expenses in cash and then banks the remainder, leaving a float of £200.

Peter has only been keeping cash book records as he does not understand the double entry process.

His cash book for the three months to 30 June 20X7, in summary, shows the following:

Receipts	Received from sales £	Banking £	Payments	Cash £	Bank £
Per till rolls	34,164		Suppliers	12,950	6,500
Per pay-in slips		12,450	Drawings	6,000	2,000
			Wages	2,850	935
			Sundry expenses	100	

Peter is able to give you the following additional information:

- A cheque received in refund from a supplier for £450 was included in bankings but not put through the till.

- Cash in hand at 30 June 20X7 was £200.

- Customers who had received goods on credit, owed him £320 at 30 June 20X7.

Required:

(a) Balance the cash account at 30 June 20X7 (giving workings and explanations).

(10 marks)

(b) Calculate the sales for the three months to 30 June 20X7. **(2 marks)**

(Total: 12 marks)

60 MARKET TRADER

Another client who has been in business as a market trader for two years has stated that she knows that her record keeping is not as good as it should be. Nevertheless she is able to provide the following information:

- During the year to 30 April 20X8 the client's bank statements show that she lodged £65,000. This came from two sources:

  Sales for cash

  Proceeds of the sale of her husband's car   (£7,000)

- All money received was in the form of cash.

- In the same period, she paid the following expenses:

	By cheque £	In cash £
Suppliers	54,000	5,200
Motor expenses	3,985	156
Rental of premises	1,560	-
Drawings	3,600	11,700
Wages to helper	-	3,380

- She maintains a float of £500, and on a daily basis banks all cash received with the exception of the expenses noted above. Apart from these payments she makes no other payments in cash.

- Her reconciled bank balance at 30 April 20X7 was £1,500. At 30 April 20X8 her bank statement showed a balance of £3,969. On checking the statements you discover that the following cheques had not been presented:

Cheque No.	£
705834	125
705837	422
705838	67

- Her suppliers' statements show that at 30 April 20X7 she owed £3,750. At 30 April 20X8 the figure was £3,429.

- Her stock at 30 April 20X7 had cost £2,700. At 30 April 20X8 she had stock which had cost £3,500.

Required:

(a) Complete the following ledger accounts:

- cash; **(4 marks)**

- creditors; **(2 marks)**

- bank. **(3 marks)**

(b) Confirm the balance on the bank account by completing a bank reconciliation statement. **(3 marks)**

(c) Calculate the gross profit for the year to 30 April 20X8. **(3 marks)**

(Total: 15 marks)

61   TOM WEST

Tom West has been trading part time for four years as a supplier of computer software. In the past he has not completed full accounts for his business, but has simply made a return of income and expenses to the tax authorities. He wishes to prepare full accounts in future years and has provided the following information:

(i) He began trading on I July 20X5 and prepares his income and expenses figures for the year to 30 June. When he began trading he had bought computer equipment at a cost of £4,500. He estimates that computer equipment has a useful life of five years.

(ii) His income, expenses (excluding depreciation) and drawings for the three years to 30 June 20X8 were:

	Income £	Expenses £	Drawings £
Year to 30 June 20X6	1,200	400	300
Year to 30 June 20X7	3,500	1,200	1,800
Year to 30 June 20X8	5,700	2,900	2,700

Note: All income received was paid into the bank account, and all expenses and drawings were paid by cheque.

(iii) He has no costs in respect of goods for resale as the nature of his business is to create computer software to clients' specifications.

(iv) At 30 June 20X8 he still had to collect £900 from customers. At 30 June 20X9 he still had to collect £2,700.

(v)   In the year to 30 June 20X9 he had paid £14,000 into his bank account. This had been received from clients for work completed with the exception of £3,000 which was a gift from a relative.

(vi)   During the year to 30 June 20X9 he had paid the following amounts by cheque:

	£
Stationery	250
Motor Expenses	790
Electricity	560
Repairs	425
Travel	615
Office Furniture	1,400
Drawings	4,600
	8,640

(vii) Depreciation is provided on a straight line basis at the following rates:

| Computer equipment | 20% per annum |
| Office furniture | 10% per annum |

A full year's depreciation is provided in the year of acquisition of an asset.

Required:

(a)   Calculate Tom West's capital at 30 June 20X8.   **(5 marks)**

(b)   Calculate Tom West's profit for the year to 30 June 20X9.   **(6 marks)**

(c)   Prepare Tom West's Statement of Affairs as at 30 June 20X9.   **(9 marks)**

                                                                        (Total: 20 marks)

62   SIMON MEREDITH

Simon Meredith has been trading for some years. His accounting records have been destroyed, but he has been able to provide you with some information for the year ended 30 November 20X1.

*   During the year he paid £298,000 into his business bank account.

*   Apart from £25,000 introduced as additional capital, this represented payments received from his customers.

*   All receipts were paid immediately into the bank account.

*   At 30 November 20X1 he has owed £31,500 by his customers and he owed £22,700 to his suppliers.

*   His stock at 30 November 20X1 had cost £17,500.

*   During the year he issued cheques totally £295,300.

*   Apart from payments to suppliers, the cheques issued were as follows:

    –   various business expenses   £32,000

    –   purchase of a new van   £11,000

    –   drawings   £15,000

On 30 November 20X0:

- Simon was owed £29,720 by his customers.

- He owed £23,900 to his suppliers.

- His stock was valued at £16,800.

Required:

(a)   Calculate the value of Simon's sales for the year to 30 November 20X1.   **(6 marks)**

(b)   Calculate Simon's gross profit for the year to 30 November 20X1.   **(9 marks)**

(Total: 15 marks)

63   EILEEN FIRTH

Eileen Firth does not keep full accounting records, but has been able to provide the following information for the year to 30 April 20X2:

Cash received	£78,300	(all received from customers)
Cash lodged to bank	£63,300	(after drawings)
Cheques issued:		
To suppliers	£31,900	
For expenses	£22,600	
Loan Repaid	£10,000	
Bank balance at 1 May 20X1	£4,840	(overdrawn)
Stock		
at 1 May 20X1	£6,500	
at 30 April 20X2	£6,250	
Owed to suppliers		
at 1 May 20X1	£1,950	
at 30 April 20X2	£2,320	
Owed by customers		
at 1 May 20X1	£3,800	
at 30 April 20X2	£3,350	
Depreciation charge for year	£10,000	

Required:

(a)   For the year ended 30 April 20X2, calculate:

    (i)   sales;   **(2 marks)**

    (ii)   purchases;   **(2 marks)**

    (iii)   gross profit;   **(2 marks)**

    (iv)   net profit;   **(4 marks)**

    (v)   the movement in capital.   **(2 marks)**

(b)   Calculate the bank balance at 30 April 20X2.   **(3 marks)**

(Total: 15 marks)

SOLE TRADER ACCOUNTS

64 KENDAL

Kendal, a sole trader, has provided you with the following information relating to the year ended 31 December 20X5

(i)   He has not made a note of drawings or of cash received. The following items were paid from takings prior to banking:

Purchases	£760
Sundry expenses	£400

(ii) Kendal has estimated that his gross profit percentage is 20%.

(iii) His summarised bank account was as follows:

Bank account

20X5	£	20X5	£
1 Jan Balance b/d	1,700	Rent	1,000
Bankings	16,940	Electricity	235
		Purchases	16,140
		Drawings	265
		31 Dec Balance c/d	1,000
	─────		─────
	18,640		18,640
	─────		─────

(iv) Assets and liabilities were as follows:

	31 Dec 20X5 £	31 Dec 20X4 £
Stock	4,800	5,600
Debtors	1,650	2,100
Creditors		
Goods	1,940	1,640
Electricity	65	-
Cash float	2,400	170

(v)   He started paying rent in 20X5. A year's rent was paid in advance on 1 April 20X5.

Required:

(a)   Produce a statement of opening capital for Kendal at 1 January 20X5.   **(5 marks)**

(b)   Produce ledger accounts for cash, debtors control and creditors control.   **(10 marks)**

(c)   Produce a trading and profit and loss account for Kendal for the year ended 31 December 20X5 and a balance sheet at that date.   **(10 marks)**

(Total: 25 marks)

65 J PATEL

The assets and liabilities as at the close of business on 31 October 20X8 of J Patel, retailer, are summarised as follows:

	£	£
Motor vehicles		
At cost	9,000	
Provision for depreciation	1,800	
	─────	
		7,200
Fixtures and fittings		
At cost	10,000	
Provision for depreciation	6,000	
	─────	
		4,000

Stock	16,100
Trade debtors	19,630
Cash	160
	47,090
Capital – J Patel	30,910
Bank overdraft	6,740
Trade creditors	9,440
	47,090

All receipts from credit customers are paid intact into the business bank account whilst cash sales receipts are banked after deduction of cash drawings and providing for the shop till cash float. The cash float was increased from £160 to £200 in September 20X9.

The following is a summary of the transactions in the business bank account for the year ended 31 October 20X9:

Bank account

Receipts	£	Payments	£
Credit sales	181,370	Drawings	8,500
Cash sales	61,190	Motor van (bought	
Proceeds of sale of		1 May 20X9)	11,200
land owned privately		Purchases	163,100
by J Patel	16,000	Establishment and	
		administrative expenses	33,300
		Sales and distribution	
		expenses	29,100

Additional information for the year ended 31 October 20X9

(a)   A gross profit of $33\frac{1}{3}$% has been achieved on all sales.

(b)   Bad debts of £530 have been written off during the year.

(c)   Trade debtors at 31 October 20X9 were reduced by £8,130 as compared with a year earlier.

(d)   Trade creditors at 31 October 20X9 amounted to £12,700.

(e)   Depreciation is to be provided at the following annual rates on cost

Motor vehicles   20%

Fixtures and fittings   10%

(f)   Stock at 31 October 20X9 has been valued at £23,700.

Required:

Prepare a trading and profit and loss account for the year ended 31 October 20X9 and a balance sheet as at that date for J Patel.   **(20 marks)**

66 GBA

GBA is a sole trader, supplying building materials to local builders. He prepares his accounts to 30 June each year. At 30 June 20X5, his trial balance was as follows:

	£	£
Capital at 1 July 20X4		55,550
Purchases and sales	324,500	625,000
Returns	2,300	1,700
Discounts	1,500	2,500
Stock of building materials at 1 July 20X4	98,200	
Packing materials purchased	12,900	
Distribution costs	17,000	
Rent, rates and insurance	5,100	
Telephone	3,200	
Car expenses	2,400	
Wages	71,700	
Provision for doubtful debts at 1 July 20X4		1,000
Heat and light	1,850	
Sundry expenses	6,700	
Delivery vehicles – cost	112,500	
Delivery vehicles – depreciation at 1 July 20X4		35,000
Equipment - cost	15,000	
Equipment – depreciation at 1 July 20X4		5,000
Debtors and creditors	95,000	82,000
Loan		10,000
Loan repayments	6,400	
Bank deposit account	15,000	
Bank current account	26,500	
	817,750	817,750

The following additional information at 30 June 20X5 is available:

(i) Closing stocks of building materials   £75,300
     Closing stocks of packing materials   £700

There was also an unpaid invoice of £200 for packing materials received and consumed during the year.

(ii) Prepayments:

- rent, rates and insurance   £450

(iii) Accrued expenses:

- heat and light   £400
- telephone   £500

(iv) Wages includes £23,800 cash withdrawn by GBA.

(v) Debtors have been analysed as follows:

Current month	£60,000
30 to 60 days	£20,000
60 to 90 days	£12,000
over 90 days	£3,000

and provision is to be made for doubtful debts as follows:

30 to 60 days	1%
60 to 90 days	2.5%
over 90 days	5% (writing off £600)

(vi)   Sundry expenses include £3,500 for GBA's personal tax bill.

(vii)   The loan was taken out some years ago, and is due for repayment on 31 March 20X6. The figure shown in the trial balance for 'loan repayments' includes interest of £800 for the year.

(viii) The Bank deposit account was opened on 1 January 20X5 as a short term investment; interest is credited at 31 December annually; the average rate of interest since opening the account has been 6% per annum.

(ix)   At 1 July 20X4 GBA decided to bring one of his family cars, valued at £8,000, into the business. No entries have been made in the business books for its introduction.

(x)   Depreciation is to be provided as follows:

- at 20% on cost for delivery vehicles;

- at 25% on the reducing balance for the car;

- at 25% on the reducing balance for equipment.

Required:

(a)   Prepare a trading and profit and loss account for the year ended 30 June 20X5.

(12 marks)

(b)   Prepare a balance sheet at 30 June 20X5.   **(10 marks)**

(c)   Explain to GBA why *FOUR* of the transactions which have occurred in his business during the year have affected his bank balance but have not affected the calculation of his profit for the year.   **(8 marks)**

(Total: 30 marks)

67   DRAFT BALANCE SHEET

A trainee in your office has prepared draft accounts for a client for the year to 31 March 2005, but has not dealt with the adjustments for accrued expenses, prepaid expenses, bad and doubtful debts and depreciation.

Following the preparation of the profit and loss account, the trainee prepared the balance sheet shown below. You have been asked to complete the final accounts.

Draft balance sheet as at 31 March 2005 (before adjustments)

		£	£
Fixed assets	Equipment at cost	175,000	
	Accumulated depreciation (at 31 March 2004)	(85,400)	89,600
Current assets			
Stock		42,339	
Debtors		149,411	
Bank account		6,280	
		198,030	
Current liabilities			
Creditors		(86,560)	111,470
Total net assets			201,070
Capital			201,070

The trainee has given you the following information about the remaining adjustments:

(i)   The last invoice received for electricity covered the three-month period to 31 January 2005. The invoice was for £6,870.

(ii)   Rent of £28,500 for the six months to 30 June 2005 was paid in January.

(iii)   The debtors figure of £149,411 is stated after deducting the existing allowance for doubtful debts of £7,900 from the total debtors balance of £157,311.

(iv)   The total debtors balance of £157,311 includes a balance of £660 which has been outstanding for eight months. The client has decided to write off this balance.

(v)   The client's policy is to make an allowance for doubtful debts on the basis of the length of time the debt has been outstanding.

The aged analysis of trade debtors at 31 March 2005 and the allowance required is shown below:

Age of debt	Balance £	Allowance required
0 – 30 days	125,275	nil
31 – 60 days	27,200	20% of balances
Over 60 days	4,836	75% of balances
	157,311	

(vi)   Depreciation is to be charged at a rate of 20% per annum on the reducing balance basis.

Required:

(a)   Calculate the correct balance at 31 March 2005 for each of the following:

(i)   accrued expenses;   **(2 marks)**

(ii)   prepaid expenses;   **(2 marks)**

(iii)   allowance for doubtful debts; and   **(3 marks)**

(iv)   accumulated depreciation.   **(2 marks)**

(b)   Prepare the corrected balance sheet as at 31 March 2005.   **(6 marks)**

(Total: 15 marks)

PARTNERSHIP ACCOUNTS

68   PAT AND SAM

Pat and Sam are in partnership and have the following profit-sharing arrangements:

(a)   interest on capital is to be provided at a rate of 4% pa;

(b)   Pat and Sam are to receive salaries of £14,400 and £19,200 pa respectively;

(c)   the balance of profit or loss is to be divided between Pat and Sam in the ratio 3:2.

Net profit for the year amounts to £48,000 and each partner drew cash of £10,000 from the business. Capital account balances are Pat £28,800 and Sam £21,600, and current account balances are Pat £5,700 and Sam £3,200 before drawings and appropriation of profit for the year are recorded.

You are required to prepare:

(a) a statement showing the allocation of profit between the partners; **(10 marks)**

(b) the partners' current accounts in columnar form. **(5 marks)**

(Total: 15 marks)

69 ADAM AND COLIN

A member of your team has been preparing accounts for a business which has two partners, Adam and Colin. The net profit has been calculated at £69,602. No calculations have been carried out to share the profit between the partners. You have agreed to complete the accounts.

The partnership agreement provides for the following:

(a) Salaries are due to the partners as follows:

Adam	£7,500
Colin	£3,000

(b) Interest is paid to partners at a rate of 9% per annum, based on the balances on their capital accounts at the last balance sheet date.

(c) Profits and losses are to be shared between Adam and Colin in the ratio 3:4 respectively.

(d) The balances on the capital and current accounts at the last Balance Sheet date, and the value of drawings made during the year are:

	Capital	Current	Drawings
Adam	£45,000	£11,500	£20,000
Colin	£94,000	£17,600	£18,000

Required:

(a) Prepare the profit and loss appropriation account for the partnership. **(7 marks)**

(b) Complete the partners' current accounts. **(8 marks)**

(Total: 15 marks)

70 GARY AND PAULINE

Gary and Pauline commenced trading on 1 August 20X0, introducing capital of £30,000 and £15,000 respectively.

The partnership agreement provides for:

(i) a salary of £12,000 per annum to be paid to Gary;

(ii) interest on partners' capital balances to be paid at 8% per annum;

(iii) residual profits and losses to be shared 2/3 to Gary and 1/3 to Pauline.

Gary has a basic knowledge of accounting and has prepared draft accounts for the first 15 months of trading. These accounts show a net profit of £39,790. When preparing the accounts, Gary had not dealt with the balance on the suspense account, which had a credit balance of £12,550. This balance had arisen because:

(i) A payment of £17,000 had been made to a supplier in full settlement of a balance of £17,050. The payment had been recorded by an entry of £17,050 in the supplier's account in the personal ledger. In the nominal ledger £17,050 had been entered in the purchase ledger control account, and £17,000 had been entered in the bank account.

The double entry had been completed with an entry of £50 in the suspense account. All entries had been made on the correct sides of the accounts.

(ii) During the year the partners had negotiated a loan of £15,000. The lender had forwarded a cheque for the full amount of the loan. This had been correctly recorded in the bank account and the double entry completed with an entry in the suspense account.

(iii) The loan is to be repaid over three years, with capital repayments being made every three months. Two capital repayments (totalling £2,500) had been made. These payments had been correctly entered in the bank account. The double entry had been completed in the suspense account.

(*Note:* The suspense account balance had not been included in Gary's calculation of the profit.)

Required:

(a) Show the suspense account as it would appear after making the necessary correcting entries. **(5 marks)**

(b) For each of the entries you have made, indicate whether or not the entry would alter the profit for the period. **(3 marks)**

(c) Calculate the total profit to be divided between the partners. **(2 marks)**

(d) Calculate each partner's total share of the profit. **(10 marks)**

(Total: 20 marks)

71   KEITH AND JEAN

You have been asked to complete the preparation of the accounts of Keith and Jean, who have been in partnership for one year. A colleague has carried out some preparatory work, and from the file you note:

- The partnership was established on 1 September 20X0.

- At that date, Keith introduced £45,000 of capital, and Jean introduced £20,000 of capital.

- The net profit before appropriation for the year to 31 August 20X1 is £63,600.

- Drawings during the year were: Keith   £14,000

                                                              Jean   £9,600

- Interest on capital at 12% per annum has not yet been calculated.

- Salaries of £16,000 for Keith and £10,000 for Jean are to be provided for.

- Profit and losses are to be shared: Keith   60%

                                                                 Jean   40%

Required:

(a) Show the profit and loss appropriation account for the year to 31 August 20X1. **(7 marks)**

(b) Calculate the balance on each partner's current account at 31 August 20X1. **(8 marks)**

(Total: 15 marks)

72   JOHN AND DARRYL

John and Darryl are in partnership sharing profits and losses in the ratio 60:40 respectively.

Under the terms of the partnership agreement, the partners are entitled to interest on their capital account balances at a rate of 5% per annum. The agreement also provides for a salary of £13,000 to be paid to John and a salary of £5,000 to be paid to Darryl.

At 1 November 20X2 the balances on the partners' capital and current accounts were:

	Capital account £	Current account £
John	60,000	43,250
Darryl	50,000	26,560

On 1 January 20X3 John introduced a further £60,000.

During the year to 31 October 20X3 both partners withdrew £18,000.

The draft accounts for the year to 31 October 20X3 report a net profit of £37,458. Stock was valued at its cost of £45,864. This includes damaged items which cost £5,748. The partners intend to repair these at a cost of £1,475. They will then be sold for £6,700.

Required:

(a)   Calculate the revised net profit for the year to 31 October 20X3, after making any necessary adjustments to the valuation of stock.   **(4 marks)**

(b)   Calculate each partner's total share of the profit.   **(6 marks)**

(c)   Show John's current account, including the closing balance, at 31 October 20X3.

 Note: You must use a format which clearly shows whether each entry is a debit or a credit entry.   **(5 marks)**

(Total: 15 marks)

73   ORLA AND PAULA

A trainee in your office prepared draft accounts for the year ended 30 April 20X4 for Orla Hughes and Paula Jones who are in partnership. The draft accounts report a gross profit of £157,846 and a net profit of £51,024. Cash payments of £15,000 to each partner have been included in expenses.

At 1 May 20X3 the balances on the partners' capital and current accounts were:

	Orla	Paula
Capital account	£125,000 (credit)	£70,000 (credit)
Current account	£34,568 (credit)	£23,741 (debit)

The partnership agreement includes the following terms:

	Orla	Paula
Share of profits and losses	2/3	1/3
Salary	£18,000	£12,000
Interest on capital (per annum)	8%	8%

The partnership agreement also states that the partners' capital account balances will remain fixed, and that the balances on the partners' current accounts should not be included in the calculation of interest on capital.

Required:

Calculate:

(a)   the correct gross profit and net profit to be reported in the partnership profit and loss
        account for the year to 30 April 20X4;   **(2 marks)**

(b)   the amount of profit which will be credited to each partner's current account for the
        year to 30 April 20X4;   **(8 marks)**

(c)   the balance on each partner's current account at 30 April 20X4;   **(4 marks)**

(d)   the total net assets of the partnership at 30 April 20X4.   **(1 mark)**

                                                                    (Total: 15 marks)

Section 4

ANSWERS TO OBJECTIVE TEST QUESTIONS

BASIC BOOKKEEPING

1   C

Only one set of books is kept, but a debit and a credit entry is made for each transaction and adjustment.

2   C

As in the previous question, this is a transaction that records increase in assets (car account) and increase in capital.

3   C

The £900 is a debit balance because the total value of debit entries (£1,750) exceeds the total value of credits (£850). The balance b/d is therefore a debit balance.

4   C

An increase in capital and an increase in liability both require credit entries in the appropriate accounts. Debits and credits must match each other.

5   D

The accounting equation is Assets = Capital + Liabilities. So, we can have

Assets (£14,000) = Capital (£10,000) + Liabilities (£4,000)

6   D

Stock costing £400 is sold for £1,000, giving a profit of £600. The VAT on the sale will be £175.

	Cash	Stock	Liabilities	Capital
	£	£	£	£
Start business	1,000			1,000
Buy stock		800	800	
Sell stock	1,175	(400)	175	600
	———	———	———	———
	2,175	400	975	1,600
	———	———	———	———

7   B

	£
Closing capital	4,500
Opening capital	(10,000)
Decrease in net assets	(5,500)
Drawings: profit taken out	8,000
Capital introduced	(4,000)
Loss for the year	(1,500)

8   £587.50

Harper owes the amount of the sale price including VAT.

£500 + (17.5% × £500) = £587.50

9   C

The purchase return reduces the amount owed to Rawlings by £800 plus VAT.

£800 + (17.5% × £800) = £940.00

10   B

None of the loan is repayable within 12 months of the end of the accounting period, therefore it should all be shown as a long-term liability.

11   £5,300

VAT account

	£		£
Creditors/bank (input VAT)	6,000	Balance b/d	3,400
Bank	2,600	Debtors/bank (output VAT)	10,500
Balance c/d	5,300		
	13,900		13,900
		Balance b/d	5,300

VAT on sales (outputs) = 17.5% × £60,000 = £10,500.

VAT on purchases (inputs) = (17.5/117.5) × £40,286 = £6,000

12   B

The only item of current liabilities in the list is 'creditors', which are £3,045.

13   £3,000

14   C

£18,955 – 11,334 – 2,447 – 664 – 456 – 120 – 146 – 276 – 665 – 115 = £2,732

15   A

Closing stock is debited to the stock account, and is the opening balance for the start of the next period. Closing stock also reduces the cost of sales, and so is credited to the profit and loss account.

16   B

The closing balance is a debit balance, because wages are an expense item. At the end of the financial period, the expenses are transferred to the profit and loss account, by crediting the wages account and debiting the profit and loss account

17   D

The balance sheet is a list of balances, not an account. Therefore no double entry is required.

18   D

Financial statements report transactions as they occur, which may not be when the transaction is settled in cash.

19   D

The debtors account is debited with the total amount owed, including VAT. The sales account is credited with the value of sales excluding VAT. The VAT on sales, which is payable to the government, is a liability and is credited to a VAT account.

20   B

Paying a creditor reduces cash by the amount of the payment and also reduces the total amounts owed to creditors (a current liability).

21   C

Returns inwards are sales returns from customers. They can be thought of as 'negative sales' or 'negative income', so we debit a returns inwards account. The returns reduce the amount owed by debtors, so we credit the debtors account (reducing an asset = credit entry).

22   A

Cash received is recorded by debiting the bank account, so answers C and D must be incorrect. Settlement discounts allowed (cash discounts allowed) are a form of expense and reduce the amounts due from debtors. Discounts allowed are therefore recorded by debiting a discounts allowed account and crediting debtors.

23   D

This is a question about a sales ledger control account reconciliation, which is carried out to check that the balance on the sales ledger control account equals the total of all the balances on the individual debtor accounts in the sales ledger. If a transaction has been posted to the account of the wrong debtor in the sales ledger, the total of debtor balances is not affected. This error would not be discovered by the control account reconciliation.

24   £329,750

Cash sales do not affect debtors.

Discounts received affect creditors, not debtors.

The allowance for doubtful debts does not affect the amount of debtors, but specific bad debts written off do affect debtors.

Debtors account

	£		£
Opening balance b/d	37,500	Discounts allowed	15,750
Sales (credit sales)	357,500	Bad debts written off	10,500
		Bank (balancing figure)	329,750
		Closing balance c/d	39,000
	395,000		395,000
Balance b/d	39,000		

25   A

The series of transactions might be recorded as follows.

Original purchase

> Debit Purchases

> Credit Brad (creditor)

On payment

> Debit Brad (creditor)

> Credit Bank

On cancellation of the cheque

> Debit Bank

> Credit Returns outwards

If the second and third transactions are dealt with at the same time, they simplify to debit Brad, credit Returns outwards.

ACCOUNTING STANDARDS, PRINCIPLES AND POLICIES

26   C

Accounts only record items to which a monetary value can be attributed. Internally developed intangible assets cannot be valued reliably in monetary terms, and should not be shown as an asset in the balance sheet.

27   D

There has been no sale according to the realisation concept. Prudence suggests that the profit should not be recognised until it is reasonably certain that the customer will buy the goods.

28   C

Under the prudence concept, losses must be provided for as soon as they are reasonably foreseeable. The best estimate of the amount due is £20,000.

29   A

The increase of £3,000 needs to be debited to the profit and loss account as it is an expense.

FIXED ASSETS AND DEPRECIATION

30   A

If capital expenditure is incorrectly classified as revenue expenditure, both the net profit and the net assets will be understated. Net profit is understated as the full cost of the asset is deducted, rather than just depreciation. Net assets are understated because they do not include the new capital expenditure.

31   C

Depreciation spreads the value of a fixed asset over its expected useful life.

32   £9,000

$$\frac{100,000 - 10,000}{10} = £9,000$$

33   B

Year 1 charge = £100,000 × 20% = £20,000, leaving a book value of £80,000.

Year 2 charge = £80,000 × 20% = £16,000.

34   C

Delivery and installation costs are incurred in getting the asset into working condition, and so they are capitalised. The maintenance costs merely maintain the asset, they do not improve it.   Therefore they are charged as revenue expenditure.

35   £87,500

	£
Net book value of assets at start of year (140,000 – 60,000)	80,000
Assets purchased in the year	30,000
	110,000
Depreciation at 25% of this balance: charge for the year	27,500
Opening balance, accumulated depreciation	60,000
Therefore closing balance	87,500

36   D

A fixed asset register is a detailed schedule of fixed assets, and is not another name for fixed asset ledger accounts in the nominal ledger.

37   A

The nominal ledger account for fixed assets shows a net book value that is £10,000 higher than the figure in the fixed assets register. This could be due to having omitted to deduct an asset with a NBV of £10,000 from the ledger. A fixed asset will have a NBV on disposal when it is sold for £15,000 and the profit on disposal is £5,000.

38 B

The capital expenditure consists of the basic cost of the computer and the additional memory. The maintenance costs are a revenue expense.

39 £12,450

1 Jan – 30 June: 3% of £380,000 × 6/12 = £5,700.

1 July – 31 December: 3% of £450,000 × 6/12 = £6,750.

Charge for the year: £5,700 + £6,750 = £12,450.

CONTROL ACCOUNTS, RECONCILIATIONS AND ERRORS

40 B

The creditors control account and the motor expenses account are posted from the PDB. Because the original entry in the PDB was overstated by £36 then both of the postings will also be overstated by £36.

41 A

Control accounts are useful, but they are not essential. The double entry can be directly to individual supplier or creditor accounts.

42 D

The debit and credit entries agreed (Dr Cash £1,600; Cr Sales £1,600) so the trial balance will balance and a suspense account is not needed.

43 C

The full £1,600 proceeds has been claimed as income without matching it to the £1,500 net book value of the asset sold. The actual profit is only £100.

44 A

The cancelled cheques should be entered in the bank account by debiting £642.

45 C

Listing a debit balance as a credit affects the list of balances but not the control account. The transposition error in the PDB will affect the totals posted to the control account.

46 D

This answer assumes that the individual supplier accounts are drawn up from the information in the PDB, rather than from the original invoices.

47   D

£35,776 + £900 = £36,676. The error on the list of balances does not affect the control account, but the £900 undercast on the SDB needs adjusting for.

48   B

A debit bank account balance in the books of a business represents funds in the bank. Therefore it should be shown as a current asset.

49   C

Error 1   Total sales and total debtors have been recorded £370 too much.

Error 2   Total debtors have been recorded (£940 – £490) £450 too little.

As a result of these two errors, total debtors have been under-recorded by £450 – £370 = £80.

The errors have not affected the accounts of individual debtors.

50   A

As a result of the error, total creditors are under-stated by £265,080 – £260,580 = £4,500. To correct the error, we need to increase the balance in the creditors' ledger control account, and this is done by crediting the control account.

The error has affected the control account only and not the entries in the individual creditor accounts in the purchase ledger, so the total of creditors' balances is unaffected.

51   B

The list of balances on the individual suppliers' accounts needs to be reduced by the invoice posted twice and the unrecorded payment. This will result in a figure of £75,355 (£81,649 - £4,688 – £1,606). The creditors control account needs to be reduced by the unrecorded payment to £75,355 (£76,961 – £1,606).

52   A

This is not an easy question to solve. You should prepare a debtors account and calculate the closing balance as a debit balance. You should then look for the answer that gives the same net debit balance. Here, the closing balance is £32,125, and only answer A gives this net amount.

Debtors account

	£		£
Opening balance b/d	32,750	Opening balance b/d	1,275
Sales	125,000	Bank	122,500
		Discounts allowed	550
		Sales returns	1,300
		Closing balance (net)	32,125
	———		———
	157,750		157,750
Opening balance (net)	32,125		

53   C

£1,500 of purchases is being moved from stationery into purchases.

54   B

A debit entry of £1,300 is needed to correct the error: £650 to cancel out the incorrect credit and a further £650 to make the entry that should have been made.

55   C

The adjustment is known as a 'contra entry', whereby the amount due to a supplier is reduced and the amount owed by a customer is also reduced, because the supplier and the customer are one and the same person. To reduce total debtors, we credit the sales ledger control account. To reduce total creditors, we debit the purchase ledger control account. The same adjustments should be made to the accounts of the customer/supplier in the sales ledger and the purchase ledger.

56   C

There is no need to open a separate suspense account for each error, therefore statement (i) is incorrect. A suspense account is sometimes used to complete a posting while further information is being sought, so statement (ii) is correct.

57   C

The suspense account balance will remain £280 as it is unaffected by the correction of the error. The entries needed to correct the error are debit supplier account and credit purchases with £140.

58   D

This is another example of transposition error. The debtor has been recorded at £90 more than it should be (£760 – £670). This is corrected by crediting the debtors account with £90. The corresponding debit entry is to the suspense account. Since the suspense account has a credit balance of £140, the correction of the error will reduce this balance by £90.

ADJUSTMENTS TO THE TRIAL BALANCE

ACCRUALS AND PREPAYMENTS

59   C

£850 should be provided for as the liability is fairly certain and this is the best estimate of the amount due.

60   C

Sybil still has to pay her phone bill for November and this must be reflected in her accounts ($\frac{1}{3} \times$ £1,800) = £600 (accrued expenses).

61   £6,400

(£6,000 × 8/12) + (7,200 × 4/12) = £6,400

62 D

£7,200 × 8/12 = £4,800 prepaid

63 £27,500

	£
5 months at (£24,000/12) per month	10,000
7 months at (£30,000/12) per month	17,500
Annual rent expense	27,500

64 A

Charge to the profit and loss account:

7 months: 7/12 × £1,800 = £1,050

Prepayment of rent:

5 months: 5/12 × £1,800 = £750

65 C

P & L account charge for insurance:

(7 months): 7/12 × £2,400 = £1,400

Prepayment: 5 months = 5/12 × £2,400 = £1,000

66 C

The accrual for May and June 20X3 is assumed to be 2/3 × £840 = £560.

Electricity expenses account

	£		£
Bank	600	Opening balance b/d	300
Bank	720		
Bank	900		
Bank	840		
Closing balance c/d	560	Profit and loss account	3,320
	3,620		3,620
		Opening balance b/d	560

67 A

The situation in the question is unusual because there is an opening accrual on the account, but a closing prepayment of 1/3 × £1,200 = £400.

Rent account

	£		£
Bank	4,000	Balance b/d (accrual)	300
		Profit and loss account	3,300
		Balance c/d (prepayment)	400
	4,000		4,000
Balance b/d	400		

68 **£12,600**

Insurance for the year 1 July 20X2 to 30 June 20X3 was £13,200 × 1/1.1 = £12,000.

Profit and loss account charge:

six months at £12,000 plus six months at £13,200 = £6,000 + £6,600.

69 **B**

The rent payment covers the period 1 March – 31 August. At 30 June, there is a prepayment of two months (July and August). The amount of the prepayment is 2/6 × £5,520 = £1,840.

70 **D**

There is an accrual for one month (June) during which electricity charges have been incurred but no invoice has been received yet. The best estimate of the accrual is 1/3 × £1,950 = £650.

71 **D**

There is an accrual for two months (October and November) during which electricity charges have been incurred but no invoice has been received yet. The best estimate of the accrual is 2/3 × £2,100 = £1,400.

DEPRECIATION

72 **£90,800**

Depreciation

		£			£
	Disposal	17,200	1/1/X7	Bal b/d	92,000
31/12/X7	Bal c/d	90,800	31/12/X7	P&L	16,000
		108,000			108,000
			1/1/X8	Bal b/d	90,800

73 **D**

Disposal

		£			£
	Cost	20,000		Depn	17,200
31/12/X7	P&L (gain)	2,000		Bank	4,800
		22,000			22,000

74 **£16,000**

Cost

		£			£
1/1/X7	Bal b/d	180,000		Disposal	20,000
			31/12/X7	Bal c/d	160,000
		180,000			180,000
1/1/X8	Bal b/d	160,000			

£160,000 × 10% = £16,000

75   D

The answer does not include all the required double entries, which are:

Debit Disposal account, credit Machinery account (£20,000)

Debit Accumulated depreciation, credit Disposal account (£17,200)

Debit Cash, credit Disposal account (£4,800)

This leaves a balance on the account, representing the profit on disposal.

76   C

The gain or loss on disposal is the difference between the disposal value of the asset and its net book value at the date of disposal. If the asset's life and disposal value had been forecast with 100% accuracy, there would be no gain or loss on disposal.

77   D

Depreciable amount £(52,000 – 4,000)	£48,000
Expected life	8 years
Annual depreciation charge	£6,000
Number of years' depreciation (20X2 – 20X6)	5
Accumulated depreciation at time of disposal	£30,000

	£
Cost	52,000
Accumulated depreciation at time of disposal	30,000
Net book value (NBV) at time of disposal	22,000
Disposal price	35,000
Profit on disposal	13,000

78   £510,000

	Cost	Accum dep'n	NBV
	£000	£000	£000
Opening balance	860	397	
Disposal	(80)	(43)	
	780	354	
Purchase	180		
	960		
Depreciation (10%)		96	
		450	
NBV = 960 – 450			510

79   B

	£
Cost of asset	126,000
Depreciation to 31 October 20X3 (4/12 × 15%)	6,300
	119,700
Depreciation to 31 October 20X4 (15%)	17,955
	101,745
Depreciation to 31 October 20X5 (15%)	15,262
	86,483
Depreciation to 31 October 20X6 (15%)	12,972
	73,511
Depreciation to 30 September 20X7 (11/12 × 15%)	10,108
Net book value at time of disposal	63,403
Disposal price	54,800
Loss on disposal	8,603

80   D

Do not include the road tax in the cost of the car. Road tax is a revenue expense item.

	£
Cost of asset	10,000
Depreciation 20X1 (25%)	2,500
	7,500
Depreciation 20X2 (25%)	1,875
	5,625
Depreciation 20X3 (25%)	1,406
	4,219
Depreciation 20X4 (25%)	1,055
Net book value at time of disposal	3,164
Disposal value	5,000
Profit on disposal	1,836

81   £150,000

The asset disposed of had a net book value at the time of disposal = sales proceeds + loss on sale = £25,000 + £5,000 = £30,000.

	£
Net book value at 1 August 20X2	200,000
Net book value of asset disposed of	30,000
	170,000
Depreciation charge	20,000
Net book value at 31 July 20X3	150,000

82   A

You need to know the sales proceeds to calculate the length of ownership, or you need to know the length of ownership to calculate the sales proceeds. For example, this asset might have been sold after one year (NBV = £10,000) for £5,500, or it might have been sold after two years (NBV £8,000) for £3,500, and so on.

83   B

	£
Cost of asset	2,400.0
Depreciation Year 1 (20%)	480.0
	1,920.0
Depreciation Year 2 (20%)	384.0
	1,536.0
Depreciation Year 3 (20%)	307.2
Net book value at time of disposal	1,228.8
Disposal value	1,200.0
Loss on disposal	28.8

84   A

	£
Cost of asset	9,000
Depreciation Year 1 (30%)	2,700
	6,300
Depreciation Year 2 (30%)	1,890
	4,410
Depreciation Year 3 (30%)	1,323
Net book value at time of disposal	3,087
Disposal value	3,000
Loss on disposal	87

85   £100

	£
Sale value	5,300
Net book value (10,000 – 4,800)	5,200
	100

BAD AND DOUBTFUL DEBTS

86   B

This is an example of a bad debt being written off. So, we credit the debtors account in order to clear the debt and debit the bad debts account with the amount of the debt written off.

87 A

There is a specific allowance for the debt of £900 which has still not been written off as bad, and a general allowance for which specific doubtful debts are not identified.

88 A

The net amount reported in the balance sheet is £47,744 owed less the £3,500 allowance for doubtful debts.

89 £2,400

Bad debts are written off during the year by crediting the debtor's account and debiting the bad debts account with the amount of the debts written off. From the account in the question, we can see that this is £2,400.

90 C

The balance sheet will show debtors as the total amount owed by debtors less the allowance for doubtful debts. This is £40,000 – £900 = £39,100.

91 A

When a debt is written off as bad, the transaction is recorded as:

Debit Bad debts account (expense)

Credit Debtor account.

Any subsequent change to the allowance for doubtful debts should be dealt with as a separate matter.

92 A

Debtors (5% of £2 million) = £100,000.

Required allowance for doubtful debts (4% of £100,000) = £4,000.

Current allowance for doubtful debts = £4,000 × ¾ = £3,000.

Increase in allowance = £1,000.

An increase in the allowance for doubtful debts reduces profits.

93 £2,000

The charge for bad and doubtful debts is the actual amount of bad debts written off plus the increase in the allowance for doubtful debts, or minus the decrease in the allowance.

	£
Allowance at end of year (5% of £120,000)	6,000
Allowance at start of year	9,000
Decrease in allowance	(3,000)
Bad debts written off	5,000
Charge to P & L account	2,000

94   £3,770

Debtors (4% of £3 million)	£120,000
	£
Required allowance for doubtful debts (3%)	3,600
Allowance last year (£3,600 × 100/125)	2,880
Increase in allowance	720
Bad debts written off	3,200
Bad debts recovered	(150)
Charge to P & L account	3,770

95   C

The calculations are a bit complex here. The general allowance is 2% of the total debtors after deducting the specific allowance. £13,720 therefore represents 98% of the total debtors after deducting the specific allowance. This means that total debtors before deducting the general allowance are £13,720/0.98 = £14,000.

	£
Allowance for doubtful debts at start of year:	
Specific	350
General (2% of £14,000)	280
	630
Required allowance at end of year (3% of £17,500)	525
Reduction in allowance (credit P & L account)	105

96   B

The receipt has been accounted for by:

Debit Bank, Credit Sales ledger control account.

It should have been accounted for as:

Debit Bank, Credit Bad debts.

(The debtor was removed from the accounts when the bad debt was written off. The receipt is the recovery of a bad debt, which is credited to the bad debts account.)

To correct the error:

Debit Sales ledger control account, Credit Bad debts.

97   D

A allowance for doubtful debts is a type of current liability. In the balance sheet, it is subtracted from debtors. An increase in a allowance for doubtful debts will therefore reduce net current assets, i.e. it will reduce working capital.

98   B

	£
Bad debts written off	18,000
Reduction in allowance for doubtful debts	(17,000)
Net charge for bad and doubtful debts	1,000

A charge is an expense, which is a debit balance item.

CLOSING STOCK (AND STOCK VALUATION)

99   D

£6.5m + £1.6m + £1.3m = £9.4m

100   B

The damaged items have a cost of £3,660, but a net realisable value of only £1,050 (£1,500 – £450). Therefore the cost of the stock needs to be written down by £2,610 (£3,660 – £1,050). The stock will then have a correct value of £36,140 (£38,750 – £2,610).

101   B

Stocks are valued at the lower of cost and net realisable value. The cost of repairing the clock will reduce the expected profit, but the clock's net realisable value is still greater then cost and so no reduction in value is needed.

102   B

The overvaluation in 2004 will boost profits in 2004 by reducing cost of sales. However, the opening stocks in the following year will be overstated increasing cost of sales and reducing profits.

103   D

Closing stock reduces the cost of sales figure. Therefore, if the value of closing stock is increased, cost of sales will be reduced and net profit will be increased. Net assets will also be increased.

104   C

Closing stock reduces cost of sales in the profit and loss account and is reported as an asset in the balance sheet.

105   £7,368

The net realisable value of stock items is the selling price less the 4% commission payable.

	NRV	Lower of cost or NRV
	£	£
Henry VII	2,784	2,280
Dissuasion	3,840	3,840
John Bunion	1,248	1,248
		7,368

106 B

	Net realisable value	Lower of cost or NRV	Units	Value
	£	£		£
Basic	8	6	200	1,200
Super	8	8	250	2,000
Luxury	10	10	150	1,500
Total value				4,700

107 C

22,960 – 1,950 – 400 + 900 = 21,510

108 £20,030

22,700 – 1,300 + 700 – 70 = 20,030

EXTENDED TRIAL BALANCE

109 A

Allowance required		£
30 days to 59 days	£13,800 × 5%	690
60 days and over	£6,200 × 80%	4,960
Allowance at 1.11.X1		5,650
Increase in allowance		5,200
		450

110 B

	£
Cost	105,000
Less accumulated depreciation to 1.11.X1	51,450
NBV	53,550
Charge for years at 30%	16,065

111 £21,050

£210,500 × $\frac{1}{10}$ = 21,050

112 C

This is an example of a journal entry. The action is in order to correct an error of principle.

113 C

This is a post trial balance adjustment. A prepayment is an asset, and so it is recorded as a debit entry in cell F36. The prepayment reduces the rent expense for the year, so credit the rent expense account, cell G27.

114 A

The closing stock entries are posted initially to cells F37 and G37.

115 D

Post trial balance adjustment – depreciation charge: debit depreciation charge and credit motor vehicles.

116 D

Trade creditors are liability (credit balance) in the balance sheet, so cell K31.

117 D

Accruals are liability (credit balance) in the balance sheet, so cell K35.

118 C

Having posted closing stock to cells F37 and G37, the extension of closing stock is to cell J37 because closing stock is a balance sheet asset, and I37 because closing stock reduces the cost of sales in the profit and loss account.

119 A

Website costs (row 20) are £936 less the credit journal entry of £279, which is £657. Costs are a profit and loss account expense (debit balance) so the cell for the extension of website costs is H20.

120 D

	£
Profit and loss account credit balances (income)	485,889
Profit and loss account debit balances (expenses)	473,954
Profit for the year	11,935

121 B

If there had been a loss, the profit and loss account debit balance total in cell H41 would have been higher than the credit balance total in cell I41. To balance up the two totals, the difference (loss for the year) would be entered in cell I42. Similarly, the balance sheet credit balance total in cell K41 would have been higher than the debit balance total in cell J41. To balance up the two totals, the difference (loss for the year) would be entered in cell J42.

122 C

£27,645 – £27,456 = £189. Sales have been recorded in the Sales Account at a lower amount than they should be, so the adjustment will result in an increase in sales.

123 A

The customer has paid £2,500 in full settlement of the outstanding balance. The difference is therefore a discount allowed and not a bad debt. Since £2,537 had been entered into the sales ledger control account, the difference of £37 must be part of the suspense balance.

124 B

Allowance required:

	£				£
Less than 30 days	18,205	×	nil	=	nil
31 – 60 days	4,960	×	5%	=	248
Over 61 days	3,210				
Less irrecoverable debt written off	(250)				
	2,960	×	50%	=	1,480
					1,728

	£
Allowance at start of year	1,950
Allowance required	1,728
Reduction in allowance	222 allowance no longer required

125 A

Depreciation

Vehicles	NBV b/f (22,500 − 9,844) 12,656 × 25%	= £3,164
Equipment	Equipment £61,950/7	= £8,850

126 D

The correction requires a journal entry in which the light and heat should be debited with the amount of the invoice and the motor expenses account credited. So cells D10 and E12 will be used.

127 B

A prepayment is an asset, so enter the amount of the prepayment in cell F33. The effect of recording a prepayment is to reduce the expense for the year (here, car insurance so motor expenses), and the motor expenses account should therefore be credited. This is shown in cell G12.

128 A

We begin to record closing stock by entering the value of closing stock as a post trial balance adjustment, in cells F30 and G30.

129 D

Depreciation is recorded as an expense, so debit the amount of the charge in cell F31 and it is added to the accumulated depreciation. For motor vehicles, an increase in the accumulated for depreciation is entered in cell G18.

130 K32

Accruals are a credit item in the balance sheet, so the extension of the accruals amount is put in cell K32.

131 D

Having posted closing stock into cells F30 and G30, the extension of the closing stock values requires:

(a)   an addition to balance sheet assets. This is a debit item (asset – debit balance), so enter in cell J30;

(b)   a reduction in the cost of sales. This is a credit item in the P&L account, so enter in cell I30.

132 B

Sales – 373,000 + 189 credit = 273,189. Note: A credit entry indicates an addition to income. This should be extended into the credit side of the P&L account, cell I3.

133 D

	£
P&L account credit balances (income)	281,917
P&L account debit balances (expenses)	231,816
Profit for the year	50,101

134 C

If the credit balance in cell I34 exceeds the debit balance in cell H34, the difference is entered in cell H35, making the totals in the debit and credit columns for the P&L account the same. This difference represents a profit. Similarly, since the debit balance in cell J34 exceeds the credit balances in cell K34, the difference is entered in cell K35, making the totals in the debit and credit columns for the balance sheet the same. Here, the required entry in cells H35 and K35 is £50,101.

135 C

To make the correction, we need to add £2,500 to the cost of equipment (increase asset = debit entry), by entering this amount in cell D19. The amount charged to equipment repairs must be reduced (reduce expense = credit entry) by entering £2,500 in cell E11.

136 B

Depreciation

		£
Motor vehicles	$(75,950 - 45,570) \times 25\% =$	7,595
Equipment	$(156,500 + 2,500) \times 1/10 =$	15,900
		23,495

137 £36,345

Stock is valued at the lower of cost and net realisable value.

Stock	£	£
Cost	38,785	
Less: slow moving items	(7,650)	
		31,135

Slow moving items:
Realisable value   5,900
Less: Expenses of sale   (690)
                            _____

Net realisable value (lower than cost)   5,210
                                            _____

                                            36,345
                                            _____

138 £169

Bad debt allowance	£	£		£
Less than 30 days		85,652	× nil =	Nil
31 – 60 days		21,400	× 7% =	1,498
61 days and over	5,178			
Written off	(750)	4,428	× 75% =	3,321
Allowance required				4,819
Existing allowance				4,650
Additional allowance				169

139 A

The accrual at the end of May is for one month (May) in which electricity expenses have been incurred but no invoice has yet been received. Best estimate of accrual ⅓ × £2,850 = £950.

140 C

The prepayment at the end of May is for the period 1 June to 30 November 20X9 (6 months). £2,472 × 6/12 = £1,236 prepaid.

141 A

When a bad debt is written off, the amount written off is treated as a bad debt expense, so debit bad debts with £750 – cell D13. The write-off reduces debtors, so the debtors account is credited with £750 – cell E23.

142 J32

Prepayments are an asset in the balance sheet. Assets are a debit balance. The extension of prepayments is therefore made in cell J32.

143 C

Closing stock is posted first of all to cells F33 and G33. From there, the extension is to J33 (asset in the balance sheet, therefore a debit entry) and to I33 (reduction in the cost of sales in the P&L account, therefore a credit entry).

144 A

Wages are an expense, so the correct cell for extending wages (debit entry in the P&L account) is cell H10. The amount to enter in this cell is £93,453 + £5,200 (debit) = £98,653.

145   C

	£
Credit balances in P&L account (income)	804,601
Debit balances in P&L account (expenses)	738,907
Profit for the year	65,694

146   C

The four totals shown in the previous question appear in cells H39, I39, J39 and K39. The amount by which the £804,601 in cell I39 exceeds the £738,907 in cell H39 is entered in cell H40, to make the P&L column totals equal. Similarly, the amount by which the £406,621 in cell J39 exceeds the £340,927 in cell K39 is entered in cell K40, to make the balance sheet totals equal.

147   D

The fixed assets (depreciation) account is for the accumulated provision for depreciation. This has a credit balance. The purchase ledger control account should also have a credit balance. The sales ledger control account should have a debit balance.

148   C

If the interest balance has been omitted, it should be entered. Interest is an expense and so has a debit balance. Complete the double entry by crediting the Suspense account.

149   A

Note (iv) says that the charge has been recorded in the relevant fixed asset account (i.e. the depreciation account), but has been omitted from the cost of sales. Therefore debit the cost of sales account and credit the suspense account.

150   D

Under-casting the sales day book means that the total of credit sales has been recorded in the nominal ledger at too low an amount. To correct, we need to increase total debtors (so debit sales ledger control account) and increase sales (so credit sales account).

151   D

We need to eliminate the incorrect debit by crediting the administration account with £1,000 and crediting it with a second £1,000 to make the entry that should have been made. The corresponding debit entry is £2,000 to the Suspense account.

152   B

A suspense account is needed when, as a result of an accounting error, total credit balances and debit balances will not be equal to each other.

Error 1   The entry should have been Credit Bank, Debt Motor Vehicles account. Instead, it was recorded as Credit Bank, Credit Motor Vehicles account. A suspense account is needed.

Error 2   The entry should have been Debit Bank, Credit Brown, but was recorded as Debit Bank, Credit Green. Total credits and debits will be equal, so a suspense account is not needed to correct the error.

Error 3   The entry has been recorded as: Credit Bank £9,500, Debit Rent £5,900. Credits and debits are unequal, so a suspense account is needed.

Error 4   The transaction has been recorded as Credit Debtors, Debit Discounts Received, but should have been recorded as Credit Debtors, Debit Discounts Allowed. Total credits and debits will be equal, so a suspense account is not needed to correct the error.

Error 5   An omission of a transaction does not need a suspense account to correct it.

153 C

Since total debits are less than total credits in the trial balance by (£1,026,480 - £992,640) £33,840, we need a debit balance of £33,840 in the suspense account to make the total debits and total credits equal.

Error 1   does not affect the suspense account, because it is an omission and omissions do not alter debits and credits.

Error 2   has treated a debit balance of £27,680 as a credit balance, as a result of which total credits will exceed total debits by 2 × £27,680 = £55,360.

Error 3   does not affect the suspense account, since the error has been to debit the motor vehicle asset account instead of the bank account with £6,160.

Error 4   has been to omit a credit balance of £21,520 for rent payable, as a result of which total debits will exceed total credits by £21,520.

	£
To correct the errors:	
Credit suspense account	55,360
Debit suspense account	21,520
To eliminate suspense account balance	33,840

154 C

This is a complex question. Remember that a suspense account is needed when, as a result of an accounting error, total credit balances and debit balances are not equal to each other.

Error 1   The original entry for the sales return would have been: Debit Sales returns, Credit Debtors. When the cash refund is paid, the entry should be Credit Cash, Debit Debtors. The error is really two errors. The wrong customer account has been used, but a debit entry has been recorded as a credit entry.

Error 5   The entry should have been Credit Bank, Debit Plant repairs, but has been Credit Bank, Credit Plant and equipment account. A suspense account is needed to correct this error.

Errors 2, 3 and 4 do not result in total debits and total credits being unequal.

Error 2   The wrong accounts have been used, but the debit entry and credit entry are equal. (The correct entry should be Credit Purchases, Debit Director's Current Account.)

Error 3   The entry has been Debit Creditors, Credit discount allowed, but should have been Debit Creditors, Credit discount received. However, total debits and total credits are equal.

Error 4   Presumably, these transactions have been omitted from the accounts entirely.

155 C

Opening stock should be a debit balance item (asset). As a result of the error with recording stock, total credit balances exceed total debit balances by $2 \times £31,763 = £63,526$. The question seems to be saying that a suspense account has already been opened for this error, and it needs a debit balance to make total debits equal to total credits.

Adding the total of debit balances incorrectly does not affect the suspense account balance. If it did, total credits would exceed total debits by a further £90, and the suspense account balance would need to be £90 higher. This is not a choice in the solutions.

156 A

Think of the other side of the double entry that is needed to correct the error. This will help you to decide whether the entry in the suspense account should be a debit or a credit entry.

Error 1   To correct, we must debit gas account £180, therefore credit suspense account.

Error 2   To correct, we need to debit discounts received £50 and debit discounts allowed £50, so we must credit the suspense account with $2 \times £50$.

Error 3   To correct, we need to credit interest receivable, therefore we debit the suspense account.

Suspense account

	£		£
Balance (balancing figure)	210	Gas expense	180
Interest received	70	Discounts allowed	50
		Discounts received	50
	280		280

157 D

Discounts received should be recorded as:

> Debit Creditors
>
> Credit Discounts received.

Here, the discount has been debited instead of credited, so that the balance in the discounts received account is $2 \times £200 = £400$ too low. To correct, we must:

> Credit Discounts received £400

Therefore Debit Suspense account £400.

158 B

The wording of this question can make it quite difficult, but the correct answer might be identified quickly.

Item B   Discounts allowed should be debited, therefore there is no error. If there is no error, we do not need a suspense account.

Item A   This is an error where a debit entry has been incorrectly recorded as a credit balance.

Item C   This might cause you a problem. If the bad debt has been omitted entirely, and no accounting entry has been made, there can be no suspense account entry. Here, it would seem that the debtors balance has been reduced for the bad debt (credit Debtors) but the bad debt expense account has not recorded the bad debt. If so, credits exceed debits and a suspense account entry is needed.

Item D The error in item D makes total debits higher by £180. These will therefore cause an entry in the suspense account.

159 A

To decide what entries are needed in the suspense account, you should think about the entry in the other account that is needed to correct the error. The entry in the suspense account is then the other side of the double entry. For example, stock (an asset) should be a debit balance, so to correct the error, we need to debit the stock account and credit suspense account. Similarly, VAT payable should be a credit balance, and to record the missing VAT, we need to credit the VAT account, debit suspense account.

Suspense account

	£		£
Balance (balancing figure)	2,050	Stock (1,475 + 1,745)	3,220
Telephone expense (2 × £190)	380		
VAT (£5,390 – £4,600)	790		
	3,220		3,220

160 A

The VAT balance for purchases should be a debit balance, because the money is recoverable from the tax authorities. The VAT recoverable has been recorded as a credit entry (liability) instead of a debit entry, so to make the correction, we need to debit the VAT account by 2 × £3,079 = £6,158. The correction is Debit VAT £6,158, Credit Suspense account £6,158.

161 B

If the suspense account shows a credit balance, the correcting entry to clear the account must be Debit Suspense account £130, credit the account with the error £130.

Purchases have been over-stated by £130, and to correct this, we need to credit the Purchases account (and so debit Suspense account) with £130.

Omissions of transactions (item A and possibly item C) do not affect total debits and credits. If item C means that total debtors have been reduced by the bad debt, but the bad debts account does not yet show the bad debt, the correcting entry would be to debit the Bad debts account and credit Suspense account. The error in item D leaves total debits and credits equal.

162 C

This is an error of principle, because an expense item (motor repairs) has been charged to a fixed asset account.

163 A

The allowance required at the end of the period is 8% of £11,700 + 75% of £4,900 = £936 + £3,675 = £4,611.

The allowance for doubtful debts at the start of the year was £5,200.

There is a reduction in the required allowance, by £589.

164   £11,000

£77,000/7 years = £11,000

165   A

The net book value of the motor vehicles at the start of the year was £37,000 - £18,870 = £18,130.

Depreciation at 30% on the reducing balance method gives a depreciation charge for the year of 30% of £18,130 = £5,439.

166   C

In the P&L, income of £136,894 exceeds expenses (£129,685) by £7,209.

FINAL ACCOUNTS

167   C

Current assets, such as stocks or trade debtors, are normally converted into cash within 12 months.

168   B

Current		£
Payments due:	1 November 20X5	3,000
	1 May 20X6	3,000
		6,000
Long term:	Balance	21,000
Total		27,000

169   B

The allowance has decreased by £500.

170   B

Current liabilities are debts that are payable within the next 12 months, long-term liabilities are debts that are payable in more than one year.

171   B

A prepaid expense will reduce the charge to the profit and loss account. It will also be shown as a current asset in the balance sheet.

172   C

The accrual should have been for £700, but was actually £1,400. Therefore it needs to be reduced by £700.

INCOMPLETE RECORDS

173   £28,500

	£
Cash owed by debtors at the year end	1,300
Cash from clients during the year	28,000
	29,300
Cash owed by debtors at the start of the year	(800)
Therefore sales in the year	28,500

174   £1,930

	£
Cash owed to suppliers at the year end	200
Payments to suppliers during the year	1,800
	2,000
Creditors at the start of the year	(70)
Therefore purchases in the year	1,930

175   B

	Net book value £		Depreciation £
Furniture		(25% of 800)	200
Computer	1,575	(× 25%)	394
Printer	844	(× 25%)	211
			805

176   £3,714

	Cost £	Aggregate dep'n £	NBV £
Furniture	800	400	400
Computer	2,800	1,619	1,181
Printer	1,500	867	633
	5,100	2,886	2,214
Stocks		900	
Debtors		1,300	
Bank (see note)		3,900	
		6,100	
Creditors		(200)	
			5,900
			8,114
Bank loans (2,400 + 2,000)			(4,400)
Net assets = Capital			3,714

Receipts = 30,000. Payments = 26,800. Cash at start of year = £700. Therefore cash at year end = 700 + 30,000 − 26,800 = 3,900.

177 B

	£
Capital at end of year	3,714
Capital at start of year	2,599
Increase in capital	1,115
Less new capital introduced	0
Add back: Drawings	24,000
Profit for the year	25,115

178 B

Discounts allowed are the balancing figure in the debtors' account, after all the other figures have been entered in the account.

Debtors

	£		£
Balance b/d	800	Bank	6,730
Sales	6,800	Bad debts	40
		Discounts allowed	**280**
		Balance c/d	550
	7,600		7,600
Balance b/d			

179 £5,450

Cost of goods sold = £5,000.

Profit mark-up = 120% = £6,000.

Sale price = £5,000 + £6,000 = £11,000.

Discounts allowed = 5% of £11,000 = £550.

	£
Gross profit	6,000
Discounts allowed	550
Net profit	5,450

180 £18,950

	£
Sales	230,000
Money banked (160,000 + 50,000)	210,000
	20,000
Increase in debtors (3,000 – 2,000)	(1,000)
Increase in cash in till (100 – 50)	(50)
Money unaccounted for = stolen	18,950

181 A

The cost of stock includes carriage inwards (carriage outwards is charged to selling and distribution).

182 D

Purchases + Opening stock – Closing stock

183 B

The debit profit and loss column exceeds the credit column by £12,081. This means that expenses have exceeded income, so the business has made a loss.

184 A

The figure of sales is calculated as follows:

	£
Receipts	29,860
Less opening debtors	(16,528)
Plus closing debtors	15,865
Sales	29,197

185 B

	£
Money banked	50,000
Money from sale of car	(5,000)
Money banked from sales	45,000
Wages paid in cash	12,000
Drawings in cash	2,000
Increase in cash in till in the month	100
Sales (all cash)	59,100

PARTNERSHIP ACCOUNTS

186 D

Neither statement is correct. 'Salaries' paid to partners are an appropriation of profits, not an expense. It is quite possible for a partner's current account to have a debit balance. This would occur if the partner had withdrawn more than the amount of profit, interest on capital and salary credited to his account.

187 B

Albert's share of the profit is calculated after deducting David's salary: (£16,000 – £8,000) × 3/5 = £4,800.

188 £430,000

£75,000 + £290,000 - £105,000 + £170,000 = £430,000

189   **£52,750**

(£170,000 – (75,000 × 5%) – 8,000) = £158,250/ 3 = £52,750

190   **£61,500**

(£15,000 × 5%) + 8,000 + £52,750 = £61,500

Section 5

ANSWERS TO SHORT-FORM QUESTIONS

1   Capital expenditure is expenditure on fixed assets, which increase the income generating capacity of a business in the longer term e.g. factory and machinery.

Revenue expenditure is expenditure incurred by a business on day-to-day running costs e.g. wages, heat and light.

2   An asset is an item of value which the business owns or controls. A liability is a requirement to transfer value to another party.

Assets include items such as buildings, or machinery used to carry on the business, stock held for resale, amounts owed by customers, and expenditure on items which have not yet been consumed by the business

Liabilities include amounts owed to suppliers and other parties, and the cost of items and services which have been consumed, but are unpaid. (*Note:* Only ONE example of each is required.)

3   A balance sheet of a business shows the value of its assets, liabilities and capital at a point in time. Assets are classified as fixed and current; liabilities are either long-term or current. The statement is simply based on the accounting equation: i.e. assets equal liabilities plus capital.

4   •   Relevance – the information must be able to influence decisions.

•   Reliability – the information must be a faithful representation.

•   Comparability – the information must provide a basis for like with like comparisons.

•   Understandability – the information must be understandable to the end user.

5   The concept applied here is the prudence concept.

6   Accruals and prepayments include provisions and adjustments covered by the matching or accruals concept.

The concept ensures that income and costs are matched to the trading period in which they were generated or incurred and not when the income is received or the expenditure paid.

7   Financial Reporting Standards set out the manner in which accounts should be prepared. They also give guidance on how certain items should be presented in the accounts.

8   The users of financial statements and their respective needs include:

User	*Need*
Investors	Investors will use financial statements to track the return on their investment, and to assess the likely future trend. They will be particularly concerned with measures of profitability and long-term performance.
Lenders	Lenders will be primarily concerned with ensuring that the entity will be able to continue meeting its obligations under the lending arrangements. They will focus their attention on measures of liquidity and cash flow.
Suppliers	Suppliers will be interested to know if the entity is likely to continue to trade and provide a source of continuing business. They will be most concerned about measures of liquidity and cash flow.
Customers	Customers may use financial statements to ascertain whether there are any indications that the entity may cease to trade, thus leading to an interruption in the supply of goods or services. They will pay most attention to measures of liquidity and cash flow.
Employees	Employees will wish to assess the prospects for continuing job security and wage levels. Their main focus will be on solvency (job security) and profitability and cash flow (wage levels).
Tax authorities	Tax authorities will use the financial statements as the basis for calculating amounts due from the entity.

Note: The question only requires TWO users to be identified.

9   The valuation of stock and depreciation policy need to be consistent year on year, so that like with like comparison can be made by the user of the accounting statements. Different ways of stock valuation give different figures for net assets and profit.

10   The going concern basis means that the business can be reasonably expected to continue to operate for the foreseeable future, without any significant reduction in the scale of its operations.

11   The main factors which cause assets to depreciate include:

- wear and tear through use e.g. vehicles;

- passage of time e.g. lease;

- depletion e.g. gravel pit;

- obsolescence e.g. high tech change.

12   Depreciation for the period will be charged to the profit and loss account. Accumulated depreciation to date will be shown on the balance sheet, offset against the assets at cost to show their net book value.

13 The amount to be capitalised would be both the costs and installation of the asset (excluding VAT).

	£
Ramp	12,000
Installation	1,400
	————
	13,400

14 The reducing balance method is the most suitable as under this method the depreciation charge is higher in the earlier years of the life of the asset.

15 The factors to consider would be the original cost less depreciation to date, compared with the proceeds from the sale.

16 Set up a purchase ledger control account. The missing figure to complete the account would be the purchases for the period.

Purchase ledger control account

	£		£
Cash paid	X	Opening creditors b/d	X
Discounts received	X	Purchases	?
Purchase returns	X		
Closing creditors c/d	X		
	X		X

17 This is an error of principle – an asset, which is a capital expenditure, has been charged to revenue expenditure account. The chairs will be used for a long period of time and should be capitalised and depreciated over their useful economic life.

18 The difference would be posted to a suspense account and the error located later, so that the preparation of the monthly accounts are not delayed.

19 A sales ledger control account can aid management because:

- an up-to-date debtors, figure is readily available;

- it is reconcilable to subsidiary ledger accounts;

- it prevents fraud;

- it is an aid to locating errors;

- it provides the debtors, figure for the final accounts.

20 The reasons for disagreement between the cashbook and bank statement balances can be: timing differences for unpresented cheques and outstanding lodgements, together with standing order and BACS receipts and payments, and bank charges and interest.

21 The profit and loss account would be credited with the reduction in the provision i.e. £450, the debtors shown in the balance sheet would be net of the current provision of £1,650.

22 They would be valued at £180 – their NRV (net realisable value) complying with the prudence concept.

23 The accruals principle means that profit is calculated by deducting the costs incurred in an accounting period from the revenue earned in that period; costs are recognised on the basis of consumption, rather than cash flow, while revenue is considered to be earned when goods are sold rather than when payment is received.

24 Debit the provision for depreciation on vehicles account and credit the disposal of asset account.

25 Set up a debtors control account. The missing figure to complete the accounts would be the sales figure for the period.

Sales ledger control account

	£		£
Opening debtors b/d	X	Cash received	X
Sales	?	Discounts allowed	X
		Sales returns	X
		Bad debt written off	X
		Closing debtors c/d	X
	——		——
	X		X
	——		——
Balance b/d	X		

26 Items include:

- drawings;
- interest on drawings;
- salary;
- share of profit.

A closing credit balance represents a partner's accumulated share of retained profits.

27 A loss for an accounting period is debited to the capital account and reduces the amount of the owner's capital in the business.

28   Mark up involves adding a percentage to cost to derive a selling price.

The margin is the relationship of gross profit to sales, i.e. gross profit divided by sales.

29   (a)   Dr   Motor van   £12,000

Dr   VAT   £2,100

Cr   Creditors   £14,100

Being purchase of a motor van

(b)   Dr   Motor car   £10,575

Cr   Creditors   £10,575

Being purchase of a motor car

Tutorial note: VAT is recoverable on the purchase of a van, but not on the purchase of a car.

30   Dr   Cash at bank a/c

Cr   Debtors ledger control a/c (and personal a/c)

Dr   Debtors ledger control a/c (and personal a/c)

Cr   Bad debts expense a/c (or bad debts recovered a/c)
which may be abbreviated to

Dr   Cash at bank a/c

Cr   Bad debts expense a/c

31   Dr   Office expenses a/c

Cr   Purchases a/c

32   Asset number: recorded on the fixed asset itself by the business

Description: from the purchase invoice/physical inspection of the asset

Location reference: physical inspection will reveal this. The original authorisation may also detail this.

Supplier: from the invoice

Date of purchase: from the invoice

Cost: from the invoice

33

	Depreciation charge £	*Cost/Net book value* £
Original cost		15,000
Year 1	$15,000 \times 25\% = 3,750$	$15,000 - 3,750 = 11,250$
Year 2	$11,250 \times 25\% = 2,813$	$11,250 - 2,813 = 8,437$
Year 3	$8,437 \times 25\% = 2,109$	$8,437 - 2,109 = 6,328$
Year 4	$6,328 \times 25\% = 1,582$	$6,328 - 1,582 = 4,746$
Year 5	$4,746 \times 25\% = 1,187$	$4,746 - 1,187 = 3,559$

34 Non-current assets are items which are held for the long term. They are items owned by the business and used to carry out the activities of the business.

Current assets are held for the short term and usually intended for conversion into cash in the short term.

35 Depreciation is the method used to allocate the cost of non-current assets to the accounting periods which will benefit from their use.

36 A balance sheet provides a statement of the financial position of a business at a particular point in time. It lists the assets, liabilities and capital at that date.

37 The main purpose of a trial balance is to ensure that debit balances and credit balances are equal. This provides a basic check on the accuracy of the postings.

38 A bad debt is a debt which is considered to be irrecoverable. Bad debts are written off as an expense in the profit and loss account. The relevant debtor's account is reduced accordingly.

Doubtful debts are debts that may or may not be collected. The business makes an allowance for doubtful debts, usually based on past experience. Any increase or decrease in the allowance is credited or debited to the profit and loss account. The full amount of the allowance is deducted from the figure of debtors shown in the balance sheet. The accounts of the individual debtors remain unaffected.

39 Accounting policies are those rules adopted by the business in drawing up its final accounts. They cover such matters as the method used to provide for depreciation.

40 There is a dual aspect to each transaction. The debit and credit entries reflect this. For example, if a business buys a car for use by an employee, the business has gained a car but lost the funds used to pay for it. Therefore the cost of the car will be shown as a fixed asset, whilst the cash paid for the car will reduce the funds in the bank account.

41 There are a number of reasons for a difference between the assets in the fixed asset register and those physically present in the business. For example, the fixed asset register may not have been updated to reflect the purchase of a new asset or the disposal of an old asset. In addition, an error may have been made when an entry was originally made in the records.

42 The trial balance will only detect an error if the debit and credit entries do not agree.

(i) Examples of errors that *will* be detected by a trial balance are:

- Single entry; only one entry has been made for a transaction.

- Both entries made on the same side; e.g. a credit sale recorded as Credit Turnover, Credit Debtors.

- One entry for a transaction recorded at the incorrect amount; e.g. a transposition error in one entry.

(ii) Examples of errors that will *not* be detected by a trial balance are:

- Error of omission; the entire transaction has been missed out and neither the debit nor the credit entry has been recorded.

- Error of commission; one entry has been posted to the wrong account. For example cleaning expenses debited to office expenses.

- Error of principle; one entry has been posted to the wrong *class* of account. For example a loan being posted to Income in the P&L instead of to Loan Creditors in the balance sheet.

- Compensating error; the chance situation where two separate errors cancel each other out.

- Error on an original entry in a Day Book; if a purchase invoice is entered into the Purchase Day Book incorrectly then both the debit and credit postings will be incorrect by the same amount.

(Only two examples needed for each part.)

43 Capital accounts record the long-term investment by the partners in the business. Normally, entries are only made when a partner joins or leaves the business, or if the partners as a whole agree to change their capital contributions.

Current accounts record the share of profits allocated to each partner and the amount of cash that each partner has taken out of the business.

Typical transactions include:

Capital account: Capital introduced and capital withdrawn.

Current account: Appropriations of profit (interest on capital, salary, profit share).

Drawings and interest on drawings.

44 The accounting principle behind prepayments:

The accruals principle states that transactions are recorded in the profit and loss account for the financial period in which they occur, even if this is different from the related cash flows. So if insurance for 20X6 is paid in December 20X5 then this will be reported as a prepayment in the balance sheet as at 31 December 20X5 and will then be charged to the P&L in 20X6, which is the period to which it relates. (At 31 December 20X5 none of the benefits of the insurance have been used up, so it is not charged to the P&L.)

45 Fixed asset register

Data	Purpose
Description	Classification of asset in balance sheet
Date of purchase	Assess age for depreciation
Cost	Initial measurement and calculation of depreciation
Residual value	Calculation of depreciation
Useful economic life	Calculation of depreciation
Location	Inspection and security
Serial numbers and asset numbers	Identification (especially if there are similar items) and security

(Only four examples required.)

Section 6

ANSWERS TO PRACTICE QUESTIONS

BASIC BOOKKEEPING

1 CAMERON FINDLAY

Cash at bank account

		£			£
(a)	Capital a/c	1,500	(b)	Rent a/c	230
(e)	Sales a/c	240	(c)	Purchases a/c	420
(g)	Sales a/c	16	(d)	Purchases a/c	180
(j)	Sales a/c	50	(f)	Purchases a/c	10
			(h)	Purchases a/c	80
			(i)	Wages a/c	95
			(k)	Sundry expenses a/c	10
				Balance c/d	781
		_____			_____
		1,806			1,806
		_____			_____
	Balance b/d	781			

Capital account

		£			£
			(a)	Cash at bank a/c	1,500

Rent account

		£			£
(b)	Cash at bank a/c	230			

Purchases account

		£		£
(c)	Cash at bank a/c	420		
(d)	Cash at bank a/c	180		
(f)	Cash at bank a/c	10		
(h)	Cash at bank a/c	80	Balance c/d	690
		——		——
		690		690
		——		——
Balance b/d		690		

Sales account

		£			£
			(e)	Cash at bank a/c	240
			(g)	Cash at bank a/c	16
Balance c/d		306	(j)	Cash at bank a/c	50
		——			——
		306			306
		——			——
			Balance b/d		306

Wages account

		£		£
(i)	Cash at bank a/c	95		

Sundry expenses account

		£		£
(k)	Cash at bank a/c	10		

Tutorial note: It is not necessary to perform the mechanics of balancing an account which contains only one entry as this entry is the balance.

2   JOHN FRY AND JAYNE GARNETT

(i)

Cash and bank account

	£		£
Capital	10,000	Van	3,600
Sales	110	Van	1,700
Sales	80	Purchases	400
Sales	170	Freezer	260
Sales	50	Purchases	190
		Wages	40
		Drawings	60
		Bal c/d	**4,160**
	⎯⎯		⎯⎯
	10,410		10,410

Capital account

	£		£
Bal c/d	**10,000**	Cash and bank	10,000
	⎯⎯		⎯⎯
	10,000		10,000

Van account

	£		£
Cash and bank	3,600		
Cash and bank	1,700	**Bal c/d**	**5,300**
	⎯⎯		⎯⎯
	5,300		5,300

Purchases account

	£		£
Cash and bank	400		
Cash and bank	190	**Bal c/d**	**590**
	⎯⎯		⎯⎯
	590		590

Sales account

	£		£
		Cash and bank	110
		Cash and bank	80
		Cash and bank	170
Bal c/d	**410**	Cash and bank	50
	___		___
	410		410
	___		___

Freezer account

	£		£
Cash and bank	260	**Bal c/d**	**260**
	___		___
	260		260
	___		___

Wages

	£		£
Cash and bank	40	**Bal c/d**	**40**
	___		___
	40		40
	___		___

Drawings

	£		£
Cash and bank	60	**Bal c/d**	**60**
	___		___
	60		60
	___		___

(ii)

MEMORANDUM

To: Jayne Garnett

From: XYZ

Subject: The profit figure in the balance sheet and the profit and loss account

Date: 6 September 20X5

The profit figure for an accounting period is relevant to both the balance sheet and the profit and loss account.

The profit and loss account gives a detailed account of how the profit for a period has arisen from trading and other incidental activities. The net profit at the foot of the profit and loss account belongs to the owner of the business and is added to the owner's capital.

The balance sheet is an accounting equation showing the net assets which represent the owner's capital:

Net assets = capital

Changes in the net assets total will occur if capital is introduced or withdrawn or if a profit is made. The balance sheet will show these changes in capital during the year, including the net profit per the profit and loss account which is transferred into capital.

Thus, the net profit for the period links these two financial statements, effectively being transferred from one to the other.

Signed: XYZ

3   ROBERT DEMPSTER

(i)

Cash at bank account

		$			$
(a)	Capital	10,000	(e)	Vans Galore	**2,000**
(f)	Woodside Rugby Club	65	(e)	Surgiplast Ltd	**150**
			(g)	**Drawings**	130
				Balance c/d	**7,785**
		10,065			
					10,065
	Balance b/d	**7,785**			

(ii)   The **separate entity** concept is the principle underlying the treatment of the owner's private expenses paid by the business. This concept requires the transactions of a **business** to be recorded separately from those of the **owner** of a business. Consequently, this payment could not be analysed as 'electricity' as it is not the electricity expense of the business. It may be thought of as a withdrawal of cash from the business by the owner.

(iii)   (a)   revenue

(b)   capital

(c)   capital

(d)   capital

(e)   revenue

(f)   revenue

(g)   revenue

(h)   capital

(i)   revenue

(j)   revenue.

4 WILSON'S BANK ACCOUNT

(a) 'T' Account in the Nominal Ledger

Bank account

	£		£
		Nominal ledger balance	113
(i) Error on cheque (760-670)	90	(ii) Bank charges for May	428
(vii) Cancelled cheque	625	(iii) Returned cheque	320
	715		861
Balance carried down	146		-
	861		861

The timing differences on the lodgements and cheques, and the bank error on the interest, do not affect the bank account.

(b) Bank reconciliation

	£
Balance in the Nominal Ledger (overdrawn)	(146)
(iv) Add deposit account interest incorrectly recorded on the bank statement	220
(v) Less lodgement not yet recorded on the bank statement	(850)
(vi) Add unpresented cheques (326 + 469 + 22 + 187)	1,004
Balance on the Bank Statement (in hand)	228

(c) Presentation

Wilson will report the £146 overdraft as a creditor falling due within 12 months. The nominal ledger balance is used in the financial statements, not the bank statement balance.

5 PETER PINDO

Cash account

	£		£
Capital	41,000.00	Purchases/VAT	6,674.00
Sales 2,640 × 1.175	3,102.00	Creditors	2,650.00
Debtors	3,110.00	Bal c/d	37,888.00
	47,212.00		47,212.00

Capital account

	£		£
Bal c/d	41,000.00	Cash	41,000.00
	41,000.00		41,000.00

Sales account

	£		£
		Debtors	3,600.00
		Cash	2,640.00
Bal c/d	9,609.00	Debtors	3,369.00
	9,609.00		9,609.00

Debtors account

	£		£
Sales 3,600 × 1.175	4,230.00	Cash	3,110.00
Sales 3,369 × 1.175	3,958.57	Bal c/d	5,078.57
	8,188.57		8,188.57

Purchases account

	£		£
Cash 6,674 × 100/117.5	5,680.00		
Creditors	3,200.00	Bal c/d	8,880.00
	8,880.00		8,880.00

Creditors account

	£		£
Cash	2,650.00		
Bal c/d	1,110.00	Purchases 3,200 × 1.175	3,760.00
	3,760.00		3,760.00

VAT account

	£		£
VAT on purchases			
$6{,}674 \times 17.5/117.5$	994.00		
VAT on purchases		VAT on sales $3{,}600 \times 17.5\%$	630.00
$3{,}200 \times 17.5\%$	560.00	VAT on sales $2{,}640 \times 17.5\%$	462.00
Bal c/d	127.57	VAT on sales $3{,}369 \times 17.5\%$	589.57
	1,681.57		1,681.57

6 PROFIT AND LOSS ACCOUNT

Profit and loss account	£	£
Sales		55,000
Cost of goods sold: purchases		(31,600)
Gross profit		23,400
Expenses		
Loan interest	125	
Sundry	40	
Motor	360	
Wages	970	
		1,495
Net profit		21,905

Drawings account

	£		£
Cash at bank account	200	Capital account	300
Cash at bank account	100		
	300		300

Owner's capital account

	£		£
Drawings	300	Balance b/d	10,000
Balance c/d	31,605	Profit	21,905
	———		———
	31,905		31,905
	———		———
		Balance b/d	31,605

7   GRAHAM WINSTON

(a)

Cash at bank account

	£		£
Capital	5,000	Wages	120
Sales	1,400	Sundry expenses	36
Debtors	1,500	Rent	175
		Motor expenses	44
		Creditors	3,000
		Drawings	300
		Balance c/d	4,225
	———		———
	7,900		7,900
	———		———
Balance b/d	4,225		

Van account

	£		£
Capital	4,600		

Capital account

	£		£
Drawings	300	Cash at bank	5,000
		Van	4,600
Balance c/d	13,825	Profit	4,525
	———		———
	14,125		14,125
	———		———
		Balance b/d	13,825

Purchases account

	£		£
Creditors	3,000	P&L a/c	4,800
Creditors	1,800		
	———		———
	4,800		4,800
	———		———

Creditors account

	£		£
Cash at bank	3,000	Purchases	3,000
Balance c/d	1,800	Purchases	1,800
	———		———
	4,800		4,800
	———		———
		Balance b/d	1,800

Sales account

	£		£
		Debtors	2,000
		Cash at bank	1,400
P&L a/c	9,700	Debtors	6,300
	———		———
	9,700		9,700
	———		———

Debtors account

	£		£
Sales	2,000	Cash at bank	1,500
Sales	6,300	Balance c/d	6,800
	———		———
	8,300		8,300
	———		———
Balance b/d	6,800		

Wages account

	£		£
Cash at bank	120	P&L a/c	120
	———		———
	120		120
	———		———

Sundry expenses account

	£		£
Cash at bank	36	P&L a/c	36
	──		──
	36		36
	──		──

Rent account

	£		£
Cash at bank	175	P&L a/c	175
	──		──
	175		175
	──		──

Motor expenses account

	£		£
Cash at bank	44	P&L a/c	44
	──		──
	44		44
	──		──

Drawings account

	£		£
Cash at bank	300	Capital	300
	──		──
	300		300
	──		──

(b) **Graham Winston**

(i) **Trading, profit and loss account for the month ending 31 March 20X5**

	£	£
Sales		9,700
Less: Cost of sales – purchases		(4,800)
		────
Gross profit		4,900
Expenses		
Wages	120	
Sundry	36	
Rent	175	
Motor expenses	44	
	──	(375)
Net profit		4,525
		────

(ii) **Balance sheet at 31 March 20X5**

	£	£
Fixed assets – van		4,600
Current assets		
Debtors	6,800	
Cash at bank	4,225	
	11,025	
Current liabilities		
Creditors	(1,800)	
Net current assets		9,225
		13,825
Capital		9,600
Add: Profit		4,525
		14,125
Less: Drawings		(300)
		13,825

(c)   See individual accounts.

8   IVES LTD

Nominal ledger accounts

Purchases

		£			£
15 Feb	Balance b/d	28,890.31			
16 Feb	PDB	963.19			

Creditors ledger control

		£			£
16 Feb	PCB	1,431.29	15 Feb	Balance b/d	17,275.49
16 Feb	PCB - discounts	30.65	16 Feb	PDB	1,131.71

VAT

		£			£
16 Feb	PDB	168.52	15 Feb	Balance b/d	1,008.37

Discounts received

		£			£
			15 Feb	Balance b/d	165.27
			16 Feb	PCB	30.65

Purchases ledger accounts

AKC Ltd   015

		£			£
16 Feb	PDB CN113	41.57	15 Feb	Balance b/d	118.39

Channer Ltd   023

		£			£
16 Feb	PCB 013972	559.29	15 Feb	Balance b/d	1,072.59
			16 Feb	PDB 19552	621.74

Cook Associates   024

		£			£
16 Feb	PCB 013975	60.27	15 Feb	Balance b/d	60.27

Haworth & Sons   029

		£			£
			15 Feb	Balance b/d	471.72
			16 Feb	PDB 2261	223.20

GL Kertin   038

		£			£
			15 Feb	Balance b/d	–
			16 Feb	PDB 123	58.48

JT Liverpool   041

		£			£
16 Feb	PCB 013976	281.59	15 Feb	Balance b/d	612.93
16 Feb	PCB - discount	14.82	16 Feb	PDB 10472	169.32

Moore Brothers   045

		£			£
			15 Feb	Balance b/d	92.69
			16 Feb	PDB 8816	117.29

E Riordan   052

		£			£
16 Feb	PCB 013974	182.49	15 Feb	Balance b/d	192.09
16 Feb	PCB – discount	9.60			

Slutar Ltd   055

		£			£
16 Feb	PDB CN992	16.75	15 Feb	Balance b/d	236.71
	PCB 013971	118.30			
	PCB – discount	6.23			

Tutors & Sons

		£			£
16 Feb	PCB 013973	229.35	15 Feb	Balance b/d	229.35

9   VICTORIA LTD

Nominal ledger

Sales

		£			£
			30 July	Balance b/d	24,379.20
			3 Aug	SDB	986.86

Debtors ledger control

		£			£
30 July	Balance b/d	1,683.08	3 Aug	RCB	1,007.29
3 Aug	SDB	1,159.50	3 Aug	Discount	17.89

Discounts allowed

		£			£
30 July	Balance b/d	138.30			
3 Aug	RCB	17.89			

VAT

		£				£
			30 July	Balance b/d		352.69
			3 Aug	SDB		172.64

Sales ledger

Stephen Williams & Co   001

		£			£
30 July	Balance b/d	38.20			
2 Aug	SDB 5109	69.00			

Monty Dee   003

		£			£
30 July	Balance b/d	73.50	2 Aug	RCB	73.50
1 Aug	SDB 5106	61.48			

Roberts Partners   007

		£			£
30 July	Balance b/d	279.30	3 Aug	RCB	111.62
2 Aug	SDB 5107	153.20			

Imogen Jones   009

		£			£
30 July	Balance b/d	137.23	30 July	RCB	73.20

Olivia Consultants   015

		£			£
30 July	Balance b/d	42.61			
1 Aug	SDB 5105	82.47			

Anna Pargeter   019

		£			£
30 July	Balance b/d	198.17	30 July	RCB	198.17
2 Aug	SDB 5108	221.78		RCB - discount	6.13

Peter Rover   026

		£			£
30 July	Balance b/d	296.38			
31 July	SDB 5104	142.03			

AM McGee   027

		£			£
30 July	Balance b/d	335.28	2 Aug	RCB	185.31
	SDB 5103	159.30		RCB - discount	5.23

Phillipa Steven   032

		£			£
30 July	Balance b/d	116.78	31 July	RCB	116.78

Clive Brown   035

		£			£
30 July	Balance b/d	35.10			
3 Aug	SDB 5111	62.70			

Owens Ltd   036

		£			£
30 July	Balance b/d	512.74	1 Aug	RCB	211.31
3 Aug	SDB 5110	159.36		RCB - discount	6.53

Cameron Associates   045

		£			£
30 July	Balance b/d	335.28	31 July	RCB	37.40
	SDB 5102	48.18			

10   MICHAEL MOORE

(a) **General ledger accounts**

Cash at bank

	£		£
CRB	2,428	CPB	2,100

Purchases

	£		£
PDB	2,223		

Creditors ledger control

	£		£
CPB	940	PDB	2,223
CPB	3		
Balance c/d	1,280		
	——		——
	2,223		2,223
	——		——
		Balance b/d	1,280

Sales

	£		£
		SDB	2,507

Debtors ledger control

	£		£
SDB	2,507	CRB	1,328
		CRB	4
		Balance c/d	1,175
	——		——
	2,507		2,507
	——		——
Balance b/d	1,175		

Capital

	£		£
		CRB	100

Loan

	£		£
		CRB	1,000

Discounts allowed

	£		£
CRB	4		

Rent

	£		£
CPB	210		

Fixed assets

	£		£
CPB	950		

Discounts received

	£		£
		CPB	3

(b)   **Creditors ledger**

Simon

	£		£
CPB	340	PDB	340
Balance c/d	801	PDB	801
	——		——
	1,141		1,141
	——		——
		Balance b/d	801

Jake

	£		£
CPB	600	PDB	603
Discount received	3		
	——		——
	603		603
	——		——

Francis

	£		£
Balance c/d	404	PDB	224
		PDB	180
	——		——
	404		404
	——		——
		Balance b/d	404

Joseph

	£		£
		PDB	75

Debtors ledger

Jill

	£		£
SDB	750	CRB	620
SDB	620	Balance c/d	750
	———		———
	1,370		1,370
Balance b/d	750		

Vivienne

	£		£
SDB	312	CRB	312
SDB	370	Balance c/d	370
	———		———
	682		682
Balance b/d	370		

Angela

	£		£
SDB	55		

Susan

	£		£
SDB	400	CRB	396
		Discounts allowed	4
	———		———
	400		400

(c)   **List of creditors ledger balances**

	£
Simon	801
Jake	nil
Francis	404
Joseph	75
	———
Total	1,280

List of debtors ledger balances

	£
Jill	750
Vivienne	370
Angela	55
Susan	nil
	1,175

(d)   Balance per debtors ledger control account and list of balances extracted from the debtors ledger = £1,175.

Balance per creditors ledger control account and list of balances extracted from the creditors ledger = £1,280.

11   SETTLEMENT DISCOUNTS

(i)

Debtor account

	£		£
Sales	900	Cash at bank account	873
		Discounts allowed	27

Sales account

	£		£
		Debtors	900

Discounts allowed account

	£		£
Debtors	27		

Creditors account

	£		£
Cash at bank account	582	Purchases of stock	600
Discounts received	18		

Discounts received account

	£		£
		Creditors	18

Purchases of stock account

	£		£
Creditors	600		

Cash at bank account

	£		£
Debtors	873	Creditors	582

(ii)   (a)   Fixed assets.

      (b)   Current assets.

      (c)   Fixed assets.

      (d)   Current assets.

      (e)   Current assets.

      (f)   Fixed assets.

      (g)   Current assets.

ACCOUNTING STANDARDS, PRINCIPLES AND POLICIES

12   FUNDAMENTAL CONCEPTS

Note: Only three of the concepts were required to be explained by the question, but all four explanations have been given for the purposes of your studies.

The going concern concept is an assumption that the business for which accounts are being prepared will continue for the foreseeable future and that the financial statements of the business will reflect this assumption. If the business is to be assumed to be continuing for the foreseeable future then any assets that are remaining at the end of the accounting period, such as fixed assets and items of stock, can validly be valued at their original cost. If, however, there is evidence that the business will not continue for the foreseeable future then such assets should be written down to their net realisable values.

As an example under the going concern concept, it is valid to value fixed assets at their historical cost less any accumulated depreciation. However, if there were evidence to suggest that the business would soon cease then it would be more appropriate to value fixed assets at the amount at which they could be sold on the open market. This may involve writing off intangible fixed assets (e.g. goodwill) entirely.

The accruals concept means that when preparing financial statements costs and revenues should be matched wherever possible and dealt with in the period in which they are earned or incurred rather than the period in which the cash is received or paid.

As an example of this concept, the amount of telephone expense that is charged to the profit and loss account for the period should be the telephone expense used in the period. This may exclude some rental paid in advance, which will be treated as a prepayment, and may include an accrual for calls that have been made but for which perhaps the bill has not yet been received or paid.

The consistency concept is an assumption that similar items in the financial statements will be treated in the same manner within a period and from one period to another. This assumption means that it is possible to compare an organisation's results from period to period in a meaningful manner. If an organisation does change its accounting treatment of an item between one accounting period and another enough information about this change, the old policy and the new policy should be given for users to be able to appreciate the effect of the change of policy.

An area where there is a need for a consistent accounting policy in order for the accounts to be validly compared from period to period is the valuation of items of stock. The stock valuation method chosen, such as first in first out or average cost, should be used consistently from period to period.

The prudence concept is a concept that the figures used in the financial statements should never overstate profits made or the assets shown in the balance sheet. Therefore any losses that are anticipated should be written off immediately and any profits should not be recognised in the financial statements, until there is reasonable certainty that they have been earned. If an item in the financial statements is uncertain then the figure taken for that item will be that which will give the lower profit.

An example of the prudence concept is that any item of stock that is expected to realise less than its original cost should be written down to its net realisable value thus recognising the expected loss immediately. However, items of stock that are expected to realise more than their original cost are still only valued at their cost thus deferring the recognition of profit until the items are actually sold.

13 PROBLEMS

(a) **Going concern**. The accountant normally prepares the accounts on the assumption that the life of the business is long-term. If it is highly likely that the company is to be liquidated in the near future, he will prepare its accounts on the expected value of the assets at the time of dissolution. This fact must be included in its statement of accounting policies.

(b) **Business entity**. This is a matter which concerns the proprietor in his private capacity. As it is of no interest to the business, such an investment would not be recorded in the books of account.

(c) **Matching (or Accruals)**. Since the business has had the benefit of the electricity, this item would normally be included in the accounts of that period, even though the amount has not actually been paid.

(d) **Historic cost**. Fixed assets are usually recorded and retained at their original cost. Some assets may be revalued, however, e.g. property, and restated in the balance sheet at the revalued amount. Sometimes also, a special reserve is created in order to allow for the replacement of assets at what is expected to be a greater cost. Nonetheless, the historic cost concept is still widely adopted.

(e) **Materiality**. Although the pencils were still in use at the end of the year, their original value was so small that it would normally be considered quite unnecessary to value them and include them in closing stock. Instead, they should be written off to the profit and loss account in the period in which they were purchased.

FIXED ASSETS AND DEPRECIATION

14   MEAD

Motor car – cost account

		£			£
20X3			*20X3*		
1 Jan	Purchase ledger control	12,000	31 Dec	Balance c/d	12,000
		———	*20X4*		
20X4			31 Dec	Balance c/d	12,000
1 Jan	Balance b/d	12,000			———
		———	*20X5*		
20X5			31 Dec	Balance c/d	12,000
1 Jan	Balance b/d	12,000			———
20X6					
1 Jan	Balance b/d	12,000			

$$\text{Annual depreciation charge} = \frac{12,000 - 2,400}{4} = £2,400$$

Motor car – provision for depreciation account

		£			£
20X3			*20X3*		
31 Dec	Balance c/d	2,400	31 Dec	Depreciation expense	2,400
		———			———
20X4			*20X4*		
31 Dec	Balance c/d	4,800	1 Jan	Balance b/d	2,400
		———	31 Dec	Depreciation expense	2,400
		4,800			———
		———			4,800
					———
20X5			*20X5*		
31 Dec	Balance c/d	7,200	1 Jan	Balance b/d	4,800
		———	31 Dec	Depreciation expense	2,400
		7,200			———
		———			7,200
					———
			20X6		
			1 Jan	Balance b/d	7,200

Depreciation (profit and loss) account

		£			£
20X3			*20X3*		
31 Dec	Motor car provision for				
	depreciation	2,400	31 Dec	P&L a/c	2,400
		——			——
20X4			*20X4*		
31 Dec	Motor car provision				
	for depreciation	2,400	31 Dec	P&L a/c	2,400
		——			——
20X5			*20X5*		
31 Dec	Motor car provision				
	for depreciation	2,400	31 Dec	P&L a/c	2,400
		——			——

Tutorial note: The depreciation account is an expense account ie, it is closed off every year to the profit and loss account. It therefore does not have a balance b/d into the 20X4 year.

The provision for depreciation account records the total amounts of depreciation that have been charged on those assets which the business owns at each balance sheet date.

15 CASTINGS AND CO LTD

(i)

Plant and machinery account

	£		£
Creditors	35,000		

Motor vehicles account

	£		£
Creditors	7,500		

Creditors account

	£		£
		Plant and machinery account	35,000
		Motor vehicles account	7,500

Fixed asset register

Asset number	Description	Location	Supplier ref	Purchase date	Useful life	Dep method	Cost £
FZAD123	Machine	Fac.2	A Denton	10.1.X4	7	S/L	35,000
SICD456	Car	Smith	C Dealer	20.4.X4	4	S/L	7,500

(ii)

Transactions	Account to be debited	Account to be credited
(a)	Bank	Capital
(b)	Purchases	Bank
(c)	Bank (or cash)	Sales
(d)	Rent	Bank
(e)	Van	Bank

16 MILTON LTD

Fixed asset register

Class/Group of Assets: *Plant and machinery*

Register prepared as at close of business: *31 Dec 20X6*

Asset:	1	2	3
Acq date:	16.2.X2	1.1.X3	30.6.X6
Further description if any:	Compressor XTI	Scrivenor	Excelsior ZXY
Location:	Walmely	Walmely	Chipping Norton
Estimated life (yrs):	5	5	5
Estimated residual value:	1,000	1,000	Nil
Depreciation method:	S/L	S/L	S/L
Cost:	5,600	11,600	7,000
Dep'n b/d:	3,680	6,360	-

Period dep'n:	$920 \left(\frac{5,600-1,000}{5}\right)$	$2,120 \left(\frac{11,600-1,000}{5}\right)$	$1,400 \left(\frac{7,000}{5}\right)$

Disposal date (if sold):

Proceeds (if sold):

P/L on sale:

C/d figures(if unsold):

Cost:	5,600	11,600	7,000
Acc dep'n:	4,600	8,480	1,400

17 MEMORANDUM

(a)   **MEMORANDUM**

To: Mr William Hayes

From: Junior Manager, Certified Accountants

Ref: Proposed manufacturing project

Date: X-X-20XX

Regarding the proposed purchase of a machine, I bring the following points to your attention:

The classification of capital and revenue expenditure

Capital expenditure relates to fixed assets that are purchased for use in the business, rather than for resale. An annual charge is made in the Profit and Loss Account for the depreciation of fixed assets over their useful lives. This aims to match their cost to the periods benefiting from their use. In the Balance Sheet, fixed assets are generally included at their cost less accumulated depreciation to date.

Revenue expenditure is the purchase of goods for resale, the maintenance of the revenue-earning capacity of fixed assets and the day to day expenses of running the business. This type of expenditure is written off to the Profit and Loss account as it is incurred.

(b) (i) **Classification of proposed costs**

The costs in the supplier's quotation would be classified as follows:

Selling price	£70,000	Capital
Delivery/Installation	£3,500	Capital
Commissioning	£1,500	Capital
Maintenance	£3,500	Revenue

(ii) **Resulting charge of proposed costs**

This would comprise two elements:

Depreciation:

$$\frac{\text{Cost}}{\text{Expected life}} = \frac{75,000}{10} = \qquad £7,500$$

(Using the straight line method.)

Maintenance cost   £3,500
                                                       _____

Total annual charge to profit and loss account   £11,000
                                                       _____

Please do not hesitate to contact me if you require any further information.

18 PURPOSE OF FIXED ASSET REGISTER

(a) **To:** IT Section
    From: Accountant
    Re: Fixed asset register
    Date: June 20X9

The fixed asset register is an accounting record. It lists the assets owned by the company and links these back to the underlying bookkeeping records in the nominal ledger. It acts as a control because it enables us to check that assets are all present and correct.

The register will have a record for each individual asset.

* Each record will show the original cost of the asset and the depreciation charged to date. This will make it easier to record disposals because we will be able to tell what amounts have to be eliminated from the accounts.

- The register will show the basis on which depreciation should be charged, including the rate and method, so that we can calculate depreciation accurately at the year end. This is particularly important for assets that are being written off using straight line depreciation, because these are likely to become written off in full and so no further depreciation should be charged against them.

- The register will show the location of the asset and a unique reference number for that asset. This will make it easier for internal and external audit to organise physical inspections of fixed assets.

- The register will be cross referenced back to the supporting documentation that supports the purchase. This will make to easier to identify the manufacturer and trace the warranty information if the asset should break down.

(b)

Asset at cost

		£			£
1 August 20X8 b/d	Bal	22,000	31 May 20X9	Disposal	22,000
31 May 20X9 Disposal		13,700			
31 May 20X9	Bank	15,800	31 July 20X9	Bal c/d	29,500
		51,500			51,500
1 August 20X9 b/d	Bal	29,500			

Provision for depreciation

		£			£
31 May 20X9 Disposal		6,105	1 August 20X8	Bal b/d	6,105
31 July 20X9	Bal c/d	4,425	31 July 20X9	P & L	4,425
		10,530			10,530
			1 August 20X9	Bal b/d	4,425

The opening balance is arrived at as follows:

	£
Cost	22,000
Depreciation for year ended 31/7/X7	3,300
Book value at 31/7/X7	18,700
Depreciation for year ended 31/7/X8	2,805
	15,895

Depreciation to date = £3,300 + 2,805 = £6,105

The charge for the year = £29,500 × 15% = £4,425

Disposal

		£			£
31 May 20X9	Cost	22,000	31 May 20X9 Depreciation		6,105
			31 May 20X9	Cost	13,700
			31 July 20X9	P & L	2,195
		———			———
		22,000			22,000
		———			———

19 SARAH LUKE

(i)   Depreciation is an application of the matching principle.

(ii) Fixed assets are purchased with the intention that they will be used over several periods and that they will contribute to the generation of revenues during that time. The matching concept requires that the cost of these assets should be recognised in the profit and loss account during those periods when the related benefits arise.

(iii) Depreciation can be recognised in relation to the age of the assets:

- straight line;
- reducing balance;
- sum of digits.

Depreciation can also be recognised in relation to wear and tear:

- units of production.

(iv) Requirements include:

- cost;
- depreciation method;
- expected useful life;
- residual value.

(v)   Capital expenditure:

- cost of machine;
- delivery cost;
- installation cost.

Revenue expenditure:

- annual maintenance cost.

20 GARY CAMPBELL

(a) (i)   Two reasons for keeping a fixed assent register are:

- to maintain specific details about individual fixed assets;
- to allow a greater level of detail to be recorded than would be practicable within the main accounting records.

(ii)   Four items of information included in a fixed asset register are:

- a description of the fixed asset;
- a date of purchase;
- the useful life of the asset;
- the cost of the asset.

Tutorial note: Other acceptable answers would include:

- an asset number;
- a location reference;
- a reference to the supplier;
- the type of depreciation method used;
- the scrap value of the asset.

(iii)
- An asset number – this is a unique number and is a means of identifying any fixed assets in the business.
- A location reference – this will indicate where the fixed asset can be found.
- A reference to a supplier – this will enable the fixed asset to be traced back to an invoice.
- The useful life – how long the asset is expected to be used.

(b)   (i)

	£
Cost of machine traded in	42,000
Depreciation to date of trade in	25,200
Net book value	16,800
Trade in value (proceeds)	17,500
Profit on disposal	700

(ii)
Machinery cost account

	£		£
Balance	42,000	Disposal account	42,000
Disposal a/c	17,500		
Loan a/c	26,000	Balance c/f	51,500
Bank a/c	8,000		
	93,500		93,500

21   JIM

(a)

		Land £	Building £	Machinery £	Total £
(i)	Cost brought forward	85,000	120,500	74,800	280,300
	Additions at cost		6,800	14,500	21,300
	Disposals at cost			(11,000)	(11,000)
		85,000	127,300	78,300	290,600
(ii)	Opening depreciation	nil	28,920	35,600	64,520
	Eliminated on disposal (w)			(5,368)	(5,368)
	Charge for year (w)	nil	5,092	9,614	14,706
	Closing depreciation	nil	34,012	39,846	73,858
(iii)	Net book value	85,000	93,288	38,454	216,742

Workings

Depreciation eliminated:

Machine bought in January 20X0. Thus depreciation for years ended 30 September 20X0, 20X1 and 20X2 = 3 years.

20X0   Cost £11,000 × 20%   = £2,200 depreciation for year
       Thus NBV c/f = £8,800

20X1   b/f £8,800 × 20%   = £1,760 depreciation for year
       Thus NBV c/f = £7,040

20X2   b/f £7,040 × 20%   = £1,408 depreciation for year
       Thus NBV c/f = £5,632

       Total depreciation   = £5,368

Depreciation charge:

Buildings   Cost   £127,300 ÷ 25 years   = £5,092 per annum

Machinery   Cost   £ 78,300

             Depn   £ 30,232

             NBV   £48,068 × 20%   = £9,614 for year

                                             (to nearest £1)

(b)

	£
Cost of machine	11,000
Depreciation to date of disposal	5,368
NBV at disposal	5,632
Proceeds	5,500
Loss	1,132

(c)   Depreciation is required to reflect the economic benefits relating to a fixed asset which have been consumed during the period.

The provision for depreciation is required under the accruals (or matching) concept, as this will match the cost of economic benefits with the revenue generated. This means that, for all assets which are consumed, depreciation must be provided. Land is therefore an exception to the rule that fixed assets must be depreciated, as it is not consumed. It should be noted that this is entirely separate to the issue of any increase in valuation.

CONTROL ACCOUNTS, RECONCILIATIONS AND ERRORS

22   ELIZABETH

(a)

DR	**Debtors Control Account**		CR
	£		£
Balance b/f	39,982	Discount allowed	9
Invoice understated	178	Credit note (£120 × 2)	240
		Direct payment	325
		Balance c/f	39,586
	40,160		40,160

(b)   Adjustments to list of personal balances

		£
	Total as listed	39,614
(i)	Invoice omitted	288
(ii)	Discount omitted	(9)
(iii)	Credit note	(240)
(iv)	Undercast	27
(v)	Credit balance	(94)
		39,586

(c)   The correct debtors' balance is £39,586. It should be shown as a current asset.

23   A NUMBER OF ERRORS

(a)   A payment has been posted to the account of M Jones rather than M James. This means that the balance on M Jones' account will be too small and the balance on M James' account too great.

This should be rectified by reversing the incorrect entry by crediting M Jones' personal account to remove the payment that has not been made and debiting M James' account to put the payment into the correct personal account.

(b)   If the electricity bill has not been entered in the purchases day book then this means that it will appear nowhere in the accounting records at all. Therefore the electricity charge and creditors will both be understated and there will be no amount shown for this bill in the electricity company's personal account in the purchase ledger.

In order to amend this error, the electricity account should be debited and the creditors ledger control account credited in the nominal ledger. In the purchases ledger the electricity company's account should also be credited.

(c)   A credit note from a supplier should normally be debited to the supplier's personal account. In this case it has been credited to the personal account. This has no effect on the accounts in the nominal ledger but will mean that the individual supplier's account in the purchase ledger will show an incorrect balance.

In order to deal with this, the supplier's account in the purchase ledger must be debited with twice the amount of the credit note. This will firstly cancel out the incorrect entry of the credit note and then enter it correctly on the debit side of the account.

(d)   The net of VAT column of the purchases account in the nominal ledger should be credited with the excess amount. Casting errors in the day book totals have no effect on the postings to the individual creditors' accounts in the purchases ledger.

(e)   If the purchases ledger column of the payments cash book was undercast then this means that the debit made to the creditors ledger account in the nominal ledger to reflect payments to creditors was too small.

Therefore an extra debit to the creditors ledger control account is required to show the correct creditors' position. Casting errors have no effect on the individual creditors' accounts in the purchases ledger.

(f)   The discount received total should have been credited to the discount received account in the nominal ledger not the discount allowed account.

This must be rectified by a debit entry being made in the discount allowed account to cancel out the incorrect entry and a credit to the discount received account to correctly record the discount.

(g)   A purchase invoice has been entered into the purchases day book at an amount that includes the trade discount. Therefore the entry is too high and both purchases and the creditors ledger control account will be overstated.

In order to amend this error, the entry in the purchases account and the creditors ledger control account must be reduced to the correct figure by crediting the purchases account and debiting the creditors ledger control account with the difference due to the trade discount.

24   GRIFFIN LTD

GRIFFIN LTD			JOURNAL	
Date	Details		Dr	Cr
			£	£
(a) 3/6/X7	Harris Ltd		179.36	
	T Harris			179.36
	Being correction of incorrect posting of invoice in purchase ledger.			

	Date	Details	Dr	Cr
(b)	3/6/X7	Creditors ledger control	9.00	
		Purchases (32.64 – 23.64)		9.00
		Being correction of credit note transposition error in the nominal ledger.		
		ZZ Ltd	9.00	
		Being correction of credit note transposition error in the purchase ledger.		
(c)	3/6/X7	Purchases	168.26	
		VAT	29.45	
		Creditors ledger control		197.71
		Being entry of purchase invoice omitted from purchase day book in the nominal ledger.		
		Price Ltd		197.71
		Being entry of purchase invoice omitted from purchase day book in the purchases ledger.		
(d)	3/6/X7	Heat and light	247.31	
		Telephone		247.31
		Being correction of incorrect nominal ledger posting from purchases day book.		
(e)	3/6/X7	Creditors ledger control	17.39	
		Discount received		17.39
		Being entry of discount received omitted from the nominal ledger.		
(f)	3/6/X7	T Thomas (purchase ledger)	126.37	
		T Thomas (sales ledger)		126.37

Date	Details	Dr	Cr
	Being contra entry in purchase and sales ledger		
	Creditors ledger control	126.37	
	Debtors ledger control		126.37
	Being contra entry in the nominal ledger.		

25 PETTY CASH

(a)

PETTY CASH BOOK

Date 20X4	Receipts £	Voucher/ reference no	Details	Total payment £	VAT £	Office expenses £	Travel expenses £	Postage £	Stationery £	Sundry £
1 Aug	126.58		Balance b/d							
1 Aug	73.42		Cash from bank							
1 Aug		279	Refreshments	11 78		11 78				
1 Aug		280	Taxi	3 90			3 90			
2 Aug		281	Window	26 00		26 00				
3 Aug		282	Client lunch	27 90	4 16					23 74
3 Aug		283	Stamps	11 00				11 00		
4 Aug		284	Stationery	19 49	2 90				16 59	
4 Aug		285	Rail fare	12 00			12 00			
4 Aug		286	Stamps	2 30				2 30		
				114 37	7 06	37 78	15 90	13 30	16 59	23 74
7 Aug	200		Balance c/d	85 63						
				200 00						
7 Aug	85.63		Balance b/d							
8 Aug	114.37		Cash from bank							

(b)   Payments out of petty cash will occur when an authorised petty cash voucher and supporting receipts are produced.

At the end of the month, the petty cash payments will equal the vouchers and their supporting documentation, and a cheque will be cashed at the bank for this amount so as to replenish the imprest.

The vouchers, etc will be removed and filed after having been recorded in the petty cash book.

26   STRONTIUM AND CO

(a)   **The payments**

		£	£
Dr:	Cleaning account	24	
Dr:	Travel and subsistence account	48	
Dr:	Sundry expenses account	20	
Cr:	Petty cash account		92

The petty cash book would be used for this posting.

Tutorial note: Some organisations may use the petty cash book as a 'nominal ledger' account in its own right, in which case the 'total' column would be the credit entry and no further credit entry would be required in the nominal ledger.

(b)   **The receipt**

		£	£
Dr:	Petty cash account	83	
Cr:	Cash at bank account		83

The cash book would be used to post this cheque cashed for petty cash use. To post from the petty cash book would be double counting.

Tutorial note: If the petty cash book is used as a nominal ledger account, the debit entry in the nominal ledger would not be required.

27   CONTROL ACCOUNTS

(a)

Sales ledger control account

	£		£
Opening balance	35,748	Contra (ii)	750
Casting error in		Discount allowed (iii)	328
sales day book (iv)	53	Casting error in sales day	
		book (iv)	29
		Revised balance	34,694
	_____		_____
	35,801		35,801

		£
(b)	Original total per list of balances	34,874
	Transposition error (£2,570 posted as £2,750)(i)	(180)
	Amended total	34,694

Note: Cash received posted to the wrong customer account in the sales ledger will have no effect on the control account or the list of balances. The sales ledger will be adjusted as follows:

Dr. Sparks and Co

Cr. Spaks Ltd

(c)

Purchases Ledger Control Account

	£		£
Contra (ii)	750	Opening balance	22,372
Credit note omitted (vi)	2,100		
Standing order omitted (vii)	1,800		
Revised balance	17,722		
	22,372		22,372

	£
(d) Original total per list of balances	21,022
Standing order omitted (vii)	(1,800)
Transposition error (£279 listed as £297) (viii)	(18)
Debit balance listed as credit (£741 × 2) (ix)	(1,482)
Amended total	17,722

28 BANK RECONCILIATION

(a) **Bank account**

DR	£	CR	£
Balance	2,983	Standing orders	780
Cheque overstated	90	Bank fees	200
Cash lodged	1,500	Balance c/d	3,593
	4,573		4,573
Bal c/d	3,593		

(b)   **Bank reconciliation statement**

	£
Balance on statement (overdrawn)	9,820 –
Outstanding cheques	2,187 –
Outstanding lodgements	15,200 +
Cheque incorrectly debited	400 +
	3,593

29   JUDITH KELLY

(a)   *Note:* The question is worded in such a way to suggest the answer should be given in *horizontal format.*

DR		Sales Ledger Control Account			CR
		£	(Item)		£
(Item)			(iv)	Goods returned	2,648
(ii)	Balance b/d	120,539	(vi)	Discount allowed	10
			(viii)	Bad debt written off	750
				Balance c/d	117,131
		120,539			120,539
	Balance b/d	117,131			

(b)   **Adjustments to list of personal balances**

(Item)	Increase/(Decrease)	£	
(i)	List of personal account balances	122,409	
(iii)	Correction of transposition £5,740 should be £7,540	1,800	increase
(v)	Reverse credit balance shown as debit balance = £3,289 × 2	(6,578)	decrease
(vii)	Include credit balance omitted	(500)	decrease
	Total of personal account balances (now agrees with control account)	117,131	

30 A CLIENT (1)

(a)

Creditors control account

		£			£
(iii)	**Credit note**	372	(i)	Balance b/f	42,578
(iv)	**Standing orders**	3,000	(vii)	**Undercast in PDB**	900
(vi)	**Discount received**	27			
	Balance c/f	40,079			
		43,478			43,478

(b) **Reconciliation of the list of balances**

			£	£
	(i)	Creditors balances per list of balances		44,833
Add:	**(iii)**	**Incorrect balance (£2,597 – £2,570**		18
				44,851
				18
				44,851
Less:	**(ii)**	**Credit note**	372	
	(iv)	**Standing order payments**	3,000	
	(v)	**Debit balance included as a credit balance (£700 × 2)**	1,400	4,772
				£40,079

31 SYLVIA AVERY

(a)

Bank account

20X2		£	20X2		£
(i)	Cheque to a supplier £(£5,495 – 4,595)	900	Balance b/f		15,503
			(iv)	Cheque not honoured	400
Balance c/f		18,603	(v)	Standing orders	3,600
		19,503			19,503

(b) Bank reconciliation statement at 30 November 20X2

	£	£
Balance per bank statement		3,628
Add: Outstanding lodgements (iii)		5,634
		9,262

Less: Unpresented cheques (ii)	22,865		
Correction of error by bank	5,000		
		27,865	
		(18,603)	

(c) A balance sheet at 30 November 20X2 would show a bank overdraft of £18,603 under the heading of current liabilities.

32 TINA

(a)

Purchase ledger control

	£		£
(i) Discount omitted	20	Balance as stated	48,395
(ii) Daybook overcast	90	(iii) Cheques issued	9
Corrected balance	48,753	(iv) Invoice omitted	459
	48,863		48,863

(b)

	£	
Total of listing as stated	46,644	
(iv) Invoice omitted	459	+
(v) Elimination of incorrect balance	780	+
(v) Include correct balance	870	+
Restated listing	48,753	

(c) The balance to be reported on Tina's balance sheet is the corrected purchase ledger control account balance of £48,753. This will be reported as a current liability.

(d) A purchase ledger reconciliation is carried out for the following reasons:

- to identify errors in the accounting records;

- to provide a corrected figure for inclusion in the final accounts;

- to calculate missing data if incomplete records are maintained.

33 HOWARD

(a) **Adjustments to net profit**

Item			Net profit affected	£
		Net profit		75,886
(i)	Sales omitted		Yes	900
(ii)	Purchases undercast		Yes	(900)
(iii)	Error in posting to supplier's account		No	-

(iv)	Discount allowed omitted	Yes	(90)
(v)	Drawings trated as expense	Yes	405
	Corrected net profit		76,201

(b)

DR	Suspense account		CR
	£		£
Balance b/d	90	Purchases undercast	900
Sales omitted	900	Discount allowed	90
	990		990

(c)	Transposition error	(iii)
	Error of omission	(i) and (iv)
	Arithmetical error	(ii)
	Error of principle	(v)

ADJUSTMENTS TO THE TRIAL BALANCE

ACCRUALS AND PREPAYMENTS

34 GAS, ELECTRICITY AND RENT

(a)

Gas account

		£			£
20X5			*20X5*		
Sept 15	Purchases day book	1,200	July 1	Balance b/d	650
Dec 14	Purchases day book	1,750			
20X6			*20X6*		
Mar 18	Purchases day book	1,695	June 30	Profit and loss	6,035
June 14	Purchases day book	1,560			
June 30	Balance c/d	480			
		6,685			6,685
			July 1	Balance b/d	480

(b)   The bill for £126 (excluding VAT as, assuming the trader is a VAT registered trader, the VAT is recoverable) paid in March 20X8 represents electricity consumed over the three months to 28 February 20X8. The part of this relating to December 20X7 would normally be arrived at by time apportionment, i.e. one-third of £126 = £42. If this is added onto the figure of £396, this gives the cost of electricity consumed as £438.

(c)

Rent receivable

20X4		£	20X4		£
30 Sept	P&L a/c	3,500	30 June	Cash at bank	2,000
			30 Sept	Bal c/d	1,500
		3,500			3,500
1 Oct	Bal b/d	1,500			

The income to the profit and loss account is increased by crediting the rental income account with the £1,500 due but not yet received. The £1,500 is also carried down as a debit balance, a debtor for rental due which would be shown under current assets in the balance sheet.

35 XY

(a) (i)

Rent payable account

		£			£
01/10/X5	Balance b/f	1,500	30/09/X6	P&L a/c	6,000
30/11/X5	Bank	1,500	30/09/X6	Balance c/f	1,500
29/02/X6	Bank	1,500			
31/05/X6	Bank	1,500			
31/08/X6	Bank	1,500			
		7,500			7,500
1/10/X6	Balance b/f	1,500			

(ii)

Electricity account

		£			£
05/11/X5	Bank	1,000	01/10/X5	Balance b/f	800
10/02/X6	Bank	1,300	30/09/X6	P&L a/c	5,000
08/05/X6	Bank	1,500			
07/08/X6	Bank	1,100			
30/09/X6	Accrual c/f	900			
		5,800			5,800
			01/10/X6	Balance b/f	900

(iii)

Interest receivable account

		£			£
01/10/X5	Balance b/f	300	02/10/X5	Bank	250
30/09/X6	P&L a/c	850	03/04/X6	Bank	600
			30/09/X6	Accrual c/f	300
		1,150			1,150
01/10/X6	Balance b/f	300			

(iv)   **Provision for doubtful debts account**

		£			£
30/09/X6	Balance c/f	6,250	01/10/X5	Balance b/f	4,800
			30/09/X6	P&L a/c	1,450
		——			——
		6,250			6,250
			01/10/X6	Balance b/f	6,250

(b)   The balance on the rent payable account is a prepayment. Prepayments appear under the heading 'current assets' in the balance sheet.

The balance on the electricity account is an accrual. Accruals appear under the heading 'current liabilities' in the balance sheet.

The balance on the interest receivable account is accrued income. Accrued income appears under the heading 'current assets' in the balance sheet.

The balance on the provision for doubtful debts account is XY's best estimate of the general level of the present debtors which will not be recovered. The estimate will be based on past experience of the recoverability of XY's debts. This provision will be deducted from the total debtors figure under the heading 'current assets' in the balance sheet.

36   RBD

Rents receivable

20X0		£	*20X0*		£
			1 June	Bal b/f	463
20X1			*20X1*		
31 May	Profit and loss	4,004	31 May	Bank	4,058
31 May	Bal c/f	517			
		——			——
		4,521			4,521
		——			——

Rent and rates payable

20X0		£	*20X0*		£
1 June	Bal b/f	1,246	1 June	Bal b/f	315
20X1			20X1		
31 May	Bank - rent	7,491			
31 May	Bank - rates	2,805	31 May	Profit and loss	10,100
31 May	Bal c/f	382	31 May	Bal c/f	1,509
		——			——
		11,924			11,924
		——			——

Creditors

20X0		£	20X0		£
			1 June	Bal b/f	5,258
20X1			20X1		
31 May	Bank	75,181	31 May	Profit and loss	
31 May	Discounts received	1,043		Purchases	75,686
31 May	Bal c/f	4,720			
		_____			_____
		80,944			80,944
		_____			_____

Provision for discounts on creditors

20X0		£	20X0		£
1 June	Bal b/f	106			
20X1			20X1		
			31 May	Profit and loss	12
			31 May	Bal c/f	94
		___			___
		106			106
		___			___

Tutorial note:

In this example the discounts received during the year of £1,043 have been debited to the creditors account and credited to discounts received, the only entry in the provision for discounts account being the decrease in provision required of £12 being debited to the profit and loss account.

An alternative treatment would be to credit the provision for discounts received account with £1,043 giving a net transfer to the profit and loss account from that account of £1,031.

37 PDS

Motor expenses account

		£			£
1 Jul	Cash – creditors	1,225	30 June	Prepaid insurance	300
30 June	Cash – insurance	1,200	30 June	Prepaid licenses	105
	Cash – licenses	220	30 June	Profit and loss a/c	4,255
	Cash – service, repairs	1,500			
30 June	Accrued petrol	165			
30 June	Accrued service, repairs	350			
		_____			_____
		4,660			4,660
		_____			_____
1 Jul	Prepayments a/c	405	1 Jul	Accruals a/c	515

Prepayments

		£			£
30 June	Motor expenses	300			
30 June	Motor expenses	105	30 June	Balance c/d	405
		———			———
		405			405
		———			———
1 Jul	Balance b/d	405	1 Jul	Motor expenses	405

Accruals

		£			£
30 June	Balance c/d	515	30 June	Motor expenses	165
			30 June	Motor expenses	350
		———			———
		515			515
		———			———
1 Jul	Motor expenses	515	1 Jul	Balance b/d	515

DEPRECIATION

38   SPANNERS LTD

(a)   Profit or loss on disposal:

	£
Cost	12,000
Depreciation	(5,000)
	———
NBV	7,000
	———

Comparing the net book value of £7,000 with the sale proceeds of £4,000, there is a loss of (7,000 – 4,000) £3,000.

(b)   T-account entries

Disposal of fixed assets account

	£		£
Car cost	12,000	Car provision for dep'n a/c	5,000
		Cash at bank a/c	
		(sales proceeds)	4,000
Balance b/d	7,000	Loss on disposal	3,000
	———		———
	12,000		12,000
	———		———

Car account

	£		£
Balance b/d	12,000	Disposal a/c	12,000

Car provision for depreciation account

	£		£
Disposal a/c	5,000	Balance b/d	5,000

Cash at bank account

	£		£
Disposal a/c	4,000		

(c) Expenditure may be classified as 'revenue' or 'capital'. Revenue expenditure is charged to the profit and loss account as incurred, but this treatment is inappropriate for capital expenditure. Capital expenditure relates to fixed assets which are used within the business over a number of accounting periods to generate sales. Rather than charging the whole of the cost of the fixed asset to the profit and loss account in the year of its acquisition, it is spread over the accounting periods benefiting from its use, by means of an annual depreciation charge. This matches the cost of the asset which is being 'used up' to the sales which it has helped to produce in accordance with the accruals concept.

Furthermore, the depreciation charge will reduce the distributable profit of an organisation. This has the effect of maintaining the capital base of an organisation, even though funds are not specifically set aside for the replacement of fixed assets.

39 SBJ

(a) **Motor vehicles**

	£
List price	24,000
Less: 20%	(I4,800)
	19,200
Add: VAT 17.5%	3,360
	22,560
Add: Cost of painting name	100
Amount to add to fixed asset register	22,660

The insurance and road fund licence are revenue costs.

Plant and machinery

	Cost	Accumulated depreciation
	£	£
Balance as per nominal ledger	120,000	30,000
Less: Disposal	(30,000)	(5,700)
	———	———
* £30,000 – £24,300	90,000	24,300
	———	———

Office equipment

	Cost	Accumulated depreciation	Net book value
	£	£	£
Motor vehicles	48,000	12,000	36,000
Plant and machinery	90,000	24,300	65,700
Office equipment	27,500	7,500	20,000
	———	———	———
	165,500	43,800	121,700
	———	———	
Revised fixed asset register (£147,500 + £22,660)			170,160
			———
Therefore purchase of office equipment			48,460
			———

(b) **Depreciation for 20X4**

Motor vehicles:

	£
25% × £48,000	12,000
25% × £22,660 × $\frac{3}{12}$	1,416 rounded
	———
	13,416
	———

Plant and machinery:

	£
10% × £90,000	9,000
	———

Office equipment:

	£
10% × £68,460	6,846
	———

40   DIAMOND PLC

Freehold land – cost

20X5		£000	20X6		£000
1 Jan	Balance b/d	1,000	31 Dec	Balance c/d	1,000
		——			——
		1,000			1,000
		——			——
20X7					
1 Jan	Balance b/d	1,000			

Freehold buildings – cost

20X5		£000	20X5		£000
1 Jan	Balance b/d	500	31 Dec	Balance c/d	550
8 Oct	Cash	50			
		——			——
		550			550
		——			——
20X6					
1 Jan	Balance b/d	550			

Freehold buildings – provision for depreciation

20X5		£000	20X5		£000
31 Dec	Balance c/d	221	1 Jan	Balance b/d	210
			31 Dec	Profit and loss	11
		——			——
		221			221
		——			——
20X6			20X6		
31 Dec	Balance c/d	232	1 Jan	Balance b/d	221
			31 Dec	Profit and loss	11
		——			——
		232			232
		——			——
			20X7		
			1 Jan	Balance b/d	232

Office equipment – cost

20X5		£000	20X5		£000
1 Jan	Balance b/d	40	10 June	Transfer – disposal	8
10 June	Cash	12	31 Dec	Balance c/d	48
	Transfer – disposal	4			
		56			56
20X6			20X6		
1 Jan	Balance b/d	48	1 Mar	Transfer – disposal	8
			31 Dec	Balance c/d	40
		48			48
20X7					
1 Jan	Balance b/d	40			

Office equipment – provision for depreciation

20X5		£000	20X5		£000
10 June	Transfer – disposal	7	1 Jan	Balance b/d	24
31 Dec	Balance c/d	23	31 Dec	Profit and loss	6
		30			30
20X6			20X6		
1 Mar	Transfer – disposal	6	1 Jan	Balance b/d	23
31 Dec	Balance c/d	22	31 Dec	Profit and loss	5
		28			28
			20X7		
			1 Jan	Balance b/d	22

Office equipment – disposal

20X5		£000	20X5		£000
10 Jun	Office equip. cost	8	10 June	Office equip. deprec.	7
31 Dec	Profit and loss – profit	3		Office equip. – cost	4
		11			11
20X6			20X6		
1 Mar	Office equip. cost	8	1 Mar	Office equip. deprec.	6
31 Dec	Profit and loss – profit	1		Cash – proceeds of sale	3
		9			9

41   A CLIENT (2)

(a)   The car was purchased during the year ended 30 April 20X3. Depreciation was charged for the seven months from October 20X2 until the year end, giving a charge for the year of 20% × £15,000 × 7/12 = £1,750.

The car was disposed of during the year ended 30 April 20X4. Depreciation was charged for the six months from May 20X3 until October 20X3, giving a charge for the year of 20% × £15,000 × 6/12 = £1,500.

The accumulated depreciation on the car = £1,750 + £1,500 = £3,250.

(b)

Disposal

	£		£
Motor vehicles – cost	15,000	Motor vehicles – cost (trade in)	10,500
		Motor vehicles – depreciation	3,250
		Profit and loss (loss)	1,250
	15,000		15,000

Note: The question did not require the preparation of a disposal account. It is, however, an efficient way to lay out the working.

(c)   The company had vehicles costing £37,200 from May 20X3 until October 20X3. This is a period of six months and depreciation for this period would be 20% × £37,200 × 6/12 = £3,720.

The company had vehicles costing £37,200 – 15,000 + 9,000 + 10,500 = £41,700 from November 20X3 until April 20X4. This is a six-month period for which depreciation would be 20% × £41,700 × 6/12 = £4,170.

Total depreciation for the year = £3,720 + 4,170 = £7,890.

(d)

Motor vehicles at cost

	£		£
Bal b/d	37,200	Disposal	15,000
Loan	9,000		
Disposal (trade in allowance)	10,500	Bal c/d	41,700
	56,700		56,700
Bal b/d	41,700		

42   DEBBIE FRASER

(a)   Depreciation charge is 25% of cost of new car

	£
Cost of new car is:	
Cheque payment	8,200
Add Trade in allowance	6,500
	14,700
Depreciation charge = 25% × £14,700 =	3,675

(b)   Calculation of NBV on disposal:

	£
Original cost @ November 20X0	12,800

Depreciation method is reducing balance

∴ Depreciation charge each year would be:

1st year to 31 October 20X1:

	£
25% × £12,800	3,200

2nd year to 31 October 20X2:

NBV = (£12,800 – £3,200) £9,600

	£
Depreciation charge is 25% × £9,600	2,400

3rd year to 31 October 20X3

NBV = (£12,800 – (£3,200 + £2,400) £7,200

Depreciation charge is nil in year of disposal.

At disposal the NBV was £7,200 and the proceeds were £6,500 (the trade in allowance).

The result being a loss on disposal of £700.

(Proceeds £6,500 – NBV £7,200)

(c)   The balance on the disposal account is transferred to the profit and loss account. A profit on disposal is shown as income but a loss (as in this case) is shown on the debit side as an expense.

(d)

Motor vehicles at cost account

	£		£
Balance b/f	12,800	Disposal account (cost)	12,800
Disposal account (trade in)	6,500	Balance c/f (new car)	14,700
Bank (proceeds)	8,200		
	27,500		27,500

(e)   The difference between the two methods is as follows:

Straight line method: Depreciation is *calculated on the cost* of the asset, giving a uniform annual rate of depreciation over its life.

Reducing balance method: Depreciation is *calculated on the net book value* of the asset (cost less depreciation charged in previous years), giving a reducing annual rate of depreciation over its life.

BAD AND DOUBTFUL DEBTS

43 DOUBTFUL DEBTS

Debtors

		£			£
1.1.20X1	Balance b/d	10,000		Sales returns	1,000
	Sales	100,000		Bank	90,000
				Bad debts	500
				Discounts allowed	400
			31.12.20X1	Balance c/d	18,100
		———			———
		110,000			110,000
		———			———
1.1.20X2	Balance b/d	18,100		Sales returns	1,800
	Sales	90,000		Bank	95,000
				Creditors	3,000
				Bad debts	1,500
				Discounts allowed	500
			31.12.20X2	Balance c/d	6,300
		———			———
		108,100			108,100
		———			———
1.1.20X3	Balance b/d	6,300			

Provision for doubtful debts

		£			£
31.12.20X1	Balance c/d:		1.1.20X1	Balance b/d	400
	Specific	200		Bad debts	695
	General				
	5% ×				
	(18,100 - 200)	895			
		———			———
		1,095			1,095
		———			———
	Bad debts	780	1.1.20X2	Balance b/d	1,095
31.12.20X2	Balance c/d				
	(5% × 6,300)	315			
		———			———
		1,095			1,095
		———			———

44 BAD DEBT TRAINING

(a) (i) **Provision for doubtful debt**

	Debtors £	% Provision	Provision
0 to 30 days	42,700	1%	427
31 to 60 days	18,728	25%	4,682
Over 60 days	4,836		
Less bad debt	900		
	3,936	75%	2,952
			£8,061

(ii)

	£
Provision for doubtful debts brought forward	8,200
Provision required (as in (a) (i))	8,061
Decrease in provision	139

(iii) Bad and doubtful debts charge

	£
Bad debt written off	900
Decrease in provision (from (a) (ii))	139
	761

(b) A provision for bad and doubtful debts follows the accruals (matching) concept in that a sale is included in the ledger accounts at the time that it is made but there may be cause for concern that there will be unpaid debts. The application of the prudence concept reflects this actual or potential loss.

(c) A bad debt is a debt which considered to be uncollectable. A doubtful debt is an amount owing to the business, the collectability of which is uncertain.

CLOSING STOCK (AND STOCK VALUATION)

45 DEBTS AND STOCK

(a) (i) A bad debt is a debt that is regarded as irrecoverable. It is therefore written off in the profit and loss account. A doubtful debt is a debt that may or may not be recovered.

(ii) Provision for doubtful debts:

	£
£18,700 × 6% =	1,122
(£9,722 – £3,574) × 50% =	3,074
Closing provision	4,196
Opening provision	4,516
Reduction in provision	320
Charge to profit and loss account:	
Bad debt written off	3,574
Less reduction in provision	(320)
	3,254

Balance sheet:	£
Debtors (£65,013 – £3,574)	61,439
Less provision for doubtful debts	(4,196)
	57,243

(b) (i) Stock must be valued at the lower of cost and net realisable value.

(ii)

Item	Cost	NRV	Balance sheet
	£	£	£
Packing machine	5,890	5,500 – 200 = 5,300	5,300
Industrial press	11,670	14,900 – 475 = 14,425	11,670
Fork lift truck	3,926	4,200 – 720 = 3,480	3,480
			20,450

46 IMELDA FROST

(a)

Debtors ledger control account

	£		£
Balance b/d	2,849	Cash at bank	35,764
Sales (credit)	37,088	Bad debts expense	1,217
		Balance c/d	2,956
	39,937		39,937
Balance b/d	2,956		

Bad debts expense account

	£		£
Debtors ledger control	1,217	Cash at bank	380
		P&L a/c	837
	1,217		1,217

(b)

Item	Raw materials costs	Labour costs	Production overheads	NRV	Balance sheet
	£	£	£	£	£
A	500	800	800	2,600	2,100 (cost)
B	1,000	-	-	1,100	1,000 (cost)
C	500	800	800	1,950	1,950 (NRV)
					5,050

47   P, Q & R

(a)   Model P

Cost	$100 + 20 + 15$	$= 135^1$
Net realisable value	$150 - 22$	$= 128^2$
Lower of cost and net realisable value		£128

Model Q

Cost	$200 + 30 + 18$	$= 248^1$
Net realisable value	$300 - 40$	$= 260^2$
Lower of cost and net realisable value		£248

^{1}purchase cost + delivery costs from supplier + packaging costs

^{2}selling price – delivery costs to customers

(b)   FIFO

Year 1	Purchases	Cost of sales	Stock	Sales
buy 10 at 300	3,000		3,000	
buy 12 at 250	3,000		6,000	
sell 8 at 400		$2,400^3$	3,600	3,200
buy 6 at 200	1,200		4,800	
sell 12 at 400		$3,100^4$	1,700	4,800
	⎯⎯⎯	⎯⎯⎯	⎯⎯⎯	⎯⎯⎯
	7,200	5,500	1,700	8,000
	⎯⎯⎯	⎯⎯⎯	⎯⎯⎯	⎯⎯⎯

Year 2				
Opening stock			1,700	
buy 10 at 200	2,000		3,700	
sell 5 at 400		$1,100^5$	2,600	2,000
buy 12 at 150	1,800		4,400	
sell 25 at 400		$4,400^6$	0	10,000
	⎯⎯⎯	⎯⎯⎯	⎯⎯⎯	⎯⎯⎯
	3,800	5,500	0	12,000
	⎯⎯⎯	⎯⎯⎯	⎯⎯⎯	⎯⎯⎯

^{3}8 at 300

^{4}2 at 300 + 10 at 250

^{5}2 at 250 + 3 at 200

^{6}3 at 200 + 10 at 200 + 12 at 150

Trading accounts	FIFO	
	£	£
Year 1		
Sales		8,000
Opening stock	0	
Purchases	7,200	
	———	
	7,200	
Closing stock	1,700	
	———	
Cost of sales		5,500
		———
Gross profit		2,500
		———
Year 2		
Sales		12,000
Opening stock	1,700	
Purchases	3,800	
	———	
	5,500	
Closing stock	0	
	———	
Cost of sales		5,500
		———
Gross profit		6,500
		———

48   THOMAS BROWN AND PARTNERS

To: Partners

From:

Date:

The general principle to be followed is that stock should be valued in the accounts at the lower of cost or net realisable value (NRV).

Charles Gray

(a)   The damaged spray gun is expected to be sold for half the normal retail price. This means its NRV is £375 and as this is less than its cost at £550, NRV should be used as the correct valuation. This treatment complies with the prudence accounting concept.

(b)   The proposed sale to K Peacock had not taken place by 30 April 20X1, despite any intention to do so. Under the prudence concept, the sale cannot be recognised as any profit has not yet been earned

Jean Kim

This business cannot be regarded as satisfying the going concern concept and it would be incorrect to consider that normal selling prices will apply to the stock.

The NRV is £10,920 ((22 × £510) – 300), and as it is less than cost £13,200 (22 × £600), should be used as the valuation on a prudent basis.

Peter Fox

(a)   Complying with the prudence concept means that it is normally unacceptable to use selling prices in determining stock valuations as profits are not yet realised.

Only with a discounting for gross profit rates could selling prices form an acceptable basis.

(b)   In applying the cost method of valuation, it is the cost to that particular business that is used. The fact that other distributors have higher costs is irrelevant as the requirement of the consistency concept is as between transactions in a period and succeeding periods, not as between different businesses.

49   STOCK LETTER

(a)   FIFO   £

45 units @ £17.80 =   801.00

\+ 100 units @ £18.00 =   1,800.00

                                                        ————

Closing stock   2,601.00

                                                        ————

(b)   Dear Sir

Thank you for your query regarding the valuation of closing stock in the accounts.

Selling price is not used for the valuation of stock as this will reflect an element of profit in its value which has not yet been earned.

Stock should be valued at the lower of cost or net realisable value (selling price less any further costs). This rule ensures the application of the fundamental accounting concept of *prudence*, which is the relevant accounting concept when valuing stock. This concept requires losses to be recognised as soon as they are foreseen, but only allows profits to be included when they have been earned. In general, stocks will be included in the accounts at cost. However, if there is any doubt as to whether the cost can be recouped when the stock is sold, perhaps because it is damaged or obsolete, the stock should be valued at its net realisable value. Thus the possible loss is recognised immediately.

The cost of stock may need to be calculated for the purpose of its valuation if prices are regularly changing. The *FIFO* (first in, first out) method of valuation assumes that the oldest purchases or production are issued from stock.

The valuation method used will have a short term effect on profit: the higher the value of stock, the greater the profit in the first year. However, in the long term, there will be no difference as the higher value of closing stock that reduces cost and increases profits this year will increase costs and reduce profits in the following year when the stock is sold.

I hope that this has clarified matters. Please do not hesitate to contact me should you require any further information.

Yours sincerely,

ACC Assistant

50 JAMES BARTON

(a) Valuing stock at selling price would lead to the recognition of profit which has not yet been earned. It is not prudent to do so.

Stock should be valued at the lower of cost or net realisable value. This means that profits are normally recognised in the period that the goods are sold, but losses may be recognised sooner if the stock suffers a decrease in value. This applies the concept of prudence to the recognition of costs relating to stock.

FIFO assumes that the oldest stock is always used first. This has the advantage of valuing closing stock in the balance sheet at the most recent prices. Cost of sales in the profit and loss account will be based on more out of date prices.

(b) **FIFO**

Month	Purchases			Sales			Stock	
	Quantity	*Unit price (£)*	*Value (£)*	*Quantity*	*Unit price (£)*	*Value (£)*	*Quantity*	*Value (£)*
March	1,500	62	93,000				1,500	93,000
				900	62	55,800	600	37,200
April	1,600	65	104,000				2,200	141,200
				1,200	600 @ 62 600 @ 65	76,200	1,000	65,000
May	1,900	67	127,300				2,900	192,300
				2,500	1,000 @ 65 1,500 @ 67	165,500	400	26,800

(c) **Calculation of gross profit**

FIFO

	£	£
Sales (900 + 1,200 + 2,500 = 4,600 @ 95)		437,000
Purchases (93,000 + 104,000 + 127,300)	324,300	
Closing stock	26,800	
Cost of sales		297,500
Gross profit		139,500

51 ANNE LOUGHLIN

(a) Stock is valued at the lower of cost and net realisable value

If an item of stock cost more than its expected selling price, a loss will be incurred when it is sold. The prudence concept says that this loss must be accounted for straight away.

(b) (i) Closing stock value of paintings

	Cost £	NRV £	Stock value £
Painting 1	700	850	700
Painting 2	850	2,500	850
Painting 3	900	400	400
Closing stock value			1,950

(ii) Closing stock value of fabric

	Purchases Metres	Issued Metres	Balances Metres	
11 November	200 @ £10		200	
14 November		180	(180)	
			20 @ £10	
19 November	120 @ £11		120 @ £11	
			140	
22 November		20 @ £10		
		40 @ £11	80 @ £11	
23 November	90 @ £9.50		90 @ £9.50	
			170	
28 November		70 @ £11	10 @ £11	110.00
			90 @ £9.50	855.00
Closing stock value				£965.00

(c) Periodic weighted average cost

Continuous weighted average cost

(Note that LIFO is no longer examinable.)

EXTENDED TRIAL BALANCE

52   SAMANTHA WRIGHT

(a)

Cash at bank

	£		£
Capital	10,000	Rent	140
Sales	380	Purchases	730
Debtors	2,575	Van	4,050
		Wages	370
		Drawings	700
		balance c/d	6,965
	———		———
	12,955		12,955
Balance b/d	6,965		

Capital

	£		£
		Cash at bank	10,000

Rent

	£		£
Cash at bank	140		

Purchases

	£		£
Cash at bank	730	Balance c/d	2,642
Creditors	1,912		
	———		———
	2,642		2,642
Balance b/d	2,642		

Van

	£		£
Cash at bank	4,050		

Sales

	£		£
Balance c/d	5,271	Debtors	2,575
		Debtors	2,316
		Cash at bank	380
	5,271		5,271
		Balance b/d	5,271

Debtors

	£		£
Sales	2,575	Cash at bank	2,575
Sales	2,316	Balance c/d	2,316
	4,891		4,891
Balance b/d	2,316		

Creditors

	£		£
		Purchases	1,912

Wages

	£		£
Cash at bank	370		

Drawings

	£		£
Cash at bank	700		

(b)   **Samantha Wright**

Trial balance

	Debit £	Credit £
Cash at bank	6,965	
Capital		10,000
Rent	140	
Purchases	2,642	
Van	4,050	
Sales		5,271
Debtors	2,316	
Creditors		1,912
Wages	370	
Drawings	700	
	17,183	17,183

53 RAMSEY

Account	Trial balance as at 31.12.20X8		Adjustments		Trading and profit and loss account		Balance sheet	
	Dr	Cr	Dr	Cr	Dr	Cr	Dr	Cr
	£	£	£	£	£	£	£	£
Capital		24,860						24,860
Sales		94,360				94,360		
Purchases	48,910				48,910			
Fixed assets at cost	32,750						32,750	
Provision for dep'n		11,500		3,275				14,775
Debtors	17,190						17,190	
Bank	18,100						18,100	
Creditors		11,075						11,075
Stock	8,620		9,180	9,180	8,620	9,180	9,180	
Rent	4,200			300	3,900			
Electricity	2,150		250		2,400			
Drawings	9,875						9,875	
Depreciation expense			3,275		3,275			
Prepayments/accruals			300	250			300	250
					67,105	103,540		
Profit for year					36,435			36,435
	141,795	141,795	13,005	13,005	103,540	103,540	87,395	87,395

54 JANE SIMPSON

(a)   **Uncorrected trial balance as at 30 April 20X9**

	£	£
Fixtures and fittings	5,000	
Motor vehicles	4,000	
Stock in trade	12,000	
Trade debtors	7,000	
Balance at bank	1,700	
Trade creditors		6,900
Sales		132,000
Cost of sales	79,200	
Establishment and administrative expenses	11,800	
Sales and distribution expenses	33,500	

Drawings	9,700	
Capital		30,000
	———	
	163,900	
Suspense account (bal fig)	5,000	
	———	———
	168,900	168,900

Tutorial note: Take care to read the requirement. An **uncorrected** trial balance is required.

(b)

Journal

	Dr	Cr
	£	£
Fixtures and fittings	4,500	
Suspense		4,500
Assets purchased but not posted from cash book		

Debtors	500	
Suspense		500
Error in recording sale of £4,700 to debtors		

Drawings	600	
Purchases		600
Goods withdrawn by proprietor for own use		

(c)   **Corrected trial balance as at 30 April 20X9**

	£	£
Fixtures and fittings	9,500	
Motor vehicles	4,000	
Stock in trade	12,000	
Trade debtors	7,500	
Balance at bank	1,700	
Trade creditors		6,900
Sales		132,000

Cost of sales	78,600	
Establishment and administrative expenses	11,800	
Sales and distribution expenses	33,500	
Drawings	10,300	
Capital		30,000
	———	———
	168,900	168,900
	———	———

55   JEFFREY

(a)   (i)   Carriage inwards needs to be increased to £1,238 (£974 + £264).

Returns inwards need to be reduced to £111 (£375 – £264).

(ii)   Sales need to be reduced to £90,470 (£90,560 – £90).

Debtors need to be reduced to £12,790 (£12,880 – £90).

(iii)   Telephone expenses need to be increased to £1,150 (£853 + £297).

Creditors and accruals need to be increased to £6,858 (£6,561 + £297).

(b)   (i)

Jeffrey

Profit and loss account for the year ended 30 September 20X4

	£	£
Sales		90,470
Less: returns inwards		(111)
		90,359
Cost of sales		
Opening stock	12,560	
Purchases	72,674	
Carriage inwards	1,238	
	86,472	
Less: closing stock	(11,875)	74,597
Gross profit		15,762
Less: expenses		
Wages	4,684	
Rent	3,200	
Stationery	382	
Travel	749	
Telephone	1,150	
General expenses	753	(10,918)
Net profit		4,844

(ii)   The closing capital balance is calculated as follows:

	£
Opening capital	30,217
Net profit	4,844
Less: drawings	(12,500)
Closing capital	22,561

FINAL ACCOUNTS

INCOMPLETE RECORDS

56   ERASMUS LTD

(a)   *Step 1*   Set up a proforma trading account to see what figures are available.

Bathroom fitter's trading account

	£	£
Sales		300,000
Opening stock	35,000	
Purchases	190,000	
Less: Closing stock	?	
Cost of sales		?
Gross profit		?

Step 2   Establish the cost structure.

	%
Cost	100
Add profit	50
Sales	150

Step 3   Use the cost structure to find profit and cost of sales from sales.

Sales	=	£300,000 (150%)
Cost of sales	=	$300,000 \times \dfrac{100}{150}$
		£200,000
Profit	=	$300,000 \times \dfrac{50}{150}$
	=	£100,000
Or		300,000 – 200,000
	=	£100,000

Step 4　　Work out closing stock.

Bathroom fitter's trading account

	£	£
Sales		300,000
Opening stock	35,000	
Purchases	190,000	
	———	
	225,000	
Less: Closing stock (bal fig 2)		
(35,000 + 190,000 – 200,000)	(25,000)	
	———	
Cost of sales		200,000
		———
Gross profit		100,000

(b)　(i)　　　　　　　　　　　**Suspense account**

		£			£
(4)	Purchases			Balance b/d	7,510
	(357,200 – 345,000)	12,200	(3)	Sundry expenses (TB	
				only) (860 + 860)	1,720
			(5)	Cash (4,360 – 3,460)	900
			(5)	Sales (6,430 – 4,360)	2,070
		———			———
		12,200			12,200
		———			———

(ii)　*Errors*

(1)　As the entry has not been made, this is an error of omission.

(2)　This is an error of commission. An expense account has been debited but it is the wrong expense account.

57　YATTON

Yatton

Trading and profit and loss account for year ended 31 December 20X8

	£	£
Sales (step 3)		7,850
Cost of sales		
Opening stock	1,400	
Purchases (step 4)	3,000	
	———	
	4,400	
Less: Closing stock	(1,700)	
	———	
		(2,700)
		———

Gross profit			5,150
Expenses (step 5)	1,350		
Bad debts (step 5)	135		
Depreciation of van (step 5)	50		
	——	(1,535)	
		——	
Net profit		3,615	
		——	

Yatton

Balance sheet as at 31 December 20X8

	£	£	£
Fixed assets			
Van at cost			1,000
Depreciation to date (step 5)			(50)
			——
			950
Current assets			
Stocks		1,700	
Debtors (step 3)	350		
Less: Provision for doubtful debts	35		
	——		
		315	
Cash at bank		500	
Cash in hand		30	
		——	
		2,545	
Current liabilities			
Trade creditors (step 4)	900		
Expense creditors	150		
	——		
		(1,050)	
		——	
			1,495
			——
			2,445
			——
Capital account			
Capital at 1 January 20X8 (step 6)			1,670
Profit for year			3,615
			——
			5,285
Drawings in year (step 5)			(2,840)
			——
			2,445
			——

Commentary

Step 1   Produce proformas, inserting main headings and certain information such as opening and closing stock. As subsequent steps are completed, insert as many figures in the proformas as possible.

Step 2   Prepare the cash account, and post the cash and bank entries to the other accounts. The question already provides a bank account so this is not required.

Cash

	£		£
Balance b/d	70	Bank	3,000
Bank	200	Purchases control account	400
Debtors control account	5,200	Expenses	500
		Drawings (bal fig)	1,540
		Balance c/d	30
	5,470		5,470

Step 3   Complete the debtors control account. Note the adjustment for bad debts.

Debtors control account

	£		£
Balance b/d	300	Bank	2,500
Trading and profit and loss			
sales (bal fig)	7,850	Cash	5,200
		Bad debts	100
		Balance c/d (£450 - £100)	350
	8,150		8,150

Tutorial note: Inclusion of the cash sales and purchases in the control accounts will produce a total sales and total purchases figure, rather than credit sales and credit purchases.

Step 4   Complete the creditors control account.

Creditors control account

	£		£
Bank	2,500	Balance b/d	800
Cash	400	Trading and profit and loss	
Balance c/d	900	- purchases (bal fig)	3,000
	3,800		3,800

Step 5   Other adjustments

Expenses

	£		£
Bank	800	Balance b/d	100
Cash	500	Trading and profit and loss	
Balance c/d	150	(bal fig)	1,350
	1,450		1,450

Drawings

	£		£
Bank	1,300	Capital	2,840
Cash	1,540		
	2,840		2,840

Van cost

	£		£
Bank	1,000	Balance c/d	1,000

Bad debts

	£		£
Debtors control account	100	Profit and loss	135
Provision for doubtful debts	35		
	135		135

Provision for doubtful debts

	£		£
Balance c/d (10% × £350)	35	Balance b/d	Nil
		Bad debts	35
	—		—
	35		35
	—		—

Van accumulated depreciation

	£		£
Balance c/d	50	Profit and loss	50
	—		—

Charge 20% × 3 months × £1,000 = £50

Step 6   Finish the balance sheet and profit and loss account

Calculate the opening balance on capital

Statement of opening capital

	Dr	Cr
	£	£
Bank	800	
Cash	70	
Debtors	300	
Trade creditors		800
Expense creditors		100
Stock	1,400	
	———	———
	2,570	900
	900	
	———	
	1,670	
	———	

Thus debits (assets) exceeds credits (liabilities) by £1,670. Accordingly Yatton's business has net assets of £1,670, represented on the balance sheet by his capital account.

58   JULIE GRAY

(a)   Four errors in the draft accounts:

(i)   Closing stock has been added to purchases instead of being deducted.

(ii)   Loan costs appear to include both loan interest and repayment of the loan. The loan repayment element should not be charged to the profit and loss account.

(iii)   Closing stock has been valued at cost before trade discount. This is incorrect and should be valued at cost less trade discount.

(iv)   There are no charges for depreciation of the equipment.

(b) and (c)

			Difference in net profit £
(i)	Closing stock should be deducted from purchases £32,580 × 2		+65,160
(ii)	Monthly interest for loan = £1,625 – £(75,000 ÷ 60) = £375. Loan costs per year = £375 × 12 = £4,500		+15,000
(iii)	Closing stock should have been valued at £32,580 × 95% = £30,951		+1,629
(iv)	Depreciation of equipment = £(75,000 – 5,000) ÷ 5 = £14,000		–14,000

59   PETER ROBIN

(a)

Cash account

		£			£
1 Apr to	Sales (till rolls)	34,164	1 Apr	Bankings	12,450
30 June	Cheque refund	450	to	Cash purchases	12,950
			30 June	Drawings	6,000
				Wages	2,850
				Sundry expenses	100
			30 June	Balance c/d	200
					34,550
			30 June	Unaccounted cash (see note)	64
		34,614			34,614

Note: This balancing figure represents an unaccounted item that should be investigated further. It could be a purchase, an expense, drawings or a cash sales refund. If no vouchers can be found to explain its nature, it would normally be analysed as drawings.

(b)   Sales for the quarter:

	£
Per till rolls	34,164
Credit sales not yet paid	320
	34,484

60   MARKET TRADER

(a)

Cash account

	£		£
Balance b/f	500	Creditors	5,200
Cash sales (bal fig)	78,436	Motor exps	156
Capital introduced	7,000	Drawings	11,700
		Wages	3,380
		Lodged	65,000
		Balance c/f	500
	_____		_____
	85,936		85,936

Bank account

	£		£
Balance b/f	1,500	Creditors	54,000
Lodged	65,000	Motor exps	3,985
		Rent	1,560
		Drawings	3,600
		Balance c/f	3,355
		(bal fig)	
	_____		_____
	66,500		66,500

Creditors account

	£		£
Paid cheque	54,000	Balance b/f	3,750
Cash	5,200		
Balance c/f	3,429	Purchases	58,879
	_____		_____
	62,629		62,629

(b) **Bank reconciliation statement**

	£	£
Balance per statement		3,969
Less: Outstanding cheques:		
705834	125	
705837	422	
705838	67	
	614	
Balance per ledger account		3,355

(c) **Trading account for year ended 31 March 20X8**

	£	£
Sales		78,436
Opening stock	2,700	
Add: purchases	58,879	
	61,579	
Les: closing stock	3,500	
Cost of goods sold		58,079
Gross profit		20,357

61 TOM WEST

(a) **Capital at 30 June 20X8**

Assets:

Bank as at 30 June 20X8

	Income	Expenses	Drawing	Net
	£	£	£	£
Year to 30 June 20X6	1,200	(400)	(300)	500
Year to 30 June 20X6	3,500	(1,200)	(1,800)	500
Year to 30 June 20X6	5,700	(2,900)	(2,700)	100
				1,100
Computer as at 30 June 20X8 = £4,500 × 2/5 =				1,800
Debtors as at 30 June 20X8				900
				3,800

Assets = Capital + Liabilities.

There were no liabilities at 30 June 20X8 and so capital = assets = £3,800.

(b)

Tom West

Profit and loss account for the year ended 30 June 20X9

	£	£
Sales		12,800
Stationery	250	
Motor expenses	790	
Electricity	560	
Repairs	425	
Travel	615	
Depreciation – computer	900	
Depreciation – office furniture	140	
	____	
		3,680
		____
		9,120
		____

Working for sales

Debtors

	£			£
1 July 20X8 Bal b/d	900	Bank		11,000
Balancing fig. Sales	12,800	30 June 20X9 Bal c/d		2,700
	____			____
	13,700			13,700
	____			____
1 July 20X9 Bal b/d	2,700			

(c) **Tom West**

Statement of affairs as at 30 June 20X9

	£	£
Fixed assets		
Computer		900
Office furniture		1,260
		____
		2,160
Current assets		
Debtors	2,700	
Bank	6,460	
	____	
		9,160
		____
		11,320
		____
Capital		
Balance as at 30 June 20X8		3,800
Invested during year		3,000
Profit for year		9,120
		____
		15,920
Drawings		4,600
		____
		11,320
		____

Working for bank

	£
Bank	
Balance as at 30 June 20X8	1,100
Receipts	14,000
Payments	8,640
Balance as at 30 June 20X9	6,460

62 SIMON MEREDITH

(a)

Debtors control account

		£		£
	Opening balance	29,720	Cash (W1)	273,000
Bal fig	Sales	274,780	Closing balance	31,500
		304,500		304,500

(W1)	Cash received	£298,000
	less Capital introduced	£25,000
		£273,000

(b)

	£	£
Sales (i)		274,780
Cost of sales		
Opening stock	16,800	
Purchases (W2)	236,100	
	252,900	
Closing stock	17,500	235,400
Gross profit		39,380

(W2)

Creditors control account

	£		£
Paid (W3)	237,300	Opening balance	23,900
Closing balance	22,700	Purchases (bal fig)	236,100
	260,000		260,000

(W3)

	£	£
Cheques issued		295,300
less Expenses	32,000	
New van	11,000	
Drawings	15,000	
		58,000
		237,300

63   EILEEN FIRTH

(a)   (i)

	£	£
Debtors at 1 May 20X1		3,800
Less: Debtors at 30 April 20X2		3,350
		450
Cash received from customers		78,300
Sales		77,850

(ii)

	£	£
Creditors at 30 April 20X2		2,320
Less: Creditors at 1 May 20X1		1,950
		370
Cheques paid to suppliers		31,900
Purchases		32,270

(iii)

	£	£
Sales (from (i))		77,850
Stock at 1 May 20X1	6,500	
Purchases (from (ii))	32,270	
	38,770	
Stock at 30 April 20X2	6,250	
		32,520
Gross profit		45,330

(iv)

	£	£
Gross profit (from (iii))		45,330
Cheques paid for expenses	22,600	
Depreciation charge	10,000	
	_____	
		32,600
		_____
Net profit		12,730
		_____

(v)

Net profit	drawings	=	Movement in capital
£12,730 (from (iv)	(£78,300 – 63,300)	=	Movement in capital
£12,730 – £15,000		=	– £2,270 reduction

(b)

	£	£
Cash lodged to bank		63,300
Less: Cheques issued – to suppliers	31,900	
– for expenses	22,600	
Loan repaid	10,000	64,500
	_____	_____
		(1,200)
Bank balance at 1 May 20X1 (overdrawn)		(4,840)
		_____
Bank balance at 30 April 20X2 (overdrawn)		(6,040)
		_____

SOLE TRADER ACCOUNTS

64 KENDAL

(a)

Statement of opening capital

	Dr	Cr
	£	£
Bank	1,700	
Stock	5,600	
Debtors	2,100	
Creditors – goods		1,640
Cash	170	
	_____	_____
	9,570	1,640
	1,640	
	_____	
	7,930	
	_____	

(b)

Cash

	£		£
Balance b/d	170	Bank	16,940
Debtors	22,950	Creditors – goods	760
		Expenses	400
		Drawings (bal fig)	2,620
		Balance c/d	2,400
	23,120		23,120

Debtors control

	£		£
Balance b/d	2,100	Cash (bal fig)	22,950
Sales (working)	22,500	Balance c/d	1,650
	24,600		24,600

Creditors control

	£		£
Bank	16,140	Balance b/d	1,640
Cash	760	Purchases (bal fig)	17,200
Balance c/d	1,940		
	18,840		18,840

Working

Insert the opening and closing balances into the control and cash accounts. At this point the figure for purchases can be calculated.

Having reached this far, a little more thought is now required.

The position as regards unknowns can be summarised as follows

Debtors   The figures for sales and receipts from debtors are unknown

Cash   The figures for drawings and receipts from debtors are unknown

This is where the cost structure is utilised as follows

	£	£	£
Sales			
Less: Cost of goods sold		22,500	100
Opening stock	5,600 (given)		
Purchases	17,200 (calculated)		
	————		
	22,800		
Less: Closing stock	4,800		
	————		
		18,000	80
		————	—
Gross profit		4,500	20 (given)
		————	—

The sales figure has now been derived, leaving only one unknown in the debtors account – receipts from debtors, which is calculated as a balancing figure.

The resulting double entry (Dr Cash £22,950, Cr Debtors £22,950) means that there is only one unknown in the cash account, the drawings figure.

	£	£
Sales		22,500
Opening stock	5,600	
Purchases	17,200	
	————	
	22,800	
Closing stock	(4,800)	
	————	
Cost of sales		(18,000)
Gross profit		4,500
Rent (1,000 – 250)	750	
Electricity (235 + 65)	300	
Sundry	400	
	————	
		(1,450)
		————
Net profit		3,050
		————

(c)   **Trading and profit and loss account for the year ended 31 December 20X5**
Balance sheet as at 31 December 20X5

	£	£
Current assets		
Stock		4,800
Debtors		1,650
Prepayment		250
Bank		1,000
Cash		2,400
		————
		10,100

Less: Current liabilities		
Creditors		
Goods	1,940	
Expenses	65	
	_____	(2,005)
		_____
		8,095
		_____
Capital account		
Opening capital (a)		7,930
Add: Net profit		3,050
		_____
		10,980
Less: Drawings (265 + 2,620)		2,885
		_____
		8,095
		_____

65   J PATEL

Trading and profit and loss account for the year ended 31 October 20X9

	£	£	£
Sales – $\dfrac{100}{66\frac{2}{3}} \times 158,760$		238,140	100
Opening stock	16,100		
Purchases (W3)	166,360		
	_____		
	182,460		
Closing stock	23,700		
	_____		
Cost of sales		158,760	$66\frac{2}{3}$
		_____	
Gross profit $\dfrac{33\frac{1}{3}}{66\frac{2}{3}} \times 158,760$		79,380	$33\frac{1}{3}$
Establishment and administrative expenses	33,300		
Sales and districution expenses	29,100		
Bad debts written off	5320		
Depreciation			
Fixtures and fittings	1,000		
Motor vehicles $(1,800 + \frac{6}{12} \times 2,240)$	2,920		
	_____		
		66,850	
		_____	
Net profit		12,530	
		_____	

Balance sheet as at 31 October 20X9

Cost depreciation

	£	£	£
Fixed assets			
Fixtures and fittings	10,000	(7,000)	3,000
Motor vehicles	20,200	(4,720)	15,480
	30,200	(11,720)	18,480
Current assets			
Stock		23,700	
Trade debtors		11,500	
Balance at bank (W4)		6,620	
Cash in hand		200	
		42,020	
Current liabilities			
Trade creditors		(12,700)	
			29,320
			47,800
Capital – At 1 November 20X8			30,910
Add: New capital – proceeds of sale of land			16,000
Net profit for year			12,530
Drawings (£8,500 + 3,140 (W2))			(11,640)
			47,800

Workings

(W1)   **Total debtors account**

	£		£
Balance b/d	19,630	Cash banked from credit sales	181,370
Credit sales (bal fig)	173,770	Bad debts written off	530
		Balance c/d	11,500
	193,400		193,400

(W2)   **Cash**

	£		£
Balance b/d	160	Bankings	61,190
Cash from cash sales	64,370	Drawings (bal fig)	3,140
(total sales – credit sales)		Balance c/d	200
(238,140 – 173,770)			
	64,530		64,530

(W3)

Total creditors account

	£		£
Cash paid (per bank)	163,100	Balance b/d	9,440
Balance c/d	12,700	Purchases (balancing figure)	166,360
	175,800		175,800

(W4)

Bank

	£		£
Receipts	258,560	Balance b/d	6,740
		Payments	245,200
		Balance c/d	6,620
	258,560		258,560

66 GBA

(a) **Trading and profit and loss account for the year ended 30 June 20X5**

	£	£
Sales		625,000
Less: Sales returns		(2,300)
		622,700
Opening stock of materials	98,200	
Purchases	324,500	
Less: Purchases returns	(1,700)	
	421,000	
Less: Closing stock of materials	(75,300)	
Cost of sales		(345,700)
Gross profit		277,000
Discounts received		2,500
Bank interest received (£15,000 × 6% × 6/12)		450
		279,950
Expenses		
Discounts allowed	1,500	
Packing materials (W1)	12,400	
Distribution costs	17,000	
Rent, rates and insurance (5,100 – 450)	4,650	
Telephone (3,200 + 500)	3,700	
Car expenses	2,400	
Wages (71,700 – 23,800)	47,900	
Provision for doubtful debts released (W2)	(380)	
Bad debts written off	600	
Heat and light (1,850 + 400)	2,250	
Sundry expenses (6,700 – 3,500)	3,200	
Loan interest	800	

Depreciation

Delivery vehicles (112,500 × 20%)	22,500	
Equipment [(15,000 – 5,000) × 25%]	2,500	
Car (8,000 × 25%)	2,000	
		123,020
Net profit for the year		156,930

(b) **Balance sheet as at 30 June 20X5**

	Cost £	Dep'n £	Net book value £
Fixed assets			
Delivery vehicles	112,500	57,500	55,000
Equipment	15,000	7,500	7,500
Car	8,000	2,000	6,000
	135,500	67,000	68,500
Current assets			
Stock of building materials		75,300	
Stock of packaging materials		700	
Debtors (95,000 – 600)	94,400		
Less: Provision	620		
		93,780	
Prepayments		450	
Accrued income (bank deposit interest)		450	
Bank deposit account		15,000	
Bank current account		26,500	
		212,180	
Creditors: Amount falling due within 1 year			
Creditors (82,000 + 200)	82,200		
Accruals (400 + 500)	900		
Loan [10,000 – (6,400 – 800)]	4,400		
		87,500	
			124,680
			193,180
Financed by			
Capital at 1 July 20X4			55,550
Capital introduced in the year			8,000
Net profit for the year			156,930
			220,480
Less: Drawings (23,800 + 3,500)			(27,300)
			193,180

Workings
(W1)

	£
Packing materials	12,900
Packing materials purchased	200
	13,100
Less: Closing stock of packing materials	(700)
	12,400

(W2) Provision for doubtful debts
   Provision required:

	£
30 – 60 days £20,000 × 1%	200
60 – 90 days £12,000 × 2.5%	300
Over 90 days (£3,000 – £600) × 5%	120
	620
Opening provision	1,000
Release of provision	380

(c)   The transactions that affect GBA's bank balance for the year are cash transactions. Example of cash transactions that do not affect the calculation of profit for the year as follows:

Receipts from debtors – These are paid into the bank account and increase the bank balance, but the profit for the year is based upon the sales made not the cash received.

Payments to suppliers – These payments come out of the bank account thereby reducing the balance. However, profit is calculated using the purchases made during the period rather than those paid for.

Drawings – The cash that GBA withdrew from the business has come out of the bank account. Drawings, however, do not affect the calculation of profit as they are an appropriation of profit and not an expense.

Payment of the tax bill – GBA's tax bill was paid out of the business bank account, thereby reducing the bank balance. However, this was a personal expense rather than an expense of the business and therefore it does not appear in the profit and loss calculation. Instead this amount is treated as part of drawings.

Loan repayment – The repayment of the loan reduces the bank balance. However, as the payment is to pay off a balance sheet liability, this does not appear in the profit and loss account and does not affect calculation of the profit for the year. Only the interest on the loan affects the profit and loss calculation.

Opening bank deposit account – When the bank deposit account was opened, cash was paid out of the current account and into the deposit account. This would reduce the bank balance and replace it with a deposit account balance. None of this has any effect on profit as it is simply a transfer of cash between one asset and another in the balance sheet. Only the interest received on the bank deposit account affects the profit and loss calculation.

67 **DRAFT BALANCE SHEET**

(a)   Balances at 31 March 20X5

    (i)   Accrued expenses: Electricity

        Bill for three months to 31 January 20X5 is £6,870.

        Therefore estimate for February and March is £6,870 × $^2/_3$ =   **£4,580**

    (ii)   Prepaid expenses: Rent

        Rent paid for six months to June 20X5 is £28,500.

        Prepaid for April, May, June; £28,500 × $^3/_6$ =   **£14,250**

    (iii)   Allowance for doubtful debts

Age		Debts	%	Allowance
		£		£
0–30 days		125,275	-	-
31–60 days		27,200	20%	5,440
Over 60 days	(4,836 – 660)	4,176	75%	3,132
Total debts	(157,311 – 660)	156,651		
Total allowance				8,572

    (iv)   Accumulated depreciation

		£
Opening balance of accumulated depreciation		85,400
Depreciation @ 20% on net book value	*(£89,600 × 20%)*	17,920
Closing balance of accumulated depreciation		103,320

(b)   **Balance sheet as at 31 March 20X5**

		£	£
Fixed assets	Equipment at cost		175,000
	Accumulated Depreciation (at 31 March 20X5)		(103,320)
			71,680
Current assets			
Stock		42,339	
Debtors	(156,651 – 8,572)	148,079	
Prepayments		14,250	
Bank account		6,280	
		210,948	

Current liabilities

Creditors	86,560	
Accruals	4,580	
	91,140	

Net current assets		119,808
Net assets		191,488
Capital		191,488

Proof of capital (not required)

		£
Capital in question		*201,070*
Less accruals		*(4,580)*
Add prepayments		*14,250*
Less increase in allowance for doubtful debts	*(8,572 – 7,900)*	*(672)*
Less bad debt expense		*(660)*
Less depreciation charges		*(17,920)*
		191,488

PARTNERSHIP ACCOUNTS

68   PAT AND SAM

(a)   **Allocation of net profit of £48,000**

	Pat £	Sam £	Total £
Interest on capital	1,152	864	2,016
Salaries	14,400	19,200	33,600
Balance of profits (48,000 – 35,616)			35,616
in ratio 3 : 2	7,430 (3/5)	4,954 (2/5)	12,384
Totals	22,982	25,018	48,000

Note: This is only a calculation of the allocation of profit and not part of the double entry bookkeeping system, merely providing the figures for the appropriation account.

(b)

Current accounts

	Pat £	Sam £		Pat £	Sam £
Drawings	10,000	10,000	Balance b/d	5,700	3,200
Balance c/d	18,682	18,218	Interest on capital	1,152	864
			Salaries	14,400	19,200
			Share of profits	7,430	4,954
	28,682	28,218		28,682	28,218

69 ADAM AND COLIN

(a)

Profit and loss appropriation account

	£	£		£
Salaries			Profit per P & L account	69,602
Adam	7,500			
Colin	3,000			
		10,500		
Interest on capital				
Adam	4,050			
Colin	8,460			
		12,510		
Share of profit				
Adam (3/7)	19,968			
Colin (4/7)	26,624			
		46,592		
		69,602		69,602

(b)

Current accounts

	Adam £	Colin £		Adam £	Colin £
Drawings	20,000	18,000	Opening balance	11,500	17,600
Closing balance	23,018	37,684	Salary	7,500	3,000
			Interest on capital	4,050	8,460
			Share of profit	19,968	26,624
	43,018	55,684		43,018	55,684

70 GARY AND PAULINE

(a)

Suspense

	£		£
(i) Discount received	50	Bal b/d	12,550
(ii) Loan	15,000	(iii) Loan	2,500
	15,050		15,050

(b) (i) Recording the discount received will alter the profit for the period.

(ii) Recording the loan received will not alter the profit for the period.

(iii) Recording the loan repayment will not alter the profit for the period.

(c) Original profit =   £39,790

+ discount received =   50
_____

Revised profit =   £39,840
_____

(d)

	Gary	Pauline	Total
	£	£	£
Revised profit			39,840
Salary (15 month period)	$12,000 \times 15/12 = 15,000$		15,000
Interest on capital (15 month period)	$30,000 \times 8\% \times 15/12 = 3,000$	$15,000 \times 8\% \times 15/12 = 1,500$	4,500
Residual profit	$20,340 \times 2/3 = 13,560$	$20,340 \times 1/3 = 6,780$	20,340
TOTAL	31,560	8,280	39,840

71 KEITH AND JEAN

(a)

Keith and Jean
Profit and loss appropriation account
for the year ended 31 August 20X1

		£		£
Interest on capital			Net profit b/f	63,600
@12%	Keith	5,400		
	Jean	2,400		
Salaries	Keith	16,000		
	Jean	10,000		
Share of residual profit:				
(£63,600 – £33,800)				
Keith (60%)		17,880		
Jean (40%)		11,920		
		63,600		63,600

(b)

Partners' current accounts

	Keith	Jean		Keith	Jean
	£	£		£	£
Drawings	14,000	9,600	Interest on capital	5,400	2,400
			Salaries	16,000	10,000
Balance c/d	25,280	14,720	Profit share	17,880	11,920
	39,280	24,320		39,280	24,320
			Balance b/d	25,280	14,720

72 JOHN AND DARRYL

(a)

	£	£
Stock – valued at cost		45,864
Less: Cost of damaged items		5,748
		40,116
Expected selling price	6,700	
Cost of repairs	1,475	
Net realisable value		5,225
Stock value		45,341
Reported net profit		37,458
Stock write down (£45,864 – £45,341)		523
Revised net profit		36,935

(b)

			£
Revised net profit			36,935
	John	Darryl	
	£	£	
Salary	13,000	5,000	(18,000)
Interest on capital	5,500	2,500	(8,000)
Residual profit			10,935
Split	6,561	4,374	
Total share	25,061	11,874	

Working: Interest on capital

John	£	£
£60,000 at 5% for 2 months =	500	
£120,000 at 5% for 10 months =	5,000	5,500

Darryl		
£50,000 at 5% for 12 months =		2,500

(c)

Current account – John

	£		£
Drawings	18,000	Opening balance	43,250
Closing balance	<u>50,311</u>	Share of profit	<u>25,061</u>
	<u>68,311</u>		<u>68,311</u>

73 ORLA AND PAULA

(a) The gross profit of £157,846 does not require adjustment. However, the net profit of £51,014 needs to be increased by the £30,000 (2 × £15,000) paid to each partner as these payments are drawings rather than expenses. The net profit is therefore £81,024 (£51,024 + £30,000).

(b) **Allocation of net profit of £81,024**

	Orla	Paula	Total
	£	£	£
Interest on capital at 8%	10,000	5,600	15,600
Salaries	18,000	12,000	<u>30,000</u>
			45,600
Balance of profits 2/3 : 1/3	<u>23,616</u>	<u>11,808</u>	<u>35,424</u>
Totals	<u>51,616</u>	<u>29,408</u>	<u>81,024</u>

(c)

Partners' current accounts

	Orla	Paula		Orla	Paula
	£	£		£	£
Balance b/d	-	23,741	Balance b/d	34,568	-
Drawings	15,000	15,000	Interest on capital	10,000	5,600
			Salaries	18,000	12,000
Balance c/d	71,184	-	Profit share	23,616	11,808
			Balance c/d		<u>9,333</u>
	86,184	38,741		<u>86,184</u>	<u>38,741</u>
Balance b/d		9,333	Balance b/d	71,184	

(d) The total net assets of the partnership are equal to the total of the partners' capital and current accounts:

	£
Capital:	
Orla	125,000
Paula	70,000
Current:	
Orla	71,184
Paula	(9,333)
	———
Total net assets	256,851
	———

Section 7

PAPER-BASED MOCK QUESTIONS AND ANSWERS

QUESTIONS

SECTION A – ALL 20 QUESTIONS ARE COMPULSORY AND MUST BE ATTEMPTED.

EACH QUESTION IS WORTH 2 MARKS.

1   In a sales ledger control account, which of the following lists consists ONLY of items that would be recorded on the credit side of the account?

A   Cash received from customers, sales returns, bad debts written off, contras against amounts due to suppliers in the purchases ledger

B   Sales, cash refunds to customers, bad debts written off, discounts allowed

C   Cash received from customers, discounts allowed, interest charged on overdue accounts, bad debts written off

D   Sales, cash refunds to customers, interest charged on overdue accounts, contras against amounts due to suppliers in the purchases ledger

2   Y purchased some machinery on 1 January 20X3 for £38,000. The payment for the machinery was correctly entered in the cash book, but was entered on the debit side of machinery repairs account.

Y charges depreciation on machinery on a straight line basis at 20% per year, with a proportionate charge in the year of acquisition and assuming no scrap value at the end of the life of the asset.

How will Y's profit for the year ended 31 March 20X3 be affected by the error?

A   Understated by £30,400

B   Understated by £36,100

C   Understated by £38,000

D   Overstated by £1,900

3   The trial balance of Z failed to agree. Total debit balances were £836,200 and total credit balances were £819,700. A suspense account was opened for the amount of the difference and the following errors were found and corrected:

1   The totals of the cash discount columns in the cash book had not been posted to the discount accounts. The figures were Discount Allowed £3,900 and Discount Received £5,100.

2   A cheque for £19,000 received from a customer was correctly entered in the cash book but was posted to the customer's account as £9,100.

What will the remaining balance on the suspense account be after the correction of these errors?

A £25,300 credit

B £7,700 credit

C £27,700 debit

D £5,400 credit

4   **The following bank reconciliation statement has been prepared for Omega by a junior clerk:**

	£
Overdraft per bank statement	68,100
Add: Deposits not credited	141,200
	209,300
Less: outstanding cheques	41,800
Overdraft per cash book	167,500

Which of the following should be the correct balance per the cash book?

A £31,300 cash at bank

B £31,300 overdrawn

C £114,900 overdrawn

D £167,500 overdrawn, as stated

5   **The sales day book of Darenth has been overcast by £800 and the purchase day book has been undercast by £1,100. Darenth maintains purchase and sales ledger control accounts as part of the double entry bookkeeping system.**

The effect of correcting these errors will be to make adjustments to the:

A Control accounts, with no effect on profit

B Control accounts, with a decrease in profit of £1,900

C Ledger balances of the individual debtors and creditors, with no effect on profit

D Ledger balances of the individual debtors and creditors, with a decrease in profit of £1,900.

6   **The entries in a sales ledger control account are:**

Sales	£250,000
Bank	£225,000
Returns	£2,500
Bad debts	£3,000
Returned unpaid cheque	£3,500
Contra purchase ledger account	£4,000

What is the balance on the sales ledger control account?

A   £12,000

B   £19,000

C   £25,000

D   £27,000

7   A car was purchased for £12,000 on 1 April 20X1 and has been depreciated at 20% each year straight line, assuming no residual value.

The company policy is to charge a full year's depreciation in the year of purchase and no depreciation in the year of sale. The car was traded in for a replacement vehicle on 1 August 20X4 for an agreed figure of £5,000.

What was the profit or loss on the disposal of the vehicle for the year ended 31 December 20X4?

A   Loss £2,200

B   Loss £1,400

C   Loss £200

D   Profit £200

8   When valuing stock at cost, which of the following shows the correct method of arriving at cost?

	Include inward transport costs	*Include production overheads*
A	Yes	No
B	No	Yes
C	Yes	Yes
D	No	No

When answering questions 9 to 20, you are to assume that you are preparing the accounts of Ann Grey for the year to 31 October 20X8. Ann's extended trial balance has been partially completed and is shown at the end of this section.

On the extended trial balance each intersection of a column and a row represents a cell. Each cell is referenced by the combination of the relevant column letter and row number. For example, the Returns Inward figure of £1,500 is located in cell B5, you should use this method to identify cells when answering questions 9 to 20.

You are not required to insert any additional figures onto the extended trial balance.

9   Depreciation for motor vehicles is to be provided at 25% per annum, using the reducing balance method.

What is the depreciation charge for motor vehicles for the year?

A   £2,800

B   £900

C   £1,600

D   £700

10   The balance on one of the supplier's statements at 31 October 20X8 was £1,975. The balance of this supplier's account in the Purchase Ledger was £1,997. The difference is due to a discount, which had been agreed with the supplier. The bookkeeper had not recorded the discount.

What adjustment should be made to the purchase ledger control account?

A   An increase of £1,997

B   A decrease of £1,997

C   An increase of £22

D   A decrease of £22

11   The last telephone invoice received was for the three months ended 31st August 20X8. Telephone invoices received during the year had been for approximately £2,700 each. Each invoice had covered a three-month period.

What is the accrual for telephone charges?

A   £900

B   £2,700

C   £1,800

D   £3,600

12   Stock had been counted on the last day of October 20X8 and had a cost value of £24,750. This valuation includes slow moving items which had cost £3,800. These items will be offered for sale at a special price of cost less 20%

What is the figure for closing stock?

A   £23,990

B   £20,950

C   £22,510

D   £24,750

13   Included in the figure of rent is a payment of £5,400 for the three months ended 31 December 20X8.

What is the rent charge for the year?

A   £19,800

B   £21,600

C   £25,200

D   £28,800

14   Into which cells should the following journal entry be posted?

Dr   Light and heat   £500

Cr   Accruals   £500

A   D14 and E14

B   D34 and E14

C   D14 and E34

D   D34 and E34

15   Into which cells should a prepayment of rates be posted?

    A   F10 and G10

    B   F35 and G10

    C   F35 and G35

    D   F10 and G35

16   Into which cells should the entries for depreciation of equipment be posted?

    A   F33 and G33

    B   F33 and G22

    C   F22 and G33

    D   F22 and G22

17   When completing the extended trial balance, which is the correct cell for the extension of the accruals account?

    A   H34

    B   I34

    C   J34

    D   K34

18   When completing the extended trial balance, which are the correct cells for the extension of closing stock?

    A   H32 and I32

    B   H32 and K32

    C   I32 and J32

    D   I32 andK32

19   Assume that the trial balance has been extended and that the totals are as follows:

	Profit and loss accounts		**Balance sheet**	
	Dr	*Cr*	*Dr*	*Cr*
	£444,860	£449,912	£157,890	£152,838

    What is the result for the year?

    A   A loss of £5,052

    B   A loss of £5,061

    C   A profit of £5,052

    D   A profit of £5,061

20   If the result were a profit, into which cells would the result be entered?

    A   H38 and J38

    B   I38 and J38

    C   H38 and K38

    D   I38 and K38

(Total: 40 marks)

	A	B	C	D	E	F	G	H	I	J	K
	Ann Grey – Trial balance as at 31 October 20X8										
1		Balances per ledger		Journal entries		Post T. B. adjustments		Profit & Loss account		Balance sheet	
2		Dr	Cr	Dr	Cr	Dr	Cr	Dr	Cr	Dr	Cr
3		£	£	£	£	£	£	£	£	£	£
4	Sales		425,000								
5	Returns inward	1,500									
6	Purchases	262,000									
7	Returns outward		900								
8	Stock at 1.11.X7	27,600									
9	Rent	25,200									
10	Rates	13,000									
11	Wages	65,000									
12	Telephone	9,000									
13	Carriage inwards	1,700									
14	Light and heat	19, 500									
15	Stationery	200									
16	Loan interest	650									
17	Assets disposal		490								
18	Fixed assets at cost										
19	Equipment	104,500									
20	Motor vehicles	6,400									
21	Provision for depreciation at 1.11.X7										
22	Equipment		41,800								
23	Motor vehicles		2,800								
24	Bank account		7,250								
25	Cash on hand	100									
26	Purchase ledger control account		26,500								
27	Loan account		3,875								
28	Capital account as at 1.11.X7		49,735								
29	Drawings	22,000									
30											
31	Discount received										
32	Closing stock										
33	Depreciation for year										
34	Accruals										
35	Prepayments										
36	Heating oil										
37	Totals	558,350	558,350								
38	Profit for year										

SECTION B – ALL QUESTIONS MUST BE ANSWERED.

1.1 The ASB's Statement of Principles outlines four characteristics of information which financial statements should have.

Required:

State what the four characteristics are and explain briefly the meaning of each. **(4 marks)**

1.2 Financial statements are prepared for a variety of 'user groups'.

Required:

List the main user groups, then select one group and explain their reporting needs.

(4 marks)

1.3 A partnership's appropriation account shows the appropriation of the profit to the partners. Explain what items would be shown in the appropriation account and also the corresponding entries in the partners' current accounts. **(3 marks)**

1.4 In order to show a fair and realistic value of debtors on a balance sheet, a provision for bad debts is often raised.

Required:

Explain which accounting concept is being applied when dealing with such a provision.

(1 mark)

1.5 FRSs are accounting standards issued by the ASB.

Required:

What is the ASB and what is its role and purpose? **(3 marks)**

2 SIMON

Simon depreciates his machinery at a rate of 20% per annum on a reducing balance basis. He provides a full year's depreciation in the year an asset is acquired, and no provision is made in the year of disposal.

At 1 November 20X3, the cost of Simon's machinery was £140,900 and the net book value was £94,570.

During the year to 31 October 20X4, a machine which had cost £35,000 and had been depreciated for four years was traded in for a new machine. The new machine cost £50,000 and the trade in value was £14,000. At 31 October 20X4 the balance of the cost of the new machine was still outstanding.

Required:

(a) Calculate the profit or loss on the machine traded in. **(3 marks)**

(b) Calculate the depreciation charge for machinery for the year to 31 October 2004.

(2 marks)

(c)   Show the following ledger accounts for the year:

   (i)   machinery at cost;   **(4 marks)**

   (ii)   accumulated depreciation.   **(3 marks)**

(d)   Calculate the total charge to be reported in the profit and loss account for the year to 31 October 20X4 in respect of machinery.   **(1 mark)**

(e)   State the balances to be reported in the balance sheet as at 31 October 20X4 as a result of these transactions.   **(2 marks)**

(Total: 15 marks)

3   SUSAN ADAMS

Susan Adams has asked you to reconcile the balance on her bank statement in her nominal ledger.

You have checked her bank statement and other records, and have noted:

(i)   Cheque number 298784 is recorded in the cash book as £560 but as £650 on the bank statement. You have confirmed that the bank statement is correct.

(ii)   Susan has paid for a number of items with a total value of £3,900 by standing order, but has not recorded these payments in her cash book.

(iii) The bank has charged £225 for bank fees and paid Susan interest of £174. These amounts have not been entered in the cash book.

(iv)   One of Susan's customers has used the BACS system to make payments totalling £3,528. Susan has not recorded these payments.

(v)   The following cheques have not been debited on the bank statement:

Number	£
297618	650
299157	315
299276	166

   The first of these is a cheque sent to a supplier almost a year ago. The supplier did not receive the cheque, and a replacement cheque was issued and cashed. Susan made no entry to cancel the original cheque.

(vi)   A lodgement for £4,870 has not been credited by the bank.

(vii) The balance on the bank statement is £2,158 (credit).

(viii) The balance in the nominal ledger is £6,410 (debit).

Required:

(a)   Show the nominal ledger bank account, incorporating the adjustments required in respect of the information above.

Note: You must use a format which clearly identifies the debit and credit entries.

(9 marks)

(b)   State whether the bank balance will be reported in Susan's final accounts as an asset or a liability.   **(1 mark)**

(c)   Prepare the bank reconciliation statement.   **(5 marks)**

(Total: 15 marks)

4   STEVE FLETCHER

One of your clients, Steve Fletcher, who does not keep full accounting records, has asked you to calculate his profit for the year to 30 April 2005 and his bank balance at that date. Your file on last year's accounts shows that his assets and liabilities at 30 April 2004 included the following:

	£
Stock	15,800
Debtors	23,750
Creditors	16,800
Cash at bank	7,500
Capital	42,900

In the year to 30 April 2005, Steve received £204,800 from his customers. Before banking the cash he used £2,900 to pay business expenses and took cash drawings of £17,900. He also banked £3,000 from the sale of some personal assets.

He wrote cheques totalling £191,650. Of this amount, £3,100 was drawings and £22,800 was for business expenses. The rest of the cheques were paid to suppliers.

At 30 April 2005 his stock was valued at £16,200. At that date he was owed £25,400 by his customers and he owed £17,900 to his suppliers. You estimate that your fee for this work will be £150.

You have already calculated that the depreciation charge on Steve's fixed assets for the year to 30 April 2005 is £2,450.

Required:

(a)   Calculate Steve's bank balance at 30 April 2005.   **(3 marks)**

(b)   For the year to 30 April 2005, calculate Steve's:

   (i)   sales;   **(2 marks)**

   (ii)   purchases; and   **(4 marks)**

   (iii)   gross profit.   **(3 marks)**

(c)   Based on the gross profit you have calculated in (b) above, calculate Steve's net profit for the year to 30 April 2005.   **(3 marks)**

(Total: 15 marks)

ANSWERS

SECTION A

1   A

In the sales ledger control account, credit entries are for items that reduce the total of debts owed. These are mainly cash receipts from debtors, but also include sales returns, bad debts written off, settlements and discounts allowed and contra entries to supplier accounts in the purchases ledger.

2   B

The transaction should have been recorded as:

Debit Fixed asset account £38,000.

The fixed asset would then be depreciated and the depreciation charge for the year should be 20% of £38,000 × (7 months/12 months) = £1,900.

In error, the transaction was recorded as:

Debit Machinery repairs account £38,000.

The entire expense would have been charged against profits in the year, therefore profits have been understated by £38,000 – £1,900 = £36,100.

3   D

Suspense account

	£		£
Discounts received	5,100	Starting balance	16,500
		(836,200 – 819,700)	
Debtor account	9,900	Discounts allowed	3,900
(19,000 – 9,100)			
Closing balance	5,400		
	———		———
	20,400		20,400
	———		———
		Balance b/d	5,400

Notes

A credit entry is needed in the suspense account to make total debit balances equal to total credit balances.

To decide whether to make a credit or debit entry in a suspense account, think about what the other side of the double entry transaction should be. We should credit the discounts received account, so we debit the suspense account. We should debit the discounts allowed account, so we credit the suspense account. We should credit the debtor account with an additional £9,900, so we debit the suspense account.

4   A

	£
Overdraft in bank statement	(68,100)
Deposits not yet credited to the account	141,200
	73,100
Cheques paid but not yet presented to the bank	(41,800)
Cash balance in cash book	31,300

5   B

The sales day book has been overcast by £800 (i.e. the total is £800 higher than it should be). As a result, the sales account has been credited and the sales ledger control account has been debited with £800 too much.

The purchase day book has been undercast by £1,100. As a result of this, the purchases account has been debited and the purchase ledger control account credited with £1,100 too little.

As a result of these errors, the control account balances need to be adjusted, and profit reduced by (£800 + £1,100) £1,900, by reducing sales and increasing purchases.

Neither error affects the entries in the accounts of individual debtors and creditors.

6   B

Presumably, there was no opening balance on this account.

Sales ledger control account

	£		£
Sales	250,000	Bank	225,000
Bank: cheque returned	3,500	Sales returns	2,500
		Bad debts	3,000
		Contra: purchase ledger	4,000
		Balance c/d	19,000
	253,500		253,500
Balance b/d	19,000		

7   D

Accumulated depreciation at the time of disposal = 3 years × 20% × £12,000 = £7,200.

Written down value = £12,000 – £7,200 = £4,800

Trade-in value of asset disposed of = £5,000.

Profit on disposal = £4,800 – £5,000 = £200.

8   C

The question presumably refers to the valuation of stock of finished goods or part-finished work in progress in a manufacturing business. Inward carriage costs (i.e. the costs of delivery of materials and components purchased from suppliers) are included in stock costs. Work in progress and finished goods should also include a share of production overhead costs.

9   B

		£	
Motor vehicles	Cost	6,400	
	Less: provision depreciation b/f	2,800	
WDV		3,600	× 25% = £900

10   D

The amount owed to the supplier should be reduced by £22 (1,997 − 1,975) because the discount received from the supplier reduces the liability.

11   C

The accrual is for two months, September and October. Telephone costs have been incurred in these months, but there has not yet been an invoice. The best estimate of the accrual is:

Telephone £2,700 × $\frac{2}{3}$ = £1,800

12   A

		£
Stock	Cost	24,750
	Less: write down for slow moving items	760
	(£3,800 × 20%)	
		23,990

13   B

Rent has been paid in advance for the three months ended 31 December, which means that at 31 October, there is a prepayment of two months for rent (November and December).

The prepayment is $\frac{2}{3}$ ×£5,400 = £3,600.

	£
Rent expenses in extended trial balance	25,200
Less prepayment	
	3,600
Rent charged for the year	21,600

14   C

The accrued expenses for light and heat should be added to the total expense for the year, so debit the accrued amount in cell D14 (debit = increase expense). The corresponding credit entry is in cell E34 (accrual = liability, so a credit entry).

15   B

A prepayment of rates reduces the rent charge for the year, so credit the rates account (cell G10). The corresponding debit entry is in cell F35 (prepayment = asset, so a debit entry).

16   B

Debit the depreciation expense account (cell F33) and credit the accumulated depreciation account for equipment (cell G22).

17   D

An accrual appears as a liability in the balance sheet. Liabilities are credit balances, so the correct cell for the extension is cell K34.

18   C

Closing stock is posted initially to cells F32 and G32. The cells for the extension are cell J32, because closing stock is an asset in the balance sheet, and cell I32, because the closing stock reduces the cost of sales in the profit and loss account (and so is a credit entry).

19   C

	£
Total credit balances, P&L account (income)	449,912
Total debit balances, P&L account (expenses)	444,860
Profit for the year	5,052

20   C

The profit figure is entered in the 'profit for year' row 38. In the previous question, where there is a profit, we would have 444,860 in cell H37 and 449,912 in cell I37. The difference (the profit) is entered in cell H38 to make the debit and credit totals equal. Similarly, we would have 157,890 in cell J37 and 152,838 in cell K37. The difference (also the profit) is entered in cell K38, to make the debit and credit totals for the balance sheet equal.

SECTION B

1.1   The four characteristics are relevance, reliability, understandability and comparability.

- **Relevance** – the information must be able to influence decisions.

- **Reliability** – the information must be a faithful representation.

- **Understandability** – the information must be understandable to the end user.

- **Comparability** – the information must provide a basis for 'like with like' comparisons.

1.2   User groups include:

- Investors;
- loan creditor (lenders);
- employees;
- the public;
- the government;
- customers;
- suppliers.

For example, lenders (loan creditor group) would focus on cash flow and measures of liquidity and the firm's ability to repay loans.

1.3   Items would include:

- interest on drawings;
- interest on capital;
- salaries;
- share of balance.

Interest on drawings would be debited to the current account, the other items credited to the partners' current accounts.

1.4   When raising a provision for bad and doubtful debts the concept of prudence is being applied.

1.5   The ASB is the Accounting Standards Board which is governed and controlled by the FRC – the Financial Reporting Council.

The ASB's role and purpose is to develop, issue and withdraw accounting standards.

2   SIMON

(a)   The loss on the machine traded in is calculated as follows:

	£
Cost	35,000
Depreciation for year 1	(7,000)
	28,000
Depreciation for year 2	(5,600)
	22,400
Depreciation for year 3	(4,480)
	17,920
Depreciation for year 4	(3,584)
Net book value	14,336
Sale proceeds	(14,000)
Loss	336

(b)   The depreciation charge for the year ended 31 October 20X4 is as follows:

	£
Cost (see part (c))	155,900
Less depreciation (£46,330 – £20,664)	(25,666)
Net book value	130,234

£130,234 × 20% = £26,047

(c)   (i)

Motor car – cost account

	£		£
Balance b/f	140,900	Disposal (cost)	35,000
Disposal (proceeds)	14,000	Balance c/f	155,900
Creditors	36,000		
	190,900		190,900
Balance b/f	155,900		

(ii)   **Motor car – accumulated depreciation**

	£		£
Disposal		Balance b/f	
(£35,000 – £14,336)	20,664	(£140,900 – £94,570)	46,330
Balance c/f	51,713	Depreciation expense account	26,047
	72,377		72,377
		Balance c/f	51,713

(d)   The total charge in the profit and loss account is:

	£
Depreciation for the year	26,047
Loss on disposal	336
	26,383

(e)   The balance sheet will show:

	£
Fixed assets:	
Cost	155,900
Less depreciation	(51,713)
Net book value	104,187
Creditors	36,000

3   SUSAN ADAMS

(a)   **Bank account**

	£		£
Balance b/d	6,410	Cheque error	90
Interest	174	Standing orders	3,900
BACS	3,528	Bank charges	225
Cancelled cheque	650	Balance c/d	6,547
	———		———
	10,762		10,762
	———		———
Balance b/d	6,547		

(b)   The bank balance would be stated on her balance sheet as a current asset.

(c)

	£
Balance on bank statement	2,158
Add lodgements	4,870
	———
	7,028
Less: Unpresented cheques	481
	———
Balance per the cash book	6,547
	———

4   STEVE FLETCHER

(a)   **Bank account**

	£		£
Opening	7,500	Payments	191,650
Trade debtors (204,800 – 2,900 – 17,900)	184,000		
Capital	3,000	**Closing balance**	**2,850**
	194,500		194,500

(b)   **Sales**

	£		£
Opening	23,750	Receipts	204,800
Sales Balancing figure	206,450	Closing	25,400
	230,200		230,200

Purchases

		£		£
Payments	(191,650 – 3,100 – 22,800)	165,750	Opening	16,800
Closing		17,900	Purchases	166,850
		183,650		183,650

(c)   Gross and net profits

		£	£
Sales			206,450
Cost of sales	Opening stock	15,800	
	Purchases	166,850	
	Closing stock	(16,200)	
			(166,450)
Gross profit			**40,000**
Expenses	Cash expenses	2,900	
	Expenses paid by cheque	22,800	
	Accounting fee	150	
	Depreciation	2,450	
			(28,300)
Net profit			**11,700**

Section 8

COMPUTER-BASED MOCK QUESTIONS AND ANSWERS

QUESTIONS

ALL QUESTIONS ARE COMPULSORY AND MUST BE ATTEMPTED.

1   What transaction is recorded by the following journal entry?

Dr   Legal fees   £463

Cr   Creditors control   £463

A   Legal fees paid by cheque

B   An invoice issued to a lawyer

C   An invoice received from a lawyer

D   A credit note received from a lawyer

2   Which two of the following errors will be revealed by extracting a trial balance?

(i)   Error of single entry

(ii)   Error of commission

(iii)   Error of omission

(iv)   Error of transposition

A   (i) and (iii)

B   (ii) and (iii)

C   (iii) and (iv)

D   (i) and (iv)

3   Which of the following is an application of an estimation technique?

A   Recording fixed assets at their historical cost

B   Depreciating motor vehicles at 20% per annum

C   Valuing stock on an actual cost basis

D   Recording stationery expenses at invoiced cost

4   Lance is entering an invoice in the purchase day book. The invoice shows the following costs:

Water treatment equipment	£39,800
Delivery	£1,100
Maintenance charge	£3,980
VAT	£7,854
Invoice total	£52,734

Assuming Lance is registered for VAT, what is the total value of capital expenditure on the invoice?

```
┌─────────┐
│         │
└─────────┘
```

5   When Fred's trial balance was extracted, the debit total was £400 less than the credit total.

Which of the following errors could have caused this difference?

A   A sales invoice for £200 was debited to both the sales account and the debtors control account

B   A cheque received for £200 was entered twice in the nominal ledger

C   A cheque to a supplier for £200 was credited to both the expense account and the creditors control account

D   The purchases account was undercast by £200

6   A business which is VAT registered purchased goods that had a net value of £700 on credit from Roper Ltd. What would be the debit to purchases if VAT is payable at a rate of 17.5%?

A   £577.50

B   £700.00

C   £822.50

D   £848.48

7   Joan's draft year end accounts were prepared including a prepayment for rent of £970. The prepayment should have been £1,170.

When the error is corrected, how will net profit be affected?

A   Net profit will decrease by £200

B   Net profit will increase by £200

C   Net profit will decrease by £1,170

D   Net profit will increase by £1,170

8   When posting an invoice for car repairs, £870 was entered on the correct side of the motor expenses account. The invoice was for £780.

What correction should be made to the motor expenses account?

A   Debit £90

B   Credit £90

C   Debit £1,650

D   Credit £1,650

9   **The balance on Amy's sales ledger control account in the nominal ledger is £100 more than the total of the listing of the balances on the personal accounts.**

Which one of the following treatments of an invoice for £100 could have caused this difference?

A   The invoice was entirely omitted

B   The invoice was entered on the credit side of the personal account

C   The invoice was not entered in the personal account

D   The invoice was entered twice in the personal account

10   **How should the balance on the sales ledger control account be reported in the final accounts?**

A   As an expense

B   As a fixed asset

C   As a current asset

D   As a current liability

11   **Colin provides for potential bad debts on the basis of the length of time the debt has been outstanding. The aged debtors analysis at 30 September 20X3 and the provisions required are:**

Age of debt	£	Provision required
0 – 30 days	56,800	1% of balances
31 – 59 days	37,700	20% of balances
60 days and over	14,900	75% of balances

At 1 October 20X2, Colin's doubtful debts provision was £18,765.

Which of the following should be reported in Colin's profit and loss account for the year to 30 September 20X3?

A   A charge of £518

B   A credit of £518

C   A charge of £19,283

D   A credit of £19,283

12   **Margaret checked her bank statement with the bank account in her nominal ledger and found the following differences:**

(i)   some cheques have not been lodged by her suppliers;

(ii)   the bank credited a personal lodgement to her business account in error;

(iii)   the bank debited fees on her account.

Which of the differences require an entry in the bank account in the nominal ledger?

A   (i)

B   (ii)

C   (iii)

D   (ii) and (iii)

13 Alan prepared his draft year end accounts, but did not adjust these for a prepayment of £1,500 and an accrual of £400.

How will Alan's profit and net assets be affected by including the prepayment and the accrual?

	Net profit will:	Net assets will:
A	Increase by £1,100	Reduce by £1,100
B	Reduce by £1,900	Increase by £1,900
C	Increase by £1,100	Increase by £1,100
D	Reduce by £1,900	Reduce by £1,900

14 In September 20X3, Bridget took out a business development loan for £15,000. This is to be repaid in three equal annual instalments. The first instalment is due for payment on 1 January 20X5.

How will the outstanding balance be reported in Bridget's balance sheet at 30 November 20X3?

A £15,000 as a current liability

B £5,000 as a current liability and £10,000 as a long-term liability

C £10,000 as a current liability and £5,000 as a long-term liability

D £15,000 as a long-term liability

15 Adele runs a restaurant. In August 20X3 she received a letter from a lawyer representing a customer who claims he suffered food poisoning after eating in the restaurant. The customer is claiming damages of £3,000. Adele offered to pay £300. Her lawyer's advice is that in the event of the case going to court, she is likely to be required to pay £1,500. The solicitor also advised that the court case is unlikely to take place before April 20X4.

What amount should be provided for in respect of the claim in Adele's final accounts for the year ended 30 September 20X3?

The following information relates to questions 16 and 17.

At 30 September 20X3 Pamela's stock was valued at £6,400 and her trial balance included the following balances:

	Debit £	Credit £
Sales		45,000
Purchases	29,500	
Stock at 1 October 20X2	5,700	
Carriage inwards	750	
Postage	340	
Wages	6,000	
Advertising	1,900	
Other expenses	2,500	

---

16 What is Pamela's gross profit?

17   What sum will be reported as expenses in Pamela's profit and loss account?

[   ]

18   In the year to 30 September 20X3 Rena paid a total of £2,850 for business car expenses. This includes £350 which Rena paid from her personal funds. There was an opening accrual of £329 on the car expenses account and the closing accrual was £464.

What is the charge for car expenses to be reported in Rena's profit and loss account for the year to 30 September 20X3?

[   ]

19   Albert does not keep full accounting records. His last accounts show that his capital balance was £42,890. At the year end he calculated that his assets and liabilities were:

	£
Fixed assets	41,700
Stock	9,860
Debtors	7,695
Creditors	4,174
Bank overdraft	5,537

On reviewing his calculations, you note that he did not include £258 of unpaid invoices for expenses.

What is the value of Albert's closing capital?

[   ]

20   In the last 12 months, Jenna's capital balance increased by £6,798. In the year her drawings totalled £14,600 and she introduced additional capital of £2,900.

What is Jenna's net profit or loss for the year?

A   £4,902 loss

B   £18,498 loss

C   £4,902 profit

D   £18,498 profit

21   Alec returned goods which were bought on credit from Peter for £473.

How will this be recorded in Alec's nominal ledger?

A	Dr		Purchase returns	£473	
		Cr	Creditors control account		£473
B	Dr		Creditors control account	£473	
		Cr	Purchase returns		£473
C	Dr		Purchase returns	£473	
		Cr	Bank		£473
D	Dr		Bank	£473	
		Cr	Purchase returns		£473

22   **Which one of the following correctly states the accounting equation?**

A   Capital + Liabilities = Assets

B   Assets + Liabilities = Capital

C   Capital + Assets = Liabilities

D   Capital − Liabilities = Assets

23   **Which one of the following costs is included in the calculation of gross profit?**

A   Depreciation of delivery vans

B   Salaries of general office staff

C   Carriage outwards

D   Carriage inwards

24   **Tania's year end trial balance includes the following balances:**

	£
Opening stock	12,964
Trade debtors	43,728
Bank overdraft	5,872
Trade creditors	28,627

Tania's closing stock is valued at £11,625.

Based on the above figures, what is the value of Tania's current assets?

```
┌──────────┐
│          │
└──────────┘
```

25   **Sophie has the following information about a new fixed asset which was financed by taking out a loan:**

(i)   Serial number

(ii)   Cost

(iii)   Provider of loan

(iv)   Date of purchase.

What information will Sophie enter in the fixed asset register?

A   (i) (ii) and (iii)

B   (ii) (iii) and (iv)

C   (i) (ii) and (iv)

D   (i) (iii) and (iv)

26   **Terry bought a new car for £12,750. He paid for the new car by taking out a loan of £8,000 and trading in his old car. The old car originally cost £8,500 and had been depreciated by £4,148 at the time of the trade in.**

What is the profit on disposal of the old car?

```
┌──────────┐
│          │
└──────────┘
```

27 **When preparing the purchase ledger reconciliation for a client, you noted the following errors:**

(i) an invoice for £215 from a supplier was not entered in the accounting records;

(ii) an invoice for £465 was recorded as £456 in the purchase day book.

Which of the errors will cause a difference between the balance on the control account in the nominal ledger and the total of the list of balances from the personal ledger?

A (i) only

B (ii) only

C Both (i) and (ii)

D Neither (i) or (ii)

28 **Bruce prepared the following purchase ledger reconciliation statement:**

Balance on nominal ledger control account	£46,865	credit
Payment entered twice in nominal ledger control account	£573	credit
	£47,438	credit
Purchase daybook overcast	£900	debit
Total of list of balances	£46,538	credit

How should the purchase ledger balance be reported on the balance sheet?

A £46,538 as a current asset

B £46,538 as a current liability

C £46,865 as a current asset

D £46,865 as a current liability

29 **Which one of the following is a reason for preparing a sales ledger reconciliation?**

A To calculate discounts allowed

B To identify overdue accounts

C To check the calculation of gross profit

D To confirm the accuracy of postings

30 **Eleanor prepared the following bank reconciliation statement:**

	£	
Balance per bank statement	12,548	(overdrawn)
Outstanding cheques	3,847	
	16,395	
Outstanding lodgements	5,424	
	10,971	
Bank charges	540	
Balance per nominal ledger	10,431	(overdrawn)

What is the correct value of the bank overdraft to be reported in the balance sheet?

[   ]

31   Which of the following correctly describe(s) why a bank reconciliation is prepared?

(i)   To identify entries which have been generated by the bank, but not recorded in the cash book.

(ii)   To identify errors in the entries in the cash book.

A   (i) only

B   (ii) only

C   Both (i) and (ii)

D   Neither (i) or (ii)

32   Steve is preparing his accounts for the year to 31 May 20X4. On 1 July 20X3 he paid £22,644 to rent a store for 18 months from that date.

What adjustment is required?

A   A prepayment of £8,806

B   An accrual of £8,806

C   A prepayment of £13,209

D   An accrual of £13,209

33   Which one of the following correctly describes the effect of adjusting draft accounts for a prepaid expense?

A   Profit will be increased and current assets will be reduced

B   Profit will be reduced and current assets will be increased

C   Both profit and current assets will be increased

D   Both profit and current assets will be reduced

34   At the start of the financial year, Wilson had a prepayment of £490 for telephone expenses. During the year he paid telephone bills with a total value of £4,784. He also received a cheque for a rebate of £215. At the end of the year he had accrued telephone expenses of £270.

What amount should be charged to the profit and loss account for the year for telephone expenses?

☐

35   Edwin does not keep full accounting records, but has provided the following information:

●   total value of sales during the year: £167,580;

●   all sales were at a mark up of 20%.

What was Edwin's cost of sales for the year?

☐

36   At the beginning of the year a business had net assets of £89,548. During the year, the owner withdrew £17,500. At the end of the year, the net assets had a value of £95,574.

What was the net profit for the year?

☐

37 When the extended trial balance is extended and completed and the result for the period is a profit, in which columns will the result be entered?

	Profit and loss columns	*Balance sheet columns*
A	Debit	Credit
B	Credit	Debit
C	Debit	Debit
D	Credit	Credit

38 At the end of the financial year, Maud's fixed assets cost £136,758 and had been depreciated by £34,864.

How will the fixed assets be recorded on the opening trial balance for the next financial year?

A £136,758 debit and £34,864 credit

B £136,758 credit and £34,864 debit

C £136,758 debit and £34,864 debit

D £136,758 credit and £34,864 credit

39 Depreciation is best described as:

A A means of spreading the payment for fixed assets over a period of years

B A decline in the market value of the assets

C A means of spreading the net cost of fixed assets over their estimated useful life

D A means of estimating the amount of money needed to replace the assets.

40 In reconciling a business cash book with the bank statement, which of the following items could require a subsequent entry in the cash book?

Error

1   Cheques presented after the date of the bank statement

2   A cheque from a customer that has been dishonoured

3   An error by the bank

4   Bank charges

5   Deposits credited after the date of the bank statement

6   Standing order payment entered in the bank statement

A   Items 2, 3, 4 and 6 only

B   Items 1, 2, 5 and 6 only

C   Items 2, 4 and 6 only

D   Items 1, 3 and 5 only

41 In Paul's books an invoice for £367 for legal fees has been posted to bank fees.

What journal entry should be made to correct the error?

A Dr   Creditors   £367

   Cr   Legal fees   £367

   Being correction of error – invoice posted to wrong account

B Dr   Legal fees   £367

   Cr   Bank fees   £367

   Being correction of error – invoice posted to wrong account

C Dr   Bank fees   £367

   Cr   Legal fees   £367

   Being correction of error – invoice posted to wrong account

D Dr   Bank fees   £367

   Cr   Creditors   £367

   Being correction of error – invoice posted to wrong account.

42 One of Paul's customers paid £500 to clear a balance of £503.76. The bookkeeper has not recorded the discount.

What journal entry should now be made?

A Dr   Discount received   £3.76

   Cr   Debtor   £3.76

   Being correction of recording of discount

B Dr   Debtor   £3.76

   Cr   Discount received   £3.76

   Being correction of recording of discount

C Dr   Debtor   £3.76

   Cr   Discount allowed   £3.76

   Being correction of recording of discount

D Dr   Discount allowed   £3.76

   Cr   Debtor   £3.76

   Being correction of recording of discount

43 When Paul's trial balance was extracted, the total debits were £400 more than the total credits.

Which of the following treatments of an invoice for £200 would cause this difference?

A   Both entries have been made to the credit side of the relevant ledger accounts

B   Both entries have been made to the debit side of the relevant ledger accounts

C   No entries have been made in the ledger accounts

D   Both entries have been made twice in the relevant ledger accounts

44 **Chris received an invoice for £280 for stationery. The invoice was posted to the postage account.**

What journal entry will correct the error?

A   Dr   Postage   £280

         Cr   Stationery   £280

         Being correction of an error of commission – invoice posted to incorrect account

B   Dr   Stationery   £280

         Cr   Postage   £280

         Being correction of an error of commission – invoice posted to incorrect account

C   Dr   Postage   £560

         Cr   Stationery   £560

         Being correction of an error of commission – invoice posted to incorrect account

D   Dr   Stationery   £560

         Cr   Postage   £560

         Being correction of an error of commission – invoice posted to incorrect account

45 **When posting an invoice for £356, Len entered the value as £365.**

What type of error is this?

A   Error of transposition

B   Error of principle

C   Compensating error

D   Error of omission

46 **The last invoice paid for telephone was for £3,474. This invoice covered the three months to 30 April 20X3.**

What adjustment is required when preparing the accounts for the year to 31 May 20X3?

A   A prepayment of £1,158

B   A prepayment of £2,316

C   An accrual of £1,158

D   An accrual of £2,316.

47 **Paul's stock at 31 May 20X3 cost £48,350. This included some items at a cost of £3,500 which had been in stock for almost a year. Paul intends to advertise these items for sale at a price of £2,500. The advertising will cost £800.**

What value should be included in Paul's balance sheet at 31 May 20X3 for closing stock?

48 On extracting a trial balance a suspense account is opened with a credit balance on it. You discover that this is caused by a single error in the nominal ledger. Which of the following could therefore have caused the imbalance?

A   The PAYE and National Insurance deductions for the current month have been entered twice in the deductions control account

B   A debtors' ledger/creditors' ledger contra has been entered on the credit side of both control accounts

C   The opening accrual for telephone charges has been brought forward at the beginning of the year on the wrong side of the ledger account

D   The figure of closing stock has been entered on both sides of the trial balance

49 Which of the following is an example of a long-term liability for Paul?

A   An amount he will receive in two years

B   An amount he will have to pay in two months

C   An amount he will have to pay in two years

D   An amount he will receive in two months

50 D, E and F are in partnership, sharing profits in the ratio 5:3:2 respectively, after charging salaries for E and F of £24,000 each per year.

On 1 July 20X3 they agreed to change the profit-sharing ratio to 3:1:1 and to increase E's salary to £36,000 per year, F's salary continuing unchanged.

For the year ended 31 December 20X3 the partnership profit amounted to £480,000.

Which of the following correctly states the partners' total profit shares for the year?

	D	E	F
A	£234,000	£136,800	£109,200
B	£213,000	£157,800	£109,200
C	£186,000	£171,600	£122,400
D	£237,600	£132,000	£110,400

ANSWERS

1 C

The cost of the legal fees shown on the invoice would be debited to the legal fees account. The lawyer supplying the service is a creditor and the amount would be credited to creditors control.

2 D

Errors of commission and omission do not cause imbalance, whereas those of single entry and transposition would cause imbalance (assuming the transposition was on one side of the double entry only).

3 B

Depreciation is an estimation technique as it involves both an estimate of the useful economic life of the asset and its expected residual value. These factors are used in determining the annual depreciation charge.

4 £40,900

The cost of the equipment and its charge for delivery would be capitalised. The VAT would not be capitalised as it is recoverable.

5 C

Crediting both the expense account and creditors control with £200 would cause an imbalance of £400.

6 B

Purchases are recorded excluding VAT, provided the business is registered for VAT.

7 B

The pre-payment had been understated by £200 and therefore profit was understated.

8 B

The motor expense account was overstated by £90 therefore the account would need to be credited with £90 to adjust the error.

9 C

By omitting the invoice from the debtor's personal account, the listing of personal account balances would be £100 less than the control account balance.

10 C

The balance on the sales ledger control account represents total debtors at the date of the balance sheet. Debtors are a current asset.

11   A

Colin's bad debts provision would comprise:

	£
£56,800 @ 1%	568
£37,700 @ 20%	7,540
£14,900 @ 75%	11,175

	19,283
Existing provision	18,765

Increase in provision	518

This would be charged to the profit and loss account.

12   C

The bank account in the nominal ledger would only need adjusting for the bank charges debited to her account by the bank.

13   C

	Effect on profit	*Effect on net assets*	
	£	£	
Prepayment	1,500	1,500	(current asset)
Accrual	(400)	(400)	(current liability)
	------	------	
Net effect	1,100	1,100	
	------	------	

14   D

The date of her balance sheet was 30 November 20X3, and the first instalment is not due until 1 January 20X5. Therefore the full £15,000 is shown as a long-term liability.

15   £1,500

It would be prudent to provide for a liability of £1,500 as there is a degree of certainty regarding the outcome.

16   £15,450

Gross profit comprises:

	£	£
Sales		45,000
Stock 1/10/X2	5,700	
Purchases	29,500	
Carriage in	750	

	35,950	
Stock 30/9/X3	6,400	

Cost of sales		29,550

Gross profit		15,450
		------

17   £10,740

Expenses comprise:

	£
Postage	340
Wages	6,000
Adverts	1,900
Other expenses	2,500
	10,740

18   £2,985

Car expenses

	£		£
Bank	2,500	Balance b/d	329
Personal funds	350	Profit and loss account	2,985
Accrual c/d	464		
	3,314		3,314

Note: The £350 paid from personal funds was for a business expense.

19   £49,286

The capital can be calculated by using the accounting equation:

Assets	–	Liabilities	=	Capital
41,700		4,174		
9,860		5,537		
7,695		258		
£59,255		£9,969		£49,286

20   D

	£
Increase in capital balance of which £2,900 was	6,798
Capital introduced	2,900
Net increase	3,898
Drawings for year	14,600
Profit for year	18,498

21   B

The creditors control account is debited with £473 (thus reducing the amount owing) and purchase returns are credited with £473.

22   A

The accounting equation is: Capital + Liabilities = Assets

23   D

Carriage inwards is included in the calculation of gross profit (i.e. it goes into the trading account). All of the other expenses are deducted from gross profit in order to arrive at net profit.

24   £55,353

Current assets include closing stock (£11,625) and debtors (£43,728). Opening stock goes into the profit and loss account, not the balance sheet. Trade creditors and the bank overdraft are current liabilities.

25   C

The fixed asset register will include the serial number, cost and date of purchase. It will not include the name of the loan provider.

26   £398

The old car had a net book value of £4,352 (£8,500 − £4,148). It was sold for £4,750 (cost of new car £12,750 − bank loan £8,000). Therefore the profit on disposal is £398 (£4,352 - £4,750).

27   D

Neither of the errors will cause a difference between the control account and the list of balances. Item (i) has been omitted completely, so it affects both the control account and the list of balances equally. Item (ii) has been entered incorrectly in the purchase day book, which is the book of original entry for both the control account and the purchase ledger.

28   B

The balance of £46,538 is a current liability.

29   D

The sales ledger reconciliation is a way of confirming the accuracy of postings.

30   £10,971

The bank charges will already have been included in arriving at the overdraft figure of £12,548 shown on the bank statement.

31   C

A bank reconciliation is prepared to identify entries which have been generated by the bank, but not recorded in the cash book, and to identify errors in the entries in the cash book.

32   A

The rent covers the period from 1 July 20X3 to 31 December 20X4. Seven months of this period falls into the following accounting period. Therefore there is a prepayment of £22,644 x 7/18 = £8,806. (You needed to be careful with your calculation here, as the temptation is to apportion by 12. This would give you a figure of £13,209.)

33   C

The profit will be increased as the prepayment reduces the amount charged in the current accounting period. Assets are increased as the amount prepaid is shown on the balance sheet as a current asset.

34   D

Amount paid £4,784 + opening prepayment £490 + closing accrual £270 – rebate £215 = £5,329.

35   £139,650

Sales £157,580 × 100/120 – £139,650 cost of sales.

36   £23,526

	£
Opening net assets	89,548
Less drawings	(17,500)
	72,048
Closing net assets	95,574
Profit	23,526

37   A

The profit and loss account is actually a type of T account. If there is a profit, it will be a debit, because credits (total income) exceed debits (total expenses). To complete the double entry, the profit is then credited to the balance sheet.

38   A

The cost of the fixed assets (£136,758) is a debit. The accumulated depreciation (£34,864) is a credit.

39   C

Answer C is the most appropriate of the four definitions given.

40   C

Items shown in the bank statement that should subsequently be recorded in the cash book are items that the business does not learn about until it receives the bank statement. These include bank charges, dishonoured cheques and standing orders and direct debit payments.

41   B

As bank fees have been debited incorrectly, the journal entry required would be credit bank fees and debit legal fees.

42   D

The amount of £3.76 is a discount allowed which needs debiting to the expense account (discount allowed) and crediting as an allowance to the debtor's account.

43   B

The error of £200 posted to the debit side of two relevant accounts would double the imbalance to £400.

44   B

Stationery expenses have been incorrectly debited to the postage account. To correct the error we credit the postage account and debit the stationery account.

45   A

A common cause of bookkeeping error is through the transposition of digits, an invoice for £356 is entered as £365 (5 and 6 have been transposed). The difference the error creates is always divisible by 9.

46   C

£3,474/3 = £1,158 per month, therefore an accrual for that amount needs to be provided for May 20X3.

47   £46,550

Net realisable value = £1,700.

Therefore reduce stock by (£3,500 – £1,700) = £1,800.

Stock valuation is £46,550.

48   C

The error you should look for is one where the correction will require:

> Debit Suspense account
>
> Credit the other account containing the error.

PAYE and National Insurance deductions are liabilities, payable to the tax authorities. If they have been recorded twice, the credit balance is too high, and the correction will need a debit entry in this account.

The contra entry has credited both the control accounts, and to correct this will require a debit entry in the account containing the error (the purchase ledger/creditors control account).

Closing stock should be a debit entry, and so a debit is needed to correct the error.

A balance for an accrual is a credit balance, but has been recorded incorrectly as a debit balance. To correct the error, the telephone expense account must be credited, and so the suspense account will be debited.

49   C

A liability is something Paul will have to pay. Two years' time is long term.

50   A

	D	E	F	Total
	£000	£000	£000	£000
First half year				
Salaries		12.0	12.0	24
Share balance of profit	108	64.8	43.2	216
				240
Second half year				
Salaries		18.0	12.0	30
Share balance of profit	126	42.0	42.0	210
				240
Total share	234	136.8	109.2	480

Section 9

DECEMBER 2005 EXAM QUESTIONS

SECTION A – ALL TWENTY QUESTIONS ARE COMPULSORY AND MUST BE ATTEMPTED

1   Which of the following is a bank overdraft an example of?

    A   An asset

    B   A liability

    C   Income

    D   An expense

2   Tony made one error when he posted the total value of invoices from the purchase daybook to the nominal ledger. He posted £274,865 to the debit side of the purchases account. The correct total was £274,685.

How is the trial balance affected by this error?

    A   The total of the debit balances and the total of the credit balances will agree, but will be overstated

    B   The total of the debit balances and the total of the credit balances will agree, but will be understated

    C   The total of the debit balances will exceed the total of the credit balances

    D   The total of the credit balances will exceed the total of the debit balances

3   What is the main purpose of a balance sheet?

    A   To report the current value of the business

    B   To indicate if the business is trading profitably

    C   To report the assets and liabilities of the business

    D   To report the personal assets of the business owner

The following information relates to questions 4 and 5:

Arnold bought a machine for use in his business on 1 November 2004. He gave the supplier a cheque for £11,570 and traded in an old machine. The supplier allowed him £4,430 in part exchange for the old machine. Arnold depreciates machinery on the reducing balance basis at a rate of 20% per annum. The old machine had cost £12,000 and had been depreciated by £5,856.

4   **What is the depreciation charge on the new machine for the year to 31 October 2005?**

A   £886

B   £1,428

C   £2,314

D   £3,200

5   **What is the profit or loss on the trade in of the old machine?**

A   a profit of £1,426

B   a profit of £1,714

C   a loss of £1,426

D   a loss of £1,714

6   **Linda found the following when carrying out her bank reconciliation:**

(i)   a cheque for £7,523 has not been presented at the bank

(ii)   a cheque for £560 has been incorrectly recorded as £650 in Linda's ledger

Which of these items will require an entry in Linda's nominal ledger?

A   (i) only

B   (ii) only

C   both (i) and (ii)

D   neither (i) nor (ii)

7   **Beth's draft accounts for the year to 31 October 2005 report a loss of £1,486. When she prepared the accounts,**

Beth did not include an accrual of £1,625 and a prepayment of £834.

What is Beth's profit or loss for the year to 31 October 2005 following the inclusion of the accrual and prepayment?

A   a loss of £695

B   a loss of £2,277

C   a loss of £3,945

D   a profit of £1,807

8   **William's trial balance at 30 September 2005 includes the following balances:**

Trade debtors   £75,943

Debtors allowance   £4,751

How should these balances be reported in William's balance sheet as at 30 September 2005?

A   An asset of £71,192

B   An asset of £75,943 and a liability of £4,751

C   A liability of £71,192

D   A liability of £75,943 and an asset of £4,751

9   At 1 November 2004 Dorothy's debtors allowance was £5,670. At 31 October 2005 she was owed £275,600 by her customers. She has determined that based on past experience an allowance equivalent to 2% of outstanding balances is required at 31 October 2005.

What should be reported in Dorothy's profit and loss account for the year to 31 October 2005?

A   a credit of £158

B   a credit of £5,512

C   a charge of £158

D   a charge of £5,512

10   Simon, who is a sole trader, made a profit of £22,860 in the year to 30 November 2005. During the year his drawings were £16,890. At 1 December 2004 the balance on his capital account was £68,920.

What is the balance on Simon's capital account at 30 November 2005?

A   £29,170

B   £62,950

C   £74,890

D   £108,670

11   Priscilla is completing her extended trial balance, which includes balances for depreciation expense and accumulated depreciation.

Into which columns should these balances be extended?

Depreciation expense Accumulated depreciation

A   Profit and loss debit   Profit and loss credit

B   Balance sheet credit   Balance sheet debit

C   Profit and loss debit   Balance sheet credit

D   Balance sheet debit   Profit and loss credit

12   At 1 November 2004 Brian owed £28,754 to his suppliers. During the year he paid his suppliers a total of £185,844. At 31 October 2005 he owed £26,189.

What was the value of Brian's credit purchases in the year to 31 October 2005?

A   £130,901

B   £183,279

C   £188,409

D   £240,787

13   During the year to 30 November 2005, Amanda bought goods for resale at a cost of £75,550. Her stock at 1 December 2004 was valued at £15,740. She did not count her stock at 30 November 2005, but she knows that her sales for the year to 30 November 2005 were £91,800. All sales were made at a mark up of 20%.

Based on the information above, what was the value of Amanda's stock at 30 November 2005?

A   £13,630

B   £14,790

C   16,690

D   £17,850

14   When Mervyn's trial balance was extracted, the total of the debit balances was £500 more than the total of the credit balances.

Which of the following errors is a possible explanation for the difference?

A   a cash sale for £250 had not been recorded

B   a cash sale for £250 had been recorded twice

C   a cash sale for £250 had been posted to the credit side of both the sales account and the cash account

D   a cash sale for £250 had been posted to the debit side of both the sales account and the cash account

15   Trevor's trial balance includes a suspense account with a debit balance of £900. He has discovered that:

–   a supplier's invoice for £16,700 was posted to the correct side of the purchases account as £17,600 (the correct entry was posted to the creditors' control account); and

–   a cheque for £900 has not been recorded in his ledger.

What is the balance on the suspense account after these errors are corrected?

A   nil

B   £900

C   £1,800

D   £2,700

16   Which of the following are desirable characteristics of financial information according to the Statement of Principles?

(i)   relevance

(ii)   reliability

A   (i) and (ii)

B   (i) only

C   neither (i) nor (ii)

D   (ii) only

17 **Which of the following is the correct journal entry to write off a bad debt?**

A	Debit	Sales	
	Credit	Bad debts
B	Debit	Bad debts	
	Credit	Bank
C	Debit	Debtors	
	Credit	Bad debts
D	Debit	Bad debts	
	Credit	Debtors

18 **At 30 November 2005 Jenny had a bank loan of £8,500 and a balance of £678 in hand in her bank account.**

How should these amounts be recorded on Jenny's opening trial balance at 1 December 2005?

A   Debit £7,822

B   Credit £7,822

C   Credit £8,500 and Debit £678

D   Debit £8,500 and Credit £678

19 **Bert has extracted the following list of balances from his nominal ledger at 31 October 2005:**

	£
Sales	258,542
Opening stock	9,649
Purchases	142,958
Expenses	34,835
Fixed assets (NBV)	63,960
Debtors	31,746
Creditors	13,864
Cash at bank	1,783
Capital	12,525

What is the total of the debit balances in Bert's trial balance at 31 October 2005?

A   £267,049

B   £275,282

C   £283,148

D   £284,931

20 **Which of the following statements is/are correct?**

(i)   the fixed asset register is part of the double entry system

(ii)   a fixed asset register is required in every organisation's accounting system

(iii)   assets should be removed from the fixed asset register when they have been fully depreciated

A (i) only

B (ii) only

C (iii) only

D none of the statements   **(40 marks)**

SECTION B – ALL FOUR QUESTIONS ARE COMPULSORY AND MUST BE ATTEMPTED

1 SHORT FORM QUESTIONS

(a) Explain the difference between a current liability and a long-term liability and give one example of each.   **(4 marks)**

(b) State why it is important to differentiate between capital expenditure and revenue expenditure, and briefly explain the accounting treatment of each type of expenditure.

(4 marks)

(c) Briefly explain the purpose of the depreciation charge in the profit and loss account.

(2 marks)

(d) Give THREE examples of errors which will NOT be revealed by extracting a trial balance.   **(3 marks)**

(e) Briefly explain the business entity concept and its impact on the recording of transactions.   **(2 marks)**

(Total: 15 marks)

2 STOCK VALUATION

You work for a wholesaler which distributes a single product. A trainee has prepared draft accounts for the month of October 2005. The accounts report a net loss of £35,580 and total net assets of £283,468. You have noted that:

1 the profit and loss account does not report a figure for gross profit;

2 the trainee has not included any value for closing stock;

3 the trainee has included £57,600 for opening stock. This was calculated on the first in, first out (FIFO) basis. There were 480 items, valued at £120 per item.

4 Purchases during the month were:

Date	Number of items	Cost per item £
9 October	1,140	145
15 October	1,310	150
24 October	620	155
	3,070	

5 Sales during the month were:

Date	Number of items	Selling price per item £
12 October	1,040	205
21 October	1,840	220
	2,880	

6   As well as purchases, the other costs deducted from sales to calculate the net loss were:

	£
Wages of staff	44,700
Premises expenses	42,750
Administrative expenses	13,620
Selling and marketing costs	17,890
Carriage inwards	3,750
Carriage outwards	4,120
Depreciation	11,250
	138,080

Required:

(a)   Calculate:

    (i)   the number of items in stock at 31 October 2005; and   **(1 mark)**

    (ii)   the value of stock at 31 October 2005 on the FIFO basis.   **(2 marks)**

(b)   Using the revised stock value calculated in (a), calculate:

    (i)   Cost of sales for October 2005;   **(4 marks)**

    (ii)   Gross profit for October 2005;   **(2 marks)**

    (iii) Net profit for October 2005; and   **(2 marks)**

    (iv)   Net assets at 31 October 2005.   **(2 marks)**

(c)   State the basic rule set out in SSAP 9 which is to be applied to the valuation of stock.

(2 marks)

(Total: 15 marks)

3   ANN AND JANE

Ann and Jane have been trading as a partnership for several years, sharing profits and losses in the ratio 3:5. Their profit and loss account for the year to 31 October 2005 reports a profit of £126,842 before taking into account the following items:

(i)   Ann is paid a salary of £22,000 per annum. Jane's salary is £8,000 per annum;

(ii)   On 1 February 2005, each of the partners paid £35,000 into the partnership bank account. Ann's payment is to be treated as capital, while Jane's is to be treated as a loan, with interest at 4% per annum to be credited to her current account;

(iii) Partners are charged interest on drawings at a rate of 16% per annum. All drawings are assumed to have been made half way through the year. During the year, Ann's drawings were £28,000 and Jane's were £24,000.

At 1 November 2004, the balances on the partners' current accounts were:

Ann £17,420 (debit)   Jane £9,547 (credit)

Required:

(a) (i) Calculate the amount of profit available for appropriation for the year to 31 October 2005; **(2 marks)**

     (ii) Calculate the total amount of profit due to each of the partners for the year to 31 October 2005. **(7 marks)**

(b) Show the partners' current accounts, including the closing balances for the year ended 31 October 2005. **(6 marks)**

(Total: 15 marks)

4   JONTY AND CO

You are employed as a Trainee Accountant in Jonty and Co. One of your tasks is to prepare the monthly reconciliation of the balance on the creditors control account in the nominal ledger (£98,524) to the list of balances from the creditors ledger (£97,264).

When preparing the reconciliation at 30 November 2005, you have noted the following:

(i) One of the suppliers agreed to accept £1,500 in payment of a balance of £1,514. The full balance of £1,514 was deducted from the supplier's personal account, but only the cheque issued was recorded in the nominal ledger.

(ii) There is an ongoing agreement to offset balances with Tim Robinson, who is both a customer and a supplier. The amount for November is £2,856. No entries have yet been made.

(iii) A credit balance of £623 on the account of Joe Coleman was listed as a debit balance.

(iv) An invoice for £462 received from Robin Wayne was incorrectly recorded in the purchase day book as a credit note.

(v) Your company makes direct payments to Bruce Robbins. The payment of £974 made in November has not been recorded.

(vi) An invoice for £760 from Hill's Haulage was entered in the purchase day book as £670.

Required:

(a) Show the creditors control account in the nominal ledger, including the necessary adjusting entries and the corrected balance.

    (*Note:* You must present your answer in a format which clearly indicates whether each entry is a debit entry or a credit entry.) **(6 marks)**

(b) Show the reconciliation of the list of balances to the corrected balance on the creditors control account in the nominal ledger. **(7 marks)**

(c) State the correct creditors balance for inclusion in the final accounts, and indicate where it should be reported on the balance sheet. **(2 marks)**

(Total: 15 marks)

Section 10

ANSWERS TO DECEMBER 2005 EXAM QUESTIONS

SECTION A

1   B

A bank overdraft represents money owed to the bank. Legally it is repayable on demand and so it is classified as a current liability.

2   C

The debit entry is overstated by £180 because of this transposition error. The credit entry (to trade creditors) is correct.

3   C

A balance sheet reports the assets and liabilities of the business. Normally it is drawn up on the historic cost basis and so it does not reflect current values.

4   D

The total cost of the asset is £16,000 (£11,570 cash plus the £4,430 trade-in allowance). £16,000 × 20% = £3,200.

5   D

	£	
Proceeds	4,430	
Less carrying value (12,000 – 5,856)	(6,144)	
	1,714	loss

6   B

Only the incorrectly recorded cheque requires a correcting entry. The unpresented cheque is just a timing difference.

7   B

	£
Loss reported in draft accounts	(1,486)
Less accrual (an additional expense)	(1,625)
Add back prepayment (a reduction in expenses)	834
Revised loss	(2,277)

8   A

£75,943 - £4,751 = £71,192

The allowance for doubtful debtors is deducted from the total trade debtors balance and the net amount is shown as a current asset in the balance sheet.

9   A

	£
Allowance required *£275,600 × 2% =*	5,512
Less: opening allowance	(5,670)
Decrease (credit) recognised in profit and loss	(158)

10   C

	£
Opening capital	68,920
Add profit for the year	22,860
Less drawings in the year	(16,890)
Closing capital	74,890

11   C

The depreciation expense is charged (debited) to the profit and loss account.

The accumulated depreciation is a credit balance in the balance sheet, reducing the carrying value of the related asset.

12   B

	£	
Opening creditors	28,754	
Add purchases during the year	183,279	*Balancing figure*
Less payments during the year	(185,844)	
Closing creditors	26,189	

13   B

		£
Opening stocks		15,740
Add purchases during the year		75,550
Less COST of goods sold during the year	$^{100}/_{120} × £91,800$	(76,500)
Closing stocks		14,790

14   D

Items A and B won't create an imbalance because the mistakes affect both sides of the trial balance.

Item C would cause the credit side to be greater than the debit side.

Item D would cause the debit side to be overstated by £250 and the credit side to be understated by £250. This means that the debit side is £500 higher than the credit side.

15   C

The correction to purchases will reduce the charge by £900, reducing the total debits by £900 and so increasing the suspense account needed to £1,800. Information about the missing cheque is sparse (is it income or an expense?) but it will have no affect on the suspense account if the transaction has been completely omitted from the TB.

16   A

Relevance and reliability are two of the four principal qualitative characteristics of financial statements, along with understandability and comparability.

17   D

Before the debt was written off it would have been recognised in debtors (with or without a related allowance for doubtful debts). To remove the debt, debtors will be credited and a charge for bad debts will be recognised in the profit and loss account.

18   C

The loan is a liability; this is shown as a credit in the balance sheet.

The cash in hand is an asset; this is shown as a debit in the balance sheet.

Assets and liabilities must be shown separately; they can only be netted-off if there is a legal right of off-set.

19   D

	Dr	Cr
	£	£
Sales		258,542
Opening stock	9,649	
Purchases	142,958	
Expenses	34,835	
Fixed assets at NBV	63,960	
Debtors	31,746	
Creditors		13,864
Cash at bank	1,783	
Capital		12,525
	£284,931	£284,931

20   D

The register is not part of the double entry system. It details and provides information on the individual fixed assets held by the business. There is no legal requirement to maintain a register, but it good accounting and corporate governance to do so.

Assets are only removed from the register when they are disposed of. Fully depreciated assets will still be recorded.

SECTION B

1   SHORT FORM QUESTIONS

(a)   A liability is an amount which the business owes to a third party.

When preparing a balance sheet, we differentiate between liabilities which must be paid in the short term and those which must be paid in the long term. Liabilities which must be paid in the short term are referred to as current liabilities. It is accepted that 'short term' is within one year of the balance sheet date. It therefore follows that long term liabilities are those which will be paid more than one year after the balance sheet date.

Examples are:

Current liabilities

> Trade creditors
>
> Bank overdraft
>
> Loan repayments falling due within 12 months

Long-term liabilities

> Loan repayments falling due in more than 12 months

(b)   It is important to differentiate between capital expenditure and revenue expenditure because the accounting treatment of each type of expenditure is different.

Capital expenditure will initially be reported on the balance sheet, while revenue expenditure will be written off in the profit and loss.

It should be noted that capital expenditure is written off to the profit and loss account, but this takes place over a number of accounting periods.

(c)   The depreciation charge spreads the cost of using fixed assets over the useful economic life of the asset. This reflects the value of economic benefits which have been consumed during the accounting period. This applies the accruals concept, by charging costs against profit in the period in which they are incurred.

(d)   The following errors will not be revealed by extracting a trial balance:

- an entry which has been completely omitted from the records (an error of complete omission).

- a posting recorded in the wrong account. This can be of two types. An error of principle occurs when the incorrect entry is made in the wrong class of account. An error of commission is when the incorrect entry is made in the correct class of account, but the wrong account is used.

- an incorrect value for a transaction entered in a daybook will lead to the debit and credit entries in the ledger being equal, but incorrect.

- two errors which have the effect of cancelling each other out (compensating errors).

(e)   The business entity concept states that no matter what the legal status of the business, in accounting terms, we always keep the business and the owner separate.

This means that when recording transactions we are only concerned with how the business is affected. For example, if the owner introduces capital, we are not concerned with the source of the capital, and apart from increasing the owner's capital balance, we do not record how the owner is affected by the transaction.

This means that when recording transactions we are only concerned with how the business is affected. For example, if the owner introduces capital, we are not concerned with the source of the capital, and apart from increasing the owner's capital balance, we do not record how the owner is affected by the transaction.

2 STOCK VALUATION

Key answer tip

The only complication in this question is identifying the expenses that should be included in cost of sales.

(a) (i) The closing stock is 670 items, calculated as follows:

Opening stock volume	480 items
Purchased	3,070 items
	3,550
Sold	2,880 items
Closing stock	670 items

(ii) Applying the FIFO basis of valuation, the stock at 31 October is taken to comprise all of the units in the last delivery (24 October) and the balance is from the previous delivery (15 October).

Thus closing stock value is:

	£
620 items at £155	96,100
50 items at £150	7,500
Total value	103,600

(b) (i) Cost of sales

	£
Opening stock	57,600
Purchases (W1)	457,900
Carriage inwards	3,750
	519,250
Closing stock (a)	(103,600)
	415,650

(ii) Gross profit

	£
Sales (W2)	618,000
Cost of sales	415,650
	202,350

(iii) Net profit

	£
Loss as reported	(35,580)
Add closing stock (a)	103,600
	68,020

Alternative calculation:

	£
Gross profit	202,350
Less expenses	134,330
	68,020

(iv)   Net assets

	£
As reported	283,468
Add closing stock (a)	103,600
	387,068

Workings

W1   **Purchases:**

Date	Items	At £	Total £
9 October	1,140	145	165,300
15 October	1,310	150	196,500
24 October	620	155	96,100
			457,900

W2   **Sales:**

Date	Items	At £	Total £
12 October	1,040	205	213,200
21 October	1,840	220	404,800
			618,000

(c)   SSAP 9 states that stock should be valued at the lower of cost or net realisable value.

3   ANN AND JANE

Key answer tip

- Partners' salaries are an appropriation of profit, not a charge against profits.

- Interest on capital is an appropriation of profit, but interest on loans is a charge against profits.

- Interest on drawings must be time apportioned. It reduces the amount owed to each partner and increases the residual profit.

- The profit share is calculated after charging/crediting the above items.

(a)

			Ann	Jane	
			£	£	£
(i)	Profit as reported				126,842
	Interest on loan (W1)			1,050	(1,050)
	Revised profit				125,792
(ii)	Revised profit				125,792
	Salary		22,000	8,000	(30,000)
	Interest on drawings (W2)		(2,240)	(1,920)	4,160
	Residual profit				99,952
	Share	Ann 3/8	37,482		
		Jane 5/8		62,470	
	Total share of profit		57,242	68,550	125,792

Working 1

Interest on loan   £35,000 × 4% × 9/12   = £1,050

for time apportionment

Working 2

Interest on drawings

Ann   £28,000 × 16% × 6/12   = £2,240

Jane   £24,000 × 16% × 6/12   = £1,920

for time apportionment

(b)

Current account

	Ann	Jane		Ann	Jane
	£	£		£	£
Opening balance	17,420				9,547
Int. on drawings	2,240	1,920	Salary	22,000	8,000
Drawings	28,000	24,000	Int. on loan		1,050
Closing balance	11,822	55,147	Residual profit	37,482	62,470
	59,482	81,067		59,482	81,067

4   JONTY & CO

Key answer tip

The key point is to identify which errors affect the control account, which affect the list of balances, and which affect both.

(a)

Creditors control account

		£			£
Discount received	(i)	14	Balance as given		98,524
Offset	(ii)	2,856	Invoice	(iv)	924
Direct payment	(v)	974	Error in invoice	(vi)	90
Corrected balance		95,694			
		99,538			99,538

(b)

		£
	Total as given	97,264
(ii)	Offset	(2,856)
(iii)	Credit balance listed as debit	1,246
(iv)	Invoice treated as credit note	924
(v)	Direct payment	(974)
(vi)	Invoice error	90
	Corrected total	95,694

Balance agreed to ledger balance

(c)   The corrected balance of £95,694 should be reported on the balance sheet as a current liability.